OAKWELL CENTURIONS

OAKWELL CENTURIONS

A collection of biographies of Barnsley FC's leading players of modern times - almost all of whom have played 100 first team games.

David Watson

1990

For two enthusiastic Barnsley supporters – my sons, Robert and Chris

Printed and bound in Great Britain by
Butler & Tanner Ltd, Frome and London

Acknowledgements

In writing this book I have been greatly assisted by the recollections and opinions of John Steele, Gordon Pallister and Norman Rimmington – three men whose combined and direct involvement in Oakwell affairs extends over more than 50 years. Their help was invaluable to me and is very much appreciated.

I am also grateful to:

the chairman and directors of Barnsley FC for their permission to proceed with the project;

Arthur Bower, the club's historian, for the willingness with which he answered my almost constant stream of queries;

Peter Brook, who supplied the results of his own research into the whereabouts of former players, thus saving me much time and effort;

Janine Evans, for the loan of her scrap-books covering 20 years' happenings at Oakwell, and

the men featured herein, and in the case of those who, sadly, are no longer with us, their families and friends, without whose co-operation this book could not have been written.

D N W
Silkstone
April 1990

Contents

Foreword

by Keith Lodge, sports editor of the *Barnsley Chronicle*

'I wonder what happened to old so-and-so? Now there was a player. He really did set the pulses racing down at Oakwell, but I lost all track of him after he left us.'

How often have you mused in similar fashion over the fate or further fortune of one of your favourite players who has worn the famous red and white of Oakwell with both distinction and pride?

Well, wonder no more. David Watson's *Oakwell Centurions* provides at least some of the answers, as well as giving a vivid insight into the careers of almost all those who have 'topped the ton' with the Reds.

There is no doubt that it has been a pure labour of love, as the author has spent three years travelling the country to meet those yesterday's heroes whose contributions to the club's progress are clouded by the mists of memory.

And, wherever possible, he has obtained the information at first hand, thereby making doubly sure that his facts are right.

The result is not only an extremely accurate and informative book which will be of particular value to statisticians, historians and journalists, but it is also eminently readable and will appeal to everyone who follows football in general, and Barnsley supporters in particular.

It is obvious that David Watson has a special affection for Oakwell. That comes across in the writing. Memories stir excitingly as chapter after chapter expertly bridges the game between the evocative past and the sometimes surprising present.

John Steele: The Legendary 'Mister Barnsley'

When John Steele arrived in Barnsley from his native Scotland in the summer of 1938 he doubted he would remain for more than a few weeks. On the first morning at his lodgings in Mottram Street he was awakened at 4 o'clock by what seemed to be the noise of an army on the march – and then realized it was the sound of coal miners' clogged feet as they walked beneath his bedroom window on their way to work. New team-mate Dan McGarry had also travelled from Glasgow on the previous day and shared the small bedroom. They were already disillusioned by their first impressions of the town and on identifying the noise which had awakened them, McGarry said, 'I'm not going to be long *here*!' John nodded in firm agreement. Yet he remained at the forefront of the Barnsley soccer scene for almost 50 years to become one of the Football League's most respected figures and one of the most readily identified and best liked men ever to live in what became his adopted home town.

The young John Steele was a pupil at Alan Glenn's Grammar School in Glasgow. There the winter sport was played with an oval ball and his prowess was such that, at 13, he played in the 17-year-old team. But soccer was his first love and for three years he represented the school at rugby on Saturday mornings and played soccer for a church team in the afternoons. He had already acquired much of the uncanny ball control which was to be a feature of his play in the professional game, but with the church team he was centre half – and leading scorer.

The dribbling skill was learned while he was a small child, from two schoolboy uncles who assumed responsibility for their nephew's soccer development while his father was a soldier serving in the First World War. John's first view of professional football was from their shoulders at Celtic Park, and the ball-skills they taught him at a tender age were to delight crowds, not only north and south of the border, but on foreign fields during World War Two. As an example of his extraordinary skill, in a game against Crewe Alexandra in 1938 he collected the ball in the Barnsley penalty-area and took it the length of the pitch – beating man after man – before dribbling it round the 'keeper to score a really superb goal. And that was his normal style of play – he relished weaving through a succession of defenders before having a crack at goal. The crowds loved it. They would shout encouragement as he set off on his mazey dribbles, and he was helped by a strong build which made him extremely difficult to knock off the ball.

His first professional club was East Fife. He joined them at 17 and still has his copy of the contract. His wage was one pound ten shillings per week, with a bonus of five shillings per point – and the directors reserved the right to determine whether or not it would be paid. Which meant, in effect, that even if the team won points, if the directors thought a player hadn't performed well enough he wouldn't be paid the bonus. But John was *always* paid! A year later he was transferred to Ayr United and was a member of the side which won the championship of the Scottish Second Division in 1937.

His transfer to Barnsley was in June 1938. The fee was £2,500 and, surprisingly, manager Angus Seed secured him without having seen him play. But the favourable impressions the youngster had created were exemplified by him being recommended to Seed by the manager of Manchester United.

In his opening Oakwell season he was a member of that tremendous team who were champions of Division Three (North) and he was second-top scorer with 17 goals. In the following September, after only three games at the higher level, the beginning of the Second World War brought about the suspension of the normal League programme. John was directed to work at Wharncliffe Woodmoor Colliery and continued to play for Barnsley in the regional league until joining the Royal Air Force in 1941. Thereafter his appearances were less frequent. He remained in the side while serving as a PT Instructor at Scarborough, but a posting to Arbroath as a Drill Instructor put an end to that and he then became a guest player with Aberdeen.

With hindsight, it might have been to his advantage to have been posted to Scotland earlier. He then would not have played in the game at Oakwell in 1942 in which he sustained a knee injury of such severity that he was hospitalized for six months. On returning to duty he was remustered into Air-Sea Rescue and posted to the Far East. He spent two years as Sergeant-coxswain of a powerful launch operating in the Bay of Bengal – and throughout that time was able to fit in only three games of football. All were representative matches and in addition to playing for the RAF's Scottish team, he also played in the teams representing England and Wales.

He returned to the UK in 1946 and resumed his career at Oakwell. Still only 29, he could have hoped for several more playing seasons but knew, in his heart-of-hearts, that the knee damaged in 1942 was like an invisible shackle on his leg. Between 1946 and 1949 he played only occasional first team games, but Angus Seed, the astute man who originally brought him to the club, had already appointed him to coach the junior players. And what an excellent appointment it proved to be. He put heart and soul into the new role, and many lads who started as juniors at Oakwell and went on to have successful careers in football – and there are literally scores of them, some even became internationals – have cause to be grateful to John Steele. In his early years as coach he could have moved to Birmingham City, who offered the job of first team coach at a wage almost triple what he was getting at Barnsley. But by then he was so obsessed with the Oakwell juniors that he wouldn't have left to join even Arsenal or Manchester United.

His philosophy was that if youngsters saw you were sincere and interested in them and trying to help, they would do anything for you. At one stage, until February 1956 when Norman Rimmington was appointed to assist him, he was dealing with up to 40 at each session single-handed and would always arrange for two to attend early for extra tuition. He admits that if he had a failing footballwise, it was that he wasn't really interested in defending. And if he'd had to be a defender, he wouldn't have been a footballer!

He became manager in 1960. He didn't really want the job, being happy in what he was doing, but a director suggested he should apply. He did – and got it. In his first season the team reached the sixth round of the FA Cup for the first time in 25 years, but 1965 brought relegation into the League's lowest division. Principally that was a result of the club's desperate financial situation which necessitated the sale of every player of value and their replacement by untried youngsters and free-transfer men. Money was owed all over the town and at one stage it seemed football at Oakwell was almost at an end. It reached the stage where Midwood Sports refused to supply further equipment and a previously used ball had to be sprayed with white paint on match days. And Belgrave Road Co-op – the local corner shop – refused to supply even a packet of soap powder until outstanding bills had been paid. However, two new directors, Ernest Dennis and Geoff Buckle, provided cash with which to pay creditors and strengthen the team.

The result was that in 1968 John led the club back into Division Three. During his administration it became one of the few without an overdraft at the bank, yet what gives a feeling of real achievement to his years of management is that there were two seasons when he was able to field teams consisting entirely of players who had been recruited by him as youngsters and began their careers under his direction in the Northern Intermediate League side. That must be the supreme objective of almost every club, but Barnsley is the only one within the Football League ever to achieve it.

Despite the almost fatherly affection he had for the players, he was as hard as the next manager. A rollicking from John Steele was something best avoided; he didn't mince his words, and many a time it seemed the dressing room door would burst from its hinges as he slammed it fiercely behind him after having given vent to his feelings.

Looking back he realizes, like most managers eventually do, that the considerable time devoted to club affairs was at the expense of his family. There was, in fact, a year when he spent only two evening at home between mid-July and Christmas.

In 1970 he was appointed general manager and later combined the post with that of secretary, which he held until reaching retirement age in 1982. He was then co-opted onto the board of directors and served for two years before becoming one of the club's life vice-presidents.

In 1977 the directors acknowledged his exceptional service by granting him a testimonial game and former players inundated the organisers with requests to take part. It was held on 15th March and there were, in fact, two matches. The main attraction was a game between an international XI selected by the then England manager, Don Revie, and the Barnsley team; the supporting event was between a side of John's own choosing and a team of ex-Oakwell players. Weatherwise, conditions couldn't have been worse. Rain fell heavily throughout the day and into the evening, yet the fans responded magnificently, more than 8,000 attending in support of a man who had done so much for their club.

In 1982 he received Bell's Service to Football Award – an impressive trophy and a sizeable cheque. The ceremony took place at London's Royal Lancaster Hotel and he felt honoured that his fellow professionals considered him a suitable recipient. But after the presentation he experienced a little sadness. He got into conversation with Bobby Robson who was then assistant to the England manager, Ron Greenwood. At that time there was general concern about the scarcity of central defenders suitable for the England squad in the World Cup Finals to be held later in the year. There was even newspaper speculation that it would be necessary to recall a 35-year-old who had not played in the national side for more than two years. During the season which had just ended, Barnsley had done exceptionally well – finishing in sixth position in Division Two, dispatching three First Division sides from the Football League Cup and earning a very creditable draw in the competition at Anfield – and centre half Mick McCarthy had been quite outstanding. John said to the England manager's assistant, 'You know, you really should come to Barnsley and look at our Mick McCarthy.' After some hesitation the reply was, 'Mick . . . who?' John's sadness was for the fact that a man with a responsibility to identify the country's best footballers had such little awareness of what good players were available outside the First Division. Needless to say, the Barnsley-born man of whom he spoke was soon to play *in* the First Division, captain the Republic of Ireland team on innumerable occasions and become Glasgow Celtic's costliest-ever signing.

It is hard to imagine anyone with John's soccer commitment having time for another sporting involvement, but there are a few weeks in early and mid-summer when even he is happy to have other interests. From boyhood to middle age, that interest was tennis. He joined a club in Glasgow when 10 years old and was soon good enough to compete with the men, retaining membership until his chosen career took him to Ayr United. He didn't play the game again until he was 30, and then joined the Huddersfield Road club in Barnsley. His attitude was, as in football, that one played to win – and he was club singles champion for 11 consecutive seasons and once champion of Barnsley.

Despite John's early misgivings about coming to Barnsley his skills helped him to quickly settle in the town. A rich Scots accent prevented the locals from understanding much of what he said, but they loved the way he played football. Fifty years on, there are now comparatively few who experienced the thrill of seeing John Steele of the corkscrew dribble and rasping shot – the man who made such great contribution to his club's tremendously successful season immediately prior to the Second World War. But in the post-war years his total dedication to Oakwell affairs has been apparent to all and he has become a legend in his own lifetime. Not only did he direct an almost endless list of young men into successful careers in football, but he served the club as player, coach, manager, general manager, secretary and director – an achievement unparalleled within the annals of the Football League. And in every role he displayed skill and integrity. Little wonder, therefore, that in his adopted home town he is referred to respectfully and with much affection as – 'Mister Barnsley'.

Bernard Harper: A Man of Granite

All but the final two years of Bernard Harper's long career in professional football were spent with his home town club and he earned himself a unique place in Barnsley's soccer history. During the Second World War he played for England against Scotland and is the only Oakwell man to have been honoured at that level, and while serving in the Royal Air Force he captained representative sides in South East Asia. Earlier he had played in two of Barnsley's promotion-winning teams and captained that which won the Third Division (North) championship in 1939 with a record total of points.

He was the twelfth of a family of fourteen children and his hard, uncompromising attitude in football perhaps reflected the early years of his working life. At 14 he worked underground at Stanhope Silkstone Colliery and at 15, after being out of work throughout the 1926 General Strike, he became a trammer at Old Silkstone Colliery. Shifts there were spent on hands and knees in a two-foot seam, pushing tubs with his head up a 200-yards slope to the coal face. A year later he moved to Woolley Colliery and worked on a coal-cutting machine until becoming a professional player at Oakwell in 1932.

His serious football had begun in the Barnsley Intermediate League as a member of Woolley Colliery's 16/18-year-old side. He quickly graduated to the first team and their games regularly attracted up to 3,000 spectators. At 18 he joined West Ward FC at Smithies, in the spring of 1932 playing two trial games with Wolverhampton Wanderers. On each occasion his day-trip to the Midlands necessitated a departure from home at 5am. On the second visit he realized the return coach journey from the practice ground to Molineux took him past the railway station, so he asked the driver to drop him off there. However, the trainer intervened and said he would have to return to the ground as manager Major Frank Buckley wanted to see him. Bernard's reply was to the effect that if the manager was to see him it would have to be in Barnsley and he insisted he be allowed to alight at the station. Even if the Major had been inclined to make the suggested journey it would have been wasted effort, for when the lad arrived home he found Barnsley manager Brough Fletcher awaiting him. The outcome was that he had become a Barnsley amateur before he placed his weary head on the pillow that night, and he became a professional player a few weeks later.

As a young man he had self confidence to match his great physical strength.

On joining the club, he asked the manager the name of the first team centre half and then said, 'You can tell him I'm after his job, I haven't come here to play in the reserves.' But, not surprisingly, his opening Oakwell season – that of 1932/33 – began in the reserves. Yet within a month he had created such good impressions that he was captaining the side. He soon realized that replacing George Henderson as first team centre half could be a long process, so he told the manager he wasn't limited to one position and could play anywhere in defence. He had, in fact, always been an attacking centre half and when with Woolley Colliery had scored more goals than the centre forward – a young man who went on to be a professional with Sheffield United. The representations had the desired effect, for in a matter of weeks he won a regular place in the team at wing half and remained in that role, operating on either flank, for the following three-and-a-half seasons.

He replaced Henderson in the number 5 shirt in 1936 and took over the captaincy in the following year. He had already been a member of the Reds' 1934 Division Three (North) championship side and he captained the team which is considered to have been one of Oakwell's finest – that which won the title again in 1939.

Soon after the start of that tremendous campaign when they ended the season miles ahead of their nearest challengers, an incident occurred in training which he immediately regretted but from which stemmed a pleasant aspect of his future life. It took place during a weekly practice game in which the first team defence opposed the first team forward line. One of the attackers was newcomer John Steele who, while displaying his uncanny dribbling skill, continually left opponents kicking thin air and seemed to think the ball belonged to him. Feeling a need to put an end to such nonsense, the tough Yorkshireman felled the young Scot with a tackle which would have been considered harsh in a Cup-tie at Millmoor or Millwall and was certainly inappropriate to a game between club-mates at Oakwell. Steele was badly shaken and justifiably aggrieved, and went at the captain with flailing fists. The skirmish was over in seconds but created such anger on the pitch that, for the first time in memory, a practice had to be abandoned. Bernard knew he had behaved appallingly and felt ashamed of what he had done. He immediately apologised to Steele and held out his hand – which the other readily accepted. And the handshake was the start of a firm friendship which continues to this day.

The opportunity for the 1939 team to display their talents in Division Two was halted by the outbreak of the Second World War. Bernard was directed to work at Barnsley Main Colliery and remained there until joining the RAF in 1940. In what were extremely difficult conditions in war-time – air raids, long working hours, shortages of food and just about everything else, and family life disrupted by menfolk serving in HM Forces – regular representative football matches were organized as a help towards maintaining the morale of the general public. The Reds' captain's appearance for England was in December 1939 – before he entered the RAF; he hadn't long been in the service when the frequency with which he was being called upon for representative games resulted in him being remustered from Policeman to PT Instructor.

The international game resulted in a 2–1 win for England and in the following week the *Barnsley Chronicle* published the national dailies' comments on Bernard's performance. These included: 'The strong part of the English team was the half back line where Harper was outstanding ... He was the man of the match ... Dodds, the Scottish leader, was completely subdued, yet Harper still had time to cover the full backs when necessary ... The highest praise that can be given him is that Cullis was not missed ... Harper was the defensive star of the day ...'

He was available for Barnsley's games during the first four war-time seasons and in 1942 he scored the winning goal in a game against Sheffield United. Receiving the ball 10 yards inside the Barnsley half, he saw the opposing goalkeeper was off his line and he kicked the ball as hard as he could towards the goal. The 'keeper was perhaps distracted by the seemingly jet-propelled Gavin Smith flashing towards him from the right wing, and the ball passed over his head for what must be the longest-range goal Oakwell has ever seen.

In the autumn of 1943 he was posted to India and his football continued as a member of South-East Asia Command's Combined Services team which played against regimental sides throughout the sub-continent. In January/February 1944 a series of games was held between English and Scottish representative sides, and Bernard's soccer scrap-book contains a photograph of him, as captain of the winning team, receiving a trophy at the Irwin Stadium, Delhi, from the Supreme Allied Commander, Lord Louis Mountbatten.

He returned to Oakwell on demobilization in 1946 but, to his dismay, was unable to have a place in the team. Despite being 35 years old his RAF duties as a PTI and regular football had kept him at the peak of condition and, after surveying the competition, he couldn't see why he was excluded from the side. In fact, he was younger than Joe Wilson who held the centre half position but manager Angus Seed wanted him to cease playing and have a role as his assistant. He did that for a few months but was unhappy about it and after qualifying as an FA coach he applied for and was appointed to the post of player-manager of Scunthorpe United in the Midland League. He remained there for two years, but resigned when he decided the directors were not making a sufficiently serious attempt to gain entry into the Football League.

The following 10 years were spent in the licensed trade. He started as steward of the Victory Club at Stocksbridge and combined the role with those of player-manager of the Stocksbridge Works side and scout for Sheffield United. From there he moved to Leeds and had premises in the city centre and on the Bradford Road, and later he held the licence of the Wheatsheaf Hotel at Sherburn-in-Elmet. While there he managed John Smith's brewery team, The Magnets, at nearby Tadcaster and obtained reinstatement as an amateur in order to play for them. He then had two years at the Wilthorpe Hotel in his home town until leaving the trade in 1959.

Thereafter he was a newsagent at Stocksbridge, a sub-postmaster at Appleton Roebuck, a general dealer at Doncaster and with the British Oxygen Company in London as a stock controller. He then worked in the same capacity with civil engineers Sir Lindsay Parkinson & Co at Temple Newsham until reaching retirement age in 1976.

His second sporting love is golf, which he learned as part of the Oakwell training programme in the 1930s. He played at Staincross and took to the game so much that on Mondays – the players' day off – he would play a round in the morning and another in the afternoon. He was at his peak with a handicap of 6 when he was 65 – and for 20 years he played at the renowned Wentworth course in Surrey in the annual match between Sir Lindsay Parkinson's offices in England and Wales. More locally, he has been a member of the Silkstone Golf Club for 23 years and, although he doesn't now play as regularly as he would wish, from retirement until two years ago he played three rounds each week – which was pretty good for a 76-year-old.

The Reds' pre-war half back line of Harper, Henderson and Holley was one of the best the club has ever had. They were all six-footers and, when so inclined, were capable of frightening the opposition to death. Bernard was regarded as a Man of Granite. Opponents would literally bounce off him and he was utterly fearless, and he particularly enjoyed playing against Sheffield Wednesday at Hillsborough. There the crowd booed him every time he ran onto the pitch but, as he says, 'They never boo a bad player!' He was an ideal captain – always leading by example and covering for others – and altogether a great man to have in a side. And when one considers the achievements of the 1939 championship team – most goals scored and fewest conceded in the whole Football League, and the division's highest-ever total of points and biggest margin of success – it was appropriate for Bernard Harper to captain that strong and talented side.

Danny McGarry: As Big as the Best

In the early 1900s Danny McGarry was one of six children of a textile worker in the Renfrew village of Howood, and it seems the height the McGarry siblings were to attain as adults was dependent upon the order in which they were born. Eddie, the eldest, became a six-foot centre half with Dundee while Danny, the youngest, who was to be a member of one of Barnsley's most successful teams, stopped growing when he reached 5′ 4″.

Danny was outside left in the Reds' 1939 Division Three (North) championship side, having joined them in the previous summer from the Scottish club, Morton. From schooldays until the age of 21 he was a centre forward, in which position he made occasional appearances for Barnsley in war-time football when he must have been one of the smallest leaders the senior game has ever had. Yet when Barnsley played at Gateshead in April 1939 the home side's number 9 was Hughie Gallagher – a man acknowledged as one of the greatest centre forwards of all time – and when Danny stood beside him he was delighted that Gallagher seemed exactly the same height as himself.

On leaving school in 1925 he obtained work in a Paisley bleach factory and joined junior side Port Glasgow. At 19 he became a professional with Dunfermline and, like most Scottish footballers of the day with the exception of those with Rangers and Celtic, it was necessary for him to supplement his football income by other employment. Work at the bleach factory enabled him to do that, but not for long because when the factory began to be affected by the general recession of the late 1920s, as one of the youngest employees and in receipt of two wages, he was the first to be laid off. A few months later he was also laid off in a football sense, for after one season Dunfermline gave him a free transfer. That at least had a beneficial effect on his prospects of other employment for, as he was no longer in receipt of other remuneration, his previous employers were prepared to reinstate him and he remained with them for eight years until his football career brought him to Barnsley.

On being released by Dunfermline he joined Arthurlie and it was while there that he became a winger. Two years later he joined Morton, and four-and-a half seasons with the Clydeside club included one of their most successful periods when, in 1937, they reached the semi-finals of the Scottish Cup and won promotion into the First Division.

In the spring of 1938 the sporting press in Scotland carried regular references to his impending transfer. On one occasion the manager asked his religion, and the question would only have been put at the behest of another club. Danny is a Roman Catholic and as the matter was not pursued he is convinced the club must have been Rangers. The enquiry which did reach fruition was from Barnsley's Angus Seed. The fee was £5,000 – and full-time football at Oakwell paid double what he had received at Greenock and did away with the need to have an additional source of income.

Seed had mistakenly believed his new signing to be 22 years old. In fact, he was nearly 28 – a worldy-wise man who lived life to the full. John Steel, the sharer of his digs, was almost always in bed by the time Danny returned each night, having taken full advantage of what nocturnal activities were available within the town.

He had a leading role in what became one of his club's most successful seasons. On 5th September 1938 he opened his goal scoring before almost 20,000 spectators in a 2 – 0 defeat of Rotherham United. Another goal came in the following match at New Brighton and a week later he was among the scorers at Barrow when a sixth consecutive victory took the team to the top of the division. Over the festive season he scored on Christmas Day in a 4 – 1 beating of Accrington Stanley and on New Year's Eve he was among the goals in an identical score at Halifax Town. In Oakwell's penultimate game, by which time the championship had long been secured, he got the two goals which defeated Rochdale and the season ended with him being third-top scorer, behind Beau Asquith and John Steele.

When the Football League programme was suspended in September 1939 he returned to Scotland, but six weeks later he answered Angus Seed's summons to present himself in Barnsley on the formation of the regional leagues. The club arranged a job for him on the pit top at Old Carlton Colliery but he quickly formed the opinion that the work was only temporary while his hands hardened, and he would then be sent underground. That was something he was determined to avoid, and in mid-November he returned to his home at Johnstone, near Paisley, to obtain employment in the engineering industry at Linwood. Initially the work was combined with his various football activities, and he continued in it for nearly 40 years until reaching retirement age in 1976.

Throughout the early and middle war years his games for Barnsley were infrequent. During that time he played for St Mirren and was in their team which won the 1943 Scottish Summer Cup.

At the beginning of 1944 Seed insisted he made regular attendances at Oakwell. From then until his transfer in late 1945, despite the great inconvenience inherent in long journeys during war-time, he was rarely out of the side. A Friday departure from Glasgow got him as far as Leeds by 3 am on Saturday; what was left of the night was spent in the city at the Griffin Hotel before continuing the journey to Barnsley. After the game there wasn't a suitable train until 1 am on Sunday – and his shift at the Linwood factory began at 10 o'clock on the same morning!

A match fee in Scotland was £2 – appreciably more than the £1.10s. paid in

England, but Danny was willing to make the long, tiring journey because Seed, keen to have the services of one of his most valued players, was generous in the payment of expenses. On one occasion he received telegraphed instructions to report on the Saturday at Bradford City's ground – an unexpected venue as the Reds were due to play at Oakwell. On the appointed day he arrived at Valley Parade to learn he had been loaned to Bradford City for their match against Leeds United. And further surprise was in store, for when the teams lined up he saw the opposing full back was a club-mate, Bob Shotton. The two travelled together to Barnsley after the game – Bob with six stitches in a chin cut when his and Danny's heads clashed in the Leeds goal-mouth. On arrival Danny immediately sought out Angus Seed and told him in no uncertain terms that while he was prepared to make regular 500-mile return journeys to play for *him*, he certainly didn't intend to do it ever again for the benefit of anyone else!

In the autumn of 1945 he gave the manager notice of an intention to seek a transfer to a Scottish club. He was then 34 and Seed, who wouldn't have expected to have him for much longer and knew the player's awareness of the Scottish scene, asked if he could recommend a winger to replace him. Danny knew exactly who to suggest: it was Johnny Kelly, who had already followed him into the outside left position at Arthurlie and Morton. Seed watched Morton's next game and later told Danny that in the first five minutes he realized he'd chosen a winner for him.

The two players switched clubs, with a cash adjustment in Morton's favour, in December 1945. Danny's second spell at Greenock lasted for two-and-a-half years and he then moved to Stirling Albion for a final season before retiring from the game in 1949.

He has two other sporting interests which began about the same time as his football and which, by their nature, have allowed his participation to continue into old age. They are angling and bowls. Now nearly 80 but as trim as when he sped down the wing at Oakwell, he still casts a fly expertly onto rivers and lochs in the vicinity of Johnstone. But he long since discontinued the regular practise he had as a young footballer of fishing right through the night. He has bowled since schooldays, and an indoor competition in Glasgow in the winter of 1987 brought about a chance meeting with Johnny Kelly. The reunion prompted an invitation to accompany Johnny on a visit to Barnsley which took place in the following April. Then, for the first time in 43 years, Danny was reunited with former team-mates and shared for a few days a house – but not, this time, a bedroom – with John Steele. He also made a sentimental return to Oakwell and watched a game against Birmingham City from a seat in the directors' box.

Danny McGarry was a two-footed player which, for an outside left, was rather exceptional. Indeed, his opening games for the Reds were as an outside right. While with Barnsley he more often than not took corners on both left and right, and his fast inswingers caused maximum disruption in opposing defences. Sometimes he scored directly from them, and one such occasion was in a war-time game at Maine Road, Manchester, against no less a goalkeeper than England's Frank Swift.

He spent 20 seasons in professional football but his career might have ended before reaching the half-way stage. In the last game of Morton's promotion campaign in 1937 he had the misfortune to fracture a leg – an injury which in those days almost always prevented further participation at senior level. Yet he was back in the side soon after the start of the following season and within a year was able to further his career by moving to Barnsley and then into the English Second Division. His ability to operate on either wing and at centre forward was allied to a terrific burst of speed. Consequently, during war-time soccer when he and Gavin Smith were the two wingers, there can be little doubt that the Reds fielded the fastest pair of flank players in the country.

Johnny Logan: The Memory Man's Mistake

In March 1937 Barnsley FC paid £750 to Darlington in order to obtain wing half Johnny Logan. But it was a surprising transaction, for when manager Angus Seed had earlier been in charge at Aldershot he had declined Charlton Athletic's suggestion to have the player for nothing when he was available on a free transfer. Time proved it to be a worthwhile change of mind, for Johnny played more than 300 games before moving to Sheffield Wednesday in 1946.

A Durham man, born at Horden Colliery, he was a miner there and played football for the colliery team prior to joining Charlton as a 21-year-old in 1933. Two years later he was released without having appeared in the first team; he then returned to the North-East and was unemployed for several weeks before being taken on at Darlington. There he quickly won a place in the League side and 18 months later became the first player to be signed for Barnsley by new manager Seed.

At 5′ 6½″, he was short in height but stocky and strong, with enough self-confidence for three men. New players stepping up a grade usually want to make certain assessments before expressing their views – but this one didn't. His debut was on 6th March in a 2 – 1 defeat at Chesterfield and afterwards Beau Asquith declared, 'He's come from *Darlington* but you'd think he's an international from Arsenal, the way he wants to boss everybody about!'

But that was Johnny Logan. His attitude and manner of speech were as forceful and direct as the way he played football. And he rarely smiled – perhaps a legacy from a boyhood in an impoverished area in the 1920s – yet he had an impish sense of humour. There were occasional training days when he would be first out of the bath and turn a hosepipe on the others as they were drying themselves, but no more was seen of that little prank after someone went directly into the dressing room and then walked into the bathroom wearing a suit belonging to the chap who was spraying water over everything that moved!

He held a regular place in the side until his final weeks at Oakwell, experiencing relegation from the Second Division in 1938 and prompt return as record-breaking Northern Section champions in the following year. When the League programme was suspended on the outbreak of war he returned to Horden

Colliery and on the commencement of regional football a few weeks later he threw in his lot with Hartlepools United. But Seed wasn't having that. He travelled to Horden and persuaded Johnny to come back to Barnsley, and he worked as a miner at Wharncliffe Woodmoor Colliery until the end of hostilities.

Six months after resuming at Oakwell he returned to Hartlepool with the Reds in the second leg of a War Cup-tie. The *Barnsley Chronicle* reported that he was always in the thick of things and had no superior on the field, and he even spent 15 minutes in goal deputizing for the injured Cliff Binns. His total of 228 wartime appearances was exceeded only by Gavin Smith and, like the team's other footballing miners, he had occasional games with other clubs in the West Riding.

On the resumption of the full League programme in 1946 he was part of the side's splendid start to the season which took them to the top of Division Two by mid-October. But later in the month he lost his place following a 6 – 1 defeat at Fulham and found himself in the reserves for the first time since joining the club. Then 34, he would doubtless have expected to see out his playing days in Barnsley's second team; consequently, Sheffield Wednesday's approach for him was probably the biggest and most pleasant surprise of his whole career.

He moved to Hillsborough on 27th December with Wednesday precariously placed in the Second Division, only Newport County being below them. With Johnny at right half and 35-year-old Joe Cockroft on the other flank, the Owls must have had the oldest wing halves in the whole Football League. But their pairing was short lived. After only four games Johnny lost his place and didn't again appear in the first team. Yet he remained on the playing staff until he was 40, at which stage he became coach to the 'A' team. He was a hard taskmaster. No matter how well his young charges played, he always let them know that they could do better. Derek Dooley, who but for grievous injury would almost certainly have become one of the most prolific goalscorers the game has known, recalls scoring four times in a 6 – 1 win at Wombwell Main. And Johnny, while walking with him to the changing room, pointed out opportunities he'd had to score another three. The team cause was always uppermost in his mind but he never lost sight of what was in the players' best interests. Dooley once missed a penalty at Scunthorpe, following which Johnny told him, with great emphasis, that he would never again be entrusted with that responsibility. Yet a few weeks later when a penalty was awarded in a match against Sheffield United and Dooley had already scored twice, it was that same man who bawled from the touch-line, 'It's yours Derek, put it in!'

Wednesday's youngsters played many of their games on open, exposed grounds on the edge of the Pennines. Yet, perhaps reflecting his unflinching approach to life in general, to anyone who in the depth of winter was so unwise as to ask for a long sleeved shirt he would give the scathing response, 'You're cold? In my day they painted the stripes on our bare backs as we ran down the tunnel!' A long succession of future First Division players passed through his hands and two of them, Albert Quixall and John Fantham, went on to play for England.

He spent 20 years at Hillsborough, graduating from 'A' team duties to reserve team trainer and finally sharing first team responsibilities with Dave Smith. He was one of the staff on the bench at Wembley for the 1966 FA Cup final – an event which he no doubt placed alongside membership of Barnsley's 1939 championship team as high-points of his career in football. But less than a year later, on 8th February 1967, at the age of 54, he was made redundant. His day began normally at Hillsborough, but early in the afternoon he was called into manager Alan Brown's office to be told his services were no longer required. It was one of the saddest moments of his life. He would have even swept the terraces if he'd been allowed to stay, but that wasn't an option.

As if to lessen the blow, Brown invited him and his wife, Edna, to be guests of the directors at the next home game, against Southampton. Edna was adamant in her refusal but Johnny tried to be positive and hoped the board would use the occasion to provide him with a tangible acknowledgement of his long service. But further disappointment was in store. He was treated to drinks in the board room and viewed the game from the directors' box, and Sheffield Wednesday apparently considered that to be sufficient acknowledgement of 20 years' loyal service.

On leaving the club he obtained employment at the Wilson & Longbottom foundry in Castlereagh Street, Barnsley, remaining there for nine years before taking early retirement. During that time he involved himself in local football, coaching teams at Athersley Social WMC and the Athersley Arms Hotel.

Johnny was a supremely fit man who never had a single day's sickness until the year of his death. Then, in October 1980 at the age of 68, he died in hospital after a short illness. Throughout the preceding 13 years he had been continually rankled by what he saw as a total lack of consideration by Sheffield Wednesday in connection with his departure from the club. So much so that on the morning of his cremation Edna said to her elder daughter, 'If anything comes from Wednesday, send it back!' But unknown to her, flowers tied in blue and white ribbon with a card of condolence were already at the house.

At Oakwell, Johnny was almost always a wing half. Appearances elsewhere in the team were one at inside left in 1944 and a few at centre half in the following year when he also had one game at right full back. However, a national radio programme credited him with a versatility which, even if it was possessed, was never on display. In the 1940s a regular feature of the BBC Light Programme was *Navy Mixture* – a variety show which sometimes included among its acts Leslie Welch the Memory Man, who displayed quite amazing powers of recall by answering impromptu questions on a whole range of sports. One evening in the autumn of 1947 Johnny and Edna were at home at New Lodge listening to *Navy Mixture* when a member of the studio audience asked, 'Which Football League player has appeared in every position for his team?' Welch's answer was, 'Johnny Logan of Barnsley.' Maybe his research covered the local newspapers, for on Johnny's move to Wednesday, both the *Barnsley Chronicle* and *Sheffield Telegraph*, in reporting the transfer, referred to him having played in every position in the Barnsley team. The originators of those reports really should have been better informed. However, if the Memory Man had been asked, 'Name a Football League player who is a fearless 90-minute workhorse; a midfield destroyer who goes hard into every tackle and would run through a brick wall if to do so would be of advantage to his team' ... then the answer, 'Johnny Logan of Barnsley' would have been absolutely correct.

Beaumont Asquith: Skills as Smooth as Silk

The Barnsley club's individual record for highest number of goals in a single game is held jointly by three men – one of whom is Beau Asquith. His share of the record came during the Reds' exceptionally successful season of 1938/39 and at the end of it, and surprisingly as the team had won promotion and needed all the quality available to them, he was transferred to Manchester United. Unfortunately, the outbreak of the Second World War ended his stay in the First Division as soon as it had started. He was remarkably successful as a taker of penalties and scored from the spot on 28 consecutive occasions. His style was to roll the ball just inside the post, and after his one and only failure – at Hartlepool in November 1938 – he continued to roll them unerringly into the net for Barnsley, Manchester United and Bradford City.

He was the sixth and youngest child of a mining family at Painthorpe, near Wakefield. His scholastic abilities allied to a bright and attractive personality made him popular with staff at the village school, and the deputy headmaster, Mr Blackshaw, actually tried to adopt him. Beau's parents would not even discuss the suggestion, but the esteem in which the lad was held at school was unlikely to have been shared by his neighbours: rarely a day passed without there being a broken window in the row of miners' cottages where he lived – and the culprit was usually one of the football-mad Asquith boys. Indeed, Beau and twins Ted and Tommy were regularly out in the street with an inflated pig bladder when the day shift were on their way to work at 5 am.

Had Beau become part of the Blackshaw household his life might have taken a totally different course, for several years later, when he was 11, he won a scholarship to Wakefield Grammar School but the family finances were such that a uniform could not be afforded. He therefore remained at the village school until he was 13 and then obtained work on the pit top at Crigglestone Colliery. Soon afterwards he joined Painthorpe United FC, from where Barnsley obtained him in 1932.

He was then an inside left and won a regular place in the team in February 1937. In the following year, at Easter, his brilliant overhead kick scored the goal at Hillsborough which completed the double over the local rivals, but there were insufficient such results and at the season's end, by the merest disadvantage in goal average, the team were relegated into the Third Division.

The following campaign has to be acknowledged as 'Asquith's Season'. It began with him in his customary inside left position, but he was soon moved to centre forward and in mid-September his goal against Barrow helped the team into top place in the division. Thereafter their progress towards promotion barely faltered. His season's high-point was on 12th November against Crewe Alexandra – who went into a state of panic every time he touched the ball. Not only did he score five times but he had a hand in the others in the 7 – 1 success and equalled the club record for highest number scored in a single game. A few weeks later he was prominent in the feast of football provided for the supporters over the Christmas-New Year period. On Christmas Eve he scored twice in a defeat of Oldham Athletic; two more came on Boxing Day in a beating of Accrington Stanley and on New Year's Eve he ended 1938 in fine style with two in a victory at Halifax Town which provided a seven-point lead at the top of the division. And at Easter he was again in holiday mood with a goal at Stockport which secured promotion with four games still to play.

The championship shield was presented at his benefit match which took place on the Saturday after the season ended, when he scored a hat-trick against Newcastle United. But he was already on the transfer list. Only one Barnsley player – captain Bernard Harper – was in receipt of the maximum wage of £8, and the board's refusal to extend that entitlement to Beau resulted in a request that he be transferred. Manchester United were represented at his fine display against Newcastle and he joined them during the following week for a fee of £6,000.

At that time he was engaged to be married to his cousin Ella, and the impending requirement to live in Manchester enabled him to persuade her to name the day when she would become his wife. The marriage took place towards the end of June, and the couple moved into lodgings within walking distance of Old Trafford.

He won a place in the Manchester United team on 2nd September 1939 – and on the following day the normal League programme was abandoned for almost seven years! He retained a place in the war-time side, and at Easter 1940 the Asquiths visited Ella's parents at Middlestown, near Wakefield. On Good Friday Beau was in Barnsley when he bumped into Oakwell manager Angus Seed who invited him to play in the following day's game against Chesterfield. He did so, helped towards the 3–1 success, and at the end of an enjoyable afternoon among men with whom he had much in common he decided he'd had enough of life in Manchester. After discussing things with Ella, the two returned to the city on the following day, packed their belongings and moved in with her parents at Middlestown. He took employment as a miner at Hartley Bank Colliery and played regularly as a guest at Oakwell, journeying to Old Trafford only on occasions when his club insisted he did so. But it was difficult to enforce attendance on someone who spent six days each week mining coal on the other side of the Pennines. Eventually realizing there was little to be gained from retaining a man who didn't want to play for them, Manchester

United suggested that the situation be formalised by his transfer back to Barnsley, and that took place early in 1942.

By that time he was operating at left half and he retained the position on the resumption of the normal League programme in August 1946. In the following February in the FA Cup at First Division Huddersfield Town he scored the equalizing goal on the stroke of half-time – from which the Reds went on to a spectacular 4 – 3 victory, but that was his last season in the first team.

After the Asquiths' temporary stay at the home of Ella's parents they obtained a six-acre smallholding at Painthorpe and until the end of the war he combined the raising and selling of poultry and produce with work at the colliery and football at Oakwell. When hostilities ended in 1945 he was making a good living from the smallholding and decided to continue with that and retire from football. Yet despite him being 35 years old, chairman George Tomlinson persuaded him not only to continue to play but also to live in Barnsley – and to that end let him have the tenancy, at a nominal rent, of a large Victorian house in Park Road.

During the early summer of 1948 the chairman told Beau that he would like him to have the new post of assistant manager. It was an opportunity he was glad to have, but a few weeks later Tomlinson sought him out in training and said, 'You're going to be on your own now Beau, it looks like I'm not going to be chairman for much longer.' That proved to be the case, and when Beau took up his new duties at the start of the season it was soon apparent that the manager who had been so supportive of him as a player neither wanted nor needed an assistant. He wasn't allowed an involvement in administrative matters or decision making; consequently he assumed responsibility for the third team and was most unhappy about the uncertainty of his position.

However, during the winter trainer Tom Wilson died. This resulted in promotion for the reserve team trainer, Bob Shotton, and Beau being asked to take over his duties. But at the end of the season, to compound the earlier uncertainty, the job he had been doing was advertised. Beau was so upset that he didn't apply, and on the day after the closing date Angus Seed asked him why he hadn't done so. Then brushing the explanation aside, said, 'Never mind about that, I want you to apply now.' Seed had been in management for 20 years, but surely couldn't previously have had a job application thrust into his hand which was written on the inside of a cigarette packet! Nevertheless he took it away with him, but next day seemed to experience some embarrassment when telling Beau he hadn't got the job but the directors wanted to be fair and had granted him a maximum benefit of £750 and a free transfer.

He joined Bradford City and after two years with them he moved to Scarborough for a season in the Midland League, remaining in the professional game until 40 years old. Twelve months earlier he had bought a milk round in the Huddersfield Road area of Barnsley, and in 1951 he moved to a grocery and general store at Kendray, remaining there for more than 20 years until reaching retirement age. He was a man who could speak knowledgeably – and wittyly when the occasion allowed – on almost any subject and there were no lulls in conversation when Beau Asquith was around. It was an aspect of his personality which, particularly as a young man, provided him with a wide circle of friends. When he won a place in the Barnsley team a dozen of them travelled to games in a horse-drawn cart belonging to a Painthorpe farmer – a round trip of 20 miles at tuppence a head. He was also adept at cards and darts and, as teenagers, he and his friends won many a shilling by his exercising those skills in pubs and clubs in the area where they lived.

Away from the football pitch his main interest was greyhound racing, and he kept the dogs all his adult life until his death in 1977. He attended the first meeting at Sheffield's Owlerton Stadium when it opened in January 1932, and over the years a dozen of his animals were kennelled there. He bred and trained them himself and his favourite was Lady Barbara, named after his only child. Of the innumerable dogs he owned, the most eminent was Green Hall, whose successes included the 1976 *Sheffield Telegraph* Cup. He was a regular attender at Waterloo Cup meetings at Altcar, and was such an enthusiast that the homeward journey was usually broken at Manchester for an evening's racing at Belle Vue. In retirement the dogs were his main pastime. Indeed, it might even be said that they precipitated his death. He'd had a heart attack in 1975 and sustained another, from which he didn't recover, in February 1977, within minutes of returning home after exercising them on a cold, blustery morning. Yet he had ignored the earlier warning and wouldn't take things easy, for he had worked hard and played hard all his life – in the war years he worked underground at the pit, cultivated six acres of land and played football for Barnsley, and even had occasional games with Bradford City and Huddersfield Town.

He was a straightforward man who believed in speaking the truth as he saw it, even if feelings were going to be hurt by what he had to say. While with Bradford City he and a team-mate travelled in his car to a game at Hartlepool and found the referee to be Arthur Holland, a Barnsley man who was well known to them. Holland enquired how they had travelled there and then asked if he could return with them after the game. 'Of course you can,' said Beau, 'you could have come with us if I'd know.' However, Bradford City were refused what they felt to be a good claim for a penalty and the home team were allowed a goal which the visitors considered to be blatantly off-side. After the game the conversation was less cordial:

'You're a right referee!'

'Well, the way you played, you deserved to lose.'

'And the way you refereed, you deserve to walk back to Barnsley – you're certainly not coming with *us*!'

And the referee, who later held the centre of the national stage in an FA Cup final at Wembley Stadium, had to make his own way back to Barnsley. The incident exemplified Beau's forthrightness, but also showed Arthur Holland to be a man who did not allow his judgement to be influenced by the offer of a favour.

Beau was very much a team player and could be scathing towards those whose style was individualistic and were, in his view, 'playing for themselves'. Yet he was a generous and considerate man with an outgoing personality which made him a very popular individual. Angus Seed was fond of him from the start. Players were required to live in the town but Beau was allowed to continue living at Painthorpe. And the manager pretended not to notice his lack of punctuality: he usually arrived for training at 10.30am instead of 10 o'clock and Seed turned a blind eye, until, by prior arrangement between the remainder, the day came when everyone turned up at 10.30. Then something had to be done about it and, consequently, Beau began to arrive at the appointed hour – for all of a couple of weeks! Seed even loaned him his car to go to Doncaster Races and would sometimes give him £5 towards the afternoon's enjoyment.

He was a great header of a ball, and when anyone spoke to him about that skill he always said, 'It's because I've got such a big head.' That wasn't noticeably so, yet on a visit to Southport he tried to buy a cap at G A Dunn & Co – the country's leading retail hatters – and his companions had great amusement from there not being one in the shop large enough to fit him. His timing was so perfect he seemed to hang in the air to await the arrival of the ball, and on the day he equalled the club record there was a hat-trick of headers within the five goals. All Beau's skills were as smooth as silk and ideally suited to the quality football historically played by Manchester United – coincidentally, the team against which he made his debut for Barnsley in 1934 – and but for the Second World War he would undoubtedly have had an outstanding career in the First Division.

George Robledo: A Style Before His Time

One of the most popular footballers the Barnsley club has had was born more than 8,000 miles from the town, yet his stylish play and bronzed good looks caused the supporters to take him to their hearts in a manner they have done with few others. He was George Robledo – a man who figured prominently in Barnsley teams of the mid and late 1940s before going on to receive wide acclaim in the First Division and on the international scene in South America.

On his debut for Barnsley in war-time regional football he scored in a 3 – 1 defeat of Sheffield Wednesday, and on the day League football resumed in 1946 he did the hat-trick against Nottingham Forest. His six goals in the first four games of that season helped the Reds into top place in the Second Division, which was held until mid-October, and 40 years elapsed before another Barnsley team was in that position. In 1948 he won representative honours and in the following year his transfer to Newcastle United dismayed the Oakwell supporters but brought a record fee to the club. He was a member of Newcastle's FA Cup-winning teams of 1951 and 1952, and on returning to his native Chile he played for his country on 30 occasions.

George was born of an English mother and Chilean father in the Pacific coast town of Iquique and was five years old when the family came to England in 1931 to live at West Melton. As a pupil at Brampton Ellis School he scored 120 goals in four seasons and played in the Dearne Valley Boys team.

At 14 he won a scholarship to Barnsley Technical College for a two-year course in general subjects. That completed, he worked underground at Wath Main Colliery and studied civil engineering at night school, little realizing the work experience and schooling would later be put to good use in a post-football career on the other side of the world.

While at the Technical College he signed amateur forms for Barnsley, later having a year as a Huddersfield Town amateur before returning to Oakwell to become a professional soon after his 17th birthday. He'd actually had an outing in the first team at 15, giving an early indication of good things to come by scoring twice against an Army XI in a match in aid of Mrs Churchill's Aid to Russia Fund.

He was top scorer in each season from 1944 until his departure five years later and in 1948 he represented the FA against the RAF. Making the most of the opportunity, he scored four goals and created such good impressions that the selectors felt obliged to state that, despite his obvious merits, the fact that he had been born outside the British Commonwealth prevented him being selected for the English team.

On 22nd January 1949 he scored in a 4 – 0 win over Queen's Park Rangers in what was his last game for the Reds, and in the following week a transfer fee of £26,500 took him to Newcastle United. It was not a club he would have chosen; his preference was either Spurs or Sheffield Wednesday whom he knew had enquired about him but he was told the only offer was from Newcastle United – yet he later learned of a long standing arrangement between them and manager Angus Seed that they would have first refusal when Barnsley decided to let him go.

His seasons in the North-East were full of excitement and success. He became one of very few men to play in winning teams in consecutive FA Cup finals – in 1951 Blackpool were beaten 2 – 0 and in the following year he scored the winning goal in a victory over Arsenal. In 1952 his 33 League goals was the highest total in the First Division and that is the only occasion a non-Briton has been the division's leading scorer. The Cup competition increased his season's tally to 39 and the Wembley success of the previous year had already provided him with the distinction of being the first foreign-born player to have been in an FA Cup-winning team.

In 1953 he returned to Chile to pursue his career with the Colo-Colo club in the capital, Santiago. He joined them because they made an offer he simply couldn't refuse. Had he moved elsewhere in the English First Division he would have had a signing-on fee of £10 and a wage of £14 per week. Colo-Colo more than doubled his weekly income and he received a signing-on fee of £4,000.

George's years in the First Division in Chile were equally as successful as they had been in England, for in six seasons Colo-Colo were twice champions and three times runners-up and he was the division's leading scorer in 1953 and 1954. In 1959 he moved within the First Division to the O'Higgins club in the city of Rancagua, remaining there for two years until retiring from the game at the age of 35.

In Chile he represented his country on 30 occasions and he was a member of the team who were runners-up in the South American championship in 1955. His first international game was, in fact, while he was with Newcastle United in 1950. It was in the finals of the World Cup in Brazil, and during the competition he became the first Football League player to play against an official England team. Again on the World Cup scene, when the competition was held in Chile in 1962 he was on the organizing committee and combined that responsibility with duties of attaché to the visiting English team. The latter role required him to liaise with manager Walter Winterbottom and be on hand to solve problems and generally smooth the progress of the England party.

When his playing career ended he served as a director of the Colo-Colo and O'Higgins clubs, and for 22 years he worked in the copper mining industry. He was employed by the Braden Copper Company, owners of the largest copper mine in the world, and he worked in public relations and as manager of a mining camp. He remained in the industry until 1983 and was then appointed to the position of head of sport at St Peter's School – a British school in Viña del Mar.

The Robledos are a close family and were deeply saddened in 1970 by the unexplained disappearance of brother Ted. He and George had been footballers together at Oakwell and it was at George's insistence that Newcastle United included Ted in the 1949 transfer. That was not the club's original intention for he was only a reserve team player, but no doubt they were satisfied with what had been forced upon them when he won a place in their 1952 Wembley side. The brothers moved together to Colo-Colo and when Ted's playing career ended he was employed in the oil industry. After working for an American company in the Middle East he was en route for England where he planned to live near Lowestoft in a house bought for their mother by the youngest brother, Walter. He was last seen boarding an oil tanker in the port of Dubai. Interpol was involved in the subsequent enquiry and the ship's captain was arrested and later released, and Walter made two expensive trips with a London solicitor to Dubai but no trace of Ted was ever found.

As a young man George was a member of Staincross Tennis Club where he had a successful doubles partnership with his Oakwell team-mate, Norman Rimmington. He was also a very good table tennis player and his doubles partnership with colleague John Steele was famous throughout the district and virtually unbeatable in local leagues. He had a lot of involvement with the Barnsley community: he was one of the founders of Brampton Ellis Youth Club; frequently he opened galas and fetes in the area, gave talks at clubs and associations, and was vice president of Darton Ladies FC. Within his chosen career he had qualified as an FA coach by the time he was 21. On behalf of the Association he conducted coaching sessions at schools in the Barnsley area and he continued the work in Newcastle until returning to Chile.

George's wife, Gladys, worked at the United States Embassy in Santiago when he first met her. She was later secretary to the comptroller of his employers, the Braden Copper Company, and now manages a travel agency in the capital. Their only daughter, Elizabeth, is a PE graduate of the Catholic University in Valparaiso. Following the family's sporting traditions, she was a national junior swimming champion at 100 and 200 metres and now teaches PE in Australia.

Viña del Mar has a Mediterranean-like climate and is Chile's main tourist resort. The seventh-floor apartment in which George lived is on the sea front overlooking the Pacific Ocean, and the city's beautiful beaches, palm trees and playing fountains provide quite breathtaking views and contribute towards a life-style which verges on the luxurious.

Sadly, for George that ended in the spring of 1989. He'd been distressed by the recent deaths of former Newcastle team-mates Jackie Milburn and Joe Harvey, and he hadn't felt well for several weeks. However, two separate medical examinations had found nothing amiss but on 1st April he suffered a heart attack and died in hospital later that same day.

Except on rare occasions, George Robledo's seasons with Barnsley were as a centre forward but he had such all-round ability that during a career spanning almost 20 years, either by selection or in emergency, he played in every position except centre half. Indeed, at Old Trafford in Newcastle United's first away game of the 1951 season he scored the first goal and then replaced the injured 'keeper. He was beaten twice and his team lost 2 – 1, yet during the following week he received a letter from a Manchester United supporter who asked for a signed photograph and said George was the best goalkeeper he had ever seen! Be that as it may, he was certainly a fitness fanatic and had the powerful, loose limbed style which through the medium of television is now readily associated with footballers from the South American continent, but in England 40 years ago was quite unique. The career-heights he attained compare with the best ever to emanate from Oakwell and were well deserved, for right from the start he was determined to make the grade and drove himself to the limit. Daily he would return to the ground for extra training and the coaches spent hours crossing the ball for him to practice hitting it first time from whatever angle it arrived – on the turn and half turn, headers, overhead and scissors kicks – and from such application he became a great goal scorer. His development continued in the First Division to the extent that at his peak, at the age of 27 when he returned to Chile, he was the most effective centre forward in the country, and had he entered this world in Barnsley instead of Iquique he would almost certainly have become and English international player.

Jack Harston: A Lifetime's Enjoyment

Jack Harston's best footballing seasons were during the Second World War when he was a regular choice at full back for Barnsley between 1941 and 1945. And just as the war made big inroads into what could have been a successful League career, it was his involvement in football which perhaps prevented him from playing cricket at county level.

He was born in a cottage at Park House Farm on the Doncaster Road at Kendray – the farm and its buildings eventually making way for the development of Kendray Estate in the late 1920s. As a pupil at Ardsley Oaks School he represented Barnsley Boys at football and cricket for two years from 1933, captaining each of the sides in his final school year.

At 14 he started work at Darfield Main Colliery in the screens – the dirtiest job at the pit – sorting waste from the mined coal as it passed on a conveyer belt. After a month he was moved to the lamp room but, although the job itself was more preferable, the requirement to work on Saturday afternoons, cleaning and servicing lamps used on the day shift, meant there was no opportunity to play football. It was, therefore, a stroke of good fortune which put him on the path which led to 15 years in the professional game.

In the spring of 1936 Ardsley Athletic used an ineligible player in a local Cup-tie, a consequence of which was that the game had to be played again. And as the club was short of personnel and Jack's dad was on the committee ... The second game was won, and as it was an evening-time competition he remained in the side and played in the final at Oakwell. There a Wolves' scout spotted his potential – even though he'd played only half-a-dozen times in the preceding 18 months.

In school football he had been an inside forward, and for Ardsley Athletic he'd played on the right wing. In the trial at Wolverhampton he was at wing half; he got among the scorers and was offered a job on the ground staff. That he declined, but the club was sufficiently impressed to wait a further 12 months and sign him as a full-time professional in October 1937 when he reached 17. Then his weekly wage of £3 equated to the earnings of a miner at Darfield Main and was twice the amount he'd earned in the lamp room.

At Wolverhampton he began in the 'A' team and after a spell on loan at Dudley Town he won a place in the reserves at Easter 1938. Unfortunately, an injury sustained over the holiday put him out of the side for the remainder of the season – a consequence of which was that he was not retained.

Barnsley manager Angus Seed, who'd been annoyed by Wolves taking Jack from under his nose in the first place, promptly offered him full-time terms at Oakwell. Again he began in the 'A' team, but within a few weeks he was in the reserves and remained there for the rest of the season. The following campaign was barely a fortnight old when the declaration of war threw organized football into the melting pot for several weeks until it resumed on a regional basis. Jack returned to the mining industry, working again in a lamp room but this time at Monk Bretton Colliery. Two years later he was transferred to Mitchell's Main where he qualified as an electrician, remaining there until 1950.

The regional leagues began in October 1939 and during the first two seasons Jack played only occasionally in the first team but won a regular place in 1941. Between then and the end of hostilities he totalled 118 appearances and had frequent games as a guest of Leeds United and Bradford City. Indeed, Bradford City tried to obtain his services on a permanent basis, but at that time Angus Seed wouldn't hear of it.

Nearly 50 years on it is difficult for younger generations to envisage the difficulties which war-time conditions placed upon those on the Home Front who wished to continue with their former activities. So far as the footballing miners were concerned, missing a Saturday morning shift was the equivalent of losing half of the afternoon's football pay. Few were prepared to do that, yet when Barnsley had a game in the North-East the journey began at 9am. Therefore, whenever a visit to Sunderland or Newcastle was due, Jack would put in the required hours by working the day shift *and* the night shift on Friday, finish work at 6am on Saturday and be at Oakwell for the 9 o'clock departure. On one occasion he made that arrangement in order to play for Leeds United at Newcastle. And when the players returned to Leeds at 10pm he had to wait on the railway station for the next train to Barnsley – which was the milk train, due at 4.30am!

With the normal League programme about to resume in 1946 he had to decide whether to again become a full-time professional or continue his work at the colliery and be a part-time player. In the event he decided on the security of regular employment and part-time football and, thereafter, his appearances were rather spasmodic. One was in April 1948 against Southampton, whose goalkeeper, Ian Black, had been selected for the Scottish international side against England on the following Saturday. Yet he was powerless to stop Jack's winning goal for the Reds – a first-time volley from a few yards inside the Southampton half with the ball still rising when it hit the net – which was acclaimed as the most spectacular seen at Oakwell for as long as anyone could recall.

By then he had been at the club for 10 years and his time with it was drawing to an end, and in the summer of 1949 he was transferred to Bradford City – five years after their original approach. Twelve months later he moved into the Midland League to spend two seasons with Scarborough and Denaby United before retiring from football in 1952.

Cricketwise, all his time in the game was with Mitchell's Main. His first season was in the second XI, and after a 'duck' in his first game he went on to top the batting averages with scores which included two 77s and a 50 – pretty good for a 14-year-old in a men's league. In the spring of 1937 his club nominated him to attend county trials at Barnsley's Shaw Lane ground where youngsters from throughout the area were put through their paces under the watchful eyes of the Yorkshire coach, the legendary George Hirst. Of the 25 who attended, Jack was the only one chosen to receive coaching at the county nets at Headingley. Therefore it was most unfortunate that the appointment in Leeds clashed with pre-season training at Wolverhampton and he consequently lost a golden opportunity to display his abilities at Yorkshire's cricket headquarters.

After the initial season in the second XI and apart from war-time when he didn't play the game, he was a member of Mitchell's Yorkshire Council side. As a forceful number 4 batsman he played the kind of cricket he himself likes to watch, and until he retired in 1957 the player who headed the club's batting averages each year was usually either Jack Harston or his former Barnsley teammate, Roy Cooling.

Jack's other sporting interests are horse and dog racing which he followed for many years with his friend and one-time Oakwell colleague Beau Asquith. An indication of their closeness was that when Beau was being conveyed to hospital after suffering a heart attack from which he died, and despite the great pain he was in, he insisted that the ambulance stopped en route at Jack's home so his pal would be aware of what had happened to him. The two had pursued their interest at tracks and courses throughout the country and shared ownership of several greyhounds. When betting shops appeared on the scene in the 1960s they went into partnership as bookmakers in premises at Yews Lane, Kendray. They retained the business for four years but disposed of it because of the restrictions it placed on their attendance at meetings – they were prepared to forego the profits which the race provided for the pleasure of actually being there. Jack still visits most of the racecourses in Yorkshire, and when he feels like indulging himself he attends meetings at Newmarket and Ascot.

On leaving full-time football in 1950 he bought a newsagent-general dealer's shop in Doncaster Road, Barnsley. He kept it for 27 years before going into business as a newspaper delivery agent on a round which he had acquired some time earlier at Farm Road Estate. The work is very demanding and every day begins at 5am. Newspapers delivered to his home are divided into bags for seven separate areas; six are taken to homes of delivery boys and the seventh is delivered by himself. That takes him to 8am – then he checks that the other bags have been dealt with and, if not, he has to do that himself. On Fridays, collecting payments prolongs the working day to 7pm and further collections have to be made after deliveries on Saturday and Sunday mornings. It is therefore not surprising that on Saturday afternoons when he is at Shaw Lane to watch the cricket he can sometimes be found dozing in his deck chair.

Jack admits he lacked that extra yard of pace which is a big part of the difference between a top-flight footballer and the average professional player.

Nevertheless he was a valued member of the Oakwell staff. In the post-war years Angus Seed never wanted him as a regular in the first team – he liked to be able to fall back on him for a variety of positions whenever the need arose, in the sure knowledge that wherever he was used he would always give of his best. Indeed, the manager's appreciation was reflected in him being the highest paid part-timer at the club.

Sport in its various forms has been Jack Harston's life. And although he never quite reached the top in either football or cricket he reckons his involvement in the two games, continually giving everything he'd got, together with a love of sporting dogs and a continuing interest in horse racing, has given him the most wonderful life imaginable.

Steve Griffiths: and the Bouncing FA Cup!

It was primarily to act as coach to the reserve side that Steve Griffiths joined the Oakwell playing staff in 1947, but he quickly won a place in the first team to become part of the best post-war forward lines the club has had. He was born and bred at Stairfoot, yet, surprisingly, had been with four other League clubs before joining Barnsley and that didn't happen until he was 34 years old. Earlier he had played in a Cup final at Wembley Stadium, and in the summer of 1939 he'd had the traumatic experience of seeing the priceless FA Cup fall from his grasp and bounce down hotel steps onto a pavement in Bognor Regis.

A pupil at Ardsley Oaks School, he played football for Barnsley and Yorkshire Boys and was chosen for the England team – only for the selection to be cancelled when it was discovered he was two months past the qualifying age. On leaving school he worked as a glass blower at Tomlinson's Glassworks at Stairfoot and junior football was with Ardsley Athletic, Barnsley Main and Thurnscoe Victoria. He was always an inside forward and while with the Vics in 1934 he had a trial in Chesterfield's reserve side. He travelled to the game straight from a night shift at Tomlinson's – and on the following night the Griffiths household in Grange Lane were roused from their slumbers by the Chesterfield manager knocking on the door at midnight to obtain the signature of 19-year-old Steve.

He became a full-time professional at a weekly wage of £2 which was later doubled on condition he lived in Chesterfield. After two years there he joined Halifax Town, and in early August 1939 Everton played a friendly game at Halifax for the sole purpose of assessing Steve with a view to obtaining his transfer. But they didn't act quickly enough, for only a few days later Portsmouth – fresh from their Cup success at Wembley in May – secured him in exchange for a fee of £750. There was then a delay in him presenting himself at his new club because Halifax refused to pay the portion of the benefit entitlement which had accrued during the previous two years. When Portsmouth enquired why their new player hadn't arrived for training his father told them he wouldn't be there until Halifax paid the amount to which he was entitled. As a First Division club and FA Cup holders, Pompey had some authority in the game and the end result of Steve's stance was that on the following day he received from Halifax Town a cheque for £300.

The outbreak of the Second World War brought about the suspension of the normal League programme after only three games of the new season. Steve joined the Royal Navy and, based at Portsmouth, was available for his club until late in 1942. In the spring of that year he scored three times in a 5 – 2 beating of Brentford, and when the teams met at Wembley a fortnight later in the final of the London Cup he was in a confident frame of mind. However, Brentford had learned the earlier lesson only too well. The ace marksman was marked completely out of the game and, in front of 92,000 spectators, the favourites lost 2 – 0. Portsmouth had five men from the Barnsley area, including the Reds' former player Bert Barlow and George Bullock of the 1939 promotion team who was killed in 1943 while serving in HM Forces. The defeat was one of the most sickening experiences of Steve's life. He had had the thrill of playing in the most famous stadium in the world but all his hopes had been completely dashed. The members of the losing side were each awarded five 15-shilling National Savings Certificates which, in his utter disappointment, he gave away.

In August 1942 he joined the crew of HMS Adamant at Mombassa, Kenya. While there he played for the English Combined Services team which won an eight-nations international football competition. Later a high ranking officer of a Welsh regiment elicited from him that his grandfather was a Welshman. He then played for the Combined Services' Welsh team which he captained until late in 1944 when Adamant left Mombassa to operate from Trincomalee, Ceylon and, later, from Freemantle in Australia.

He was demobilized in 1946 and, then 32, was released by Portsmouth and joined Aldershot. Starting in the best possible way, he scored a hat-trick in his first game and was an ever-present in what was to be his final season on the South Coast.

Barnsley obtained him in July 1947. He was brought to the club in order that his wide experience could be used to the benefit of youngsters in the reserves, but towards the end of the year there were some disappointing results from the first team. Steve was drafted into the side and quickly made his presence felt – scoring in a 2 – 0 success at West Bromwich Albion and in a victory over Sheffield Wednesday. At Easter a packed Oakwell saw him score the winning goal against Newcastle United, and on the following Saturday he scored in a 2 – 1 win over Southampton.

In four weeks in September 1949 he scored five goals in victories over Coventry City, Queen's Park Rangers and Swansea Town – and scored two in a game drawn with Sheffield United. Early in the New Year he did the hat-trick in a 7 – 2 thrashing of Grimsby Town and in the next game he had a leading role in the return at Queen's Park Rangers. Then the inter-play between himself and right half Danny Blanchflower was a feature of the game and near the end, with the Reds leading 4 – 0, he felt a need to rest his ageing legs. He therefore went onto the left wing, but the ball was immediately passed to him and he took it 20 yards before crossing for Alex Wright to score a splendid fifth goal.

Despite his personal successes in what was a very good Barnsley side, the proudest moment of his long career came not on the field of play but in the privacy of the Oakwell dressing room shortly before a game against Sheffield Wednesday on 17th January 1948 – a day when skipper Gordon Pallister was absent through injury. The players were about to go on the pitch when trainer Tom Wilson threw the ball to him and said, 'Steve's captain today, and when you get out there the rest of you are going to do *exactly* as he says.' To a 34-year-old having his first season at a level higher than the Third Division it was an expression of confidence which he treasures to this day. And things couldn't have worked out better for him, for in front of more than 33,000 spectators the stand-in captain was among the scorers in a tremendous 3 – 1 victory.

Angus Seed was so impressed by Steve's aptitude for coaching that he promised him a job on the staff when his playing career came to an end. It was therefore unfortunate that he contributed towards his departure from the club. Early in 1951 he was so unwise as to openly support Danny Blanchflower in the latter's criticism of aspects of the training programme; the two were transferred within a few weeks of each other – Blanchflower moving into the First Division with Aston Villa while Steve went to the somewhat less fashionable York City.

He captained the side and in 1953 their fourth place in Division Three (North) was the highest in the club's 25-year League history. The manager left at the season's end and Steve applied for the vacant post. In view of the success the team had had under his on-the-field direction he held high hopes of getting it, but the chairman told him the board felt they couldn't appoint him as he was too young and inexperienced. Yet he had been a professional footballer for 20 years and was 39 years old! His reply was quite explicit so far as what the chairman could do with the job. He was so embittered about the manner of his rejection that he retired from the game, and in so doing declined offers of employment which ranged from player-manager in the Midland League to assistant to George Rayner, manager of the Swedish national side.

The following 11 years were spent in the licensed trade, first at the Royal Oak at Wombwell and then at the Junction Hotel in Barnsley. He was an ideal licensee – outgoing, sociable, and able to converse knowledgeably on a whole range of sports. But the job became too restrictive on family life and he disliked having to take holidays apart from his wife and children. Therefore, in 1964 he took employment with Ideal Homes as a site clerk and in 1970 he became a timekeeper at Dearne Valley Colliery, remaining there until reaching retirement age nine years later.

He has been a golfer since teenage and at Ardsley Golf Club in 1938 he won the President's Cup and the other three annual trophies. At his peak he played to a handicap of 6 and over the years he's won competitions at Silkstone, Tankersley and The Limes – and at the latter course his prize of a putter was presented by the former British Open champion, Bobby Locke. In 1939 he reached the final of a *News of the World* national competition. It was held a week after his delayed arrival at Portsmouth and when he asked for the day off in order to take part, the manager's refusal was quite scathing. 'Not likely, son, you should have been here a fortnight ago, you've had enough days off already!'

He also has an almost life-long involvement in the game of bowls. He began with Ardsley Athletic and the woods he has used since the early 1960s are one hundred years old and belonged to the club's former county player, Tom Hilton. During the season he plays almost every day and in his home at Wombwell there are almost as many trophies for bowling as from his expertise at golf.

On joining Portsmouth in 1939 he was chosen for their bowls team which was about to play in a competition at Bognor Regis, and in view of the club's recent success at Wembley the organizers had asked that the FA Cup be put on display. During the competition the team stayed at a hotel on the sea front and on arriving there Steve and Bert Barlow were detailed to carry the Cup inside. It was contained in a large glass display case but they hadn't noticed the front wasn't properly fastened . . . and as they reached the top of the hotel steps the treasured trophy fell from its case and bounced all the way down to the pavement! The damage which it sustained cost £200 to repair and now, whenever he sees the televised presentation of that same Cup, it never fails to bring back memories of the fierce verbal lashing which he and a pal received from an irate football manager more than 50 years ago.

Unlike his Oakwell team-mate Jimmy Baxter who could beat a man on a sixpence and pass in one complete movement, Steve Griffiths had to make space for himself before passing or receiving the ball. It was a skill acquired at Portsmouth, and he mastered it very quickly after his slow response to a situation put his captain, Scottish international Jimmy Guthrie, in difficulties in a game at Fratton Park. Guthrie promptly grasped him by the throat and snarled, 'If you're not where you should be next time I want you I'll bloody strangle you!' Steve made sure he was never again in that embarrassing situation and developed a sense of positional play which had much to do with him continuing in senior soccer until his fortieth year. His style dovetailed perfectly with the classy skills of Danny Blanchflower and his passes were a winger's delight, enabling Gavin Smith to use his lightning speed to maximum effect. An inside forward's role was the most demanding in the team, yet he made it look easy and seemed to almost stroll through every game. And despite the modest levels at which most of his long career was spent, while at Oakwell he was good enough to have played for any team in the land.

Danny Blanchflower: An Independent, Forward Thinker

Danny Blanchflower's first appearances for Barnsley enabled a variety of people, both inside and outside the club, to show their better than average awareness of a footballer's potential.

As a 19-year-old, Danny was a professional with Glentoran in December 1945 while serving in the Royal Air Force, spending the second half of that season as a guest of Swindon Town. Following on were three years in the Glentoran side and in February 1947 he won his first representative honour by playing for the Irish League. Yet throughout that time not a single English club showed any interest in him until April 1949, when Angus Seed paid £6,000 to bring him to Oakwell.

His first game for the club was in the reserves at Leeds United. Long before it was over, player-coach Steve Griffiths had decided Danny was one of the most talented wing halves he'd ever seen and almost certainly the best to play for Barnsley. He said as much to the manager on the following Monday, urging that the player be given a place in the first team.

That occurred two days later, on 27th April, in a County Cup semi-final against Rotherham United – at the end of which Danny received a standing ovation from the supporters. The *Barnsley Chronicle* match report verged on the ecstatic, saying Seed must have gone home a happy man after seeing his new capture produce the finest half back display seen at the ground that season. It went on to praise Danny's all-round skills and prophesied, with unerring accuracy, an international future for him. Indeed, his career became international in the fullest sense. Not only did he play for his country on 56 occasions and captain the side in World Cup Finals, he also represented Great Britain against the Rest of Europe.

Danny – christened Robert Dennis – was born in Belfast on 10th February 1926. He attributes much of his career success to encouragement from his mother, Selina, an inside forward in a ladies' football team, and many of his skills stemmed from learning to control a tennis ball on cobbled streets in the vicinity of his home.

One of his younger brothers, Jackie, was also a Northern Ireland international. Sadly, his career came to an abrupt end in 1958 when he was severely injured in the Munich Airport disaster.

At 16 Danny became an amateur with Glentoran but he was insufficiently robust for their reserve side. Consequently he drifted away to play for other teams more suited to his abilities at the time.

In 1944 he entered the RAF as a trainee navigator. While in the service he won a scholarship to St Andrew's University where he studied mathematics, physics and applied kinematics. A year later he was in Canada learning Navigation when the war in the Far East ended, thus bringing about the termination of his training and a return to the UK. At Christmas he was persuaded to sign for Glentoran, and on his release from the service in April 1946 he returned to Belfast to resume an apprenticeship to an electrical trade and his part-time professionalism in football.

He started the new season in the reserves. Until then he'd been an inside right, but after a couple of games he was switched to right half. By the middle of September he was in the first team and within six months he was chosen to represent the Irish League against the Football League. That was the first time he'd played against top class forwards and he found the changing positional magic of Mannion, Hagan and Lawton quite bewildering. Yet the experience opened his mind to new thoughts on the game and led him to the beginnings of an understanding of how football should really be played.

In the aftermath of the representative game he knew he had to get to England to benefit from full-time training and competing against players of the calibre of those who had opposed the Irish. The only trouble was, no-one seemed to want him. Maybe local newspapers had got it right with their occasional quotes from English managers to the effect that Danny could play well enough but he didn't seem sufficiently strong to be able to adapt to English football. Over the following two seasons Danny didn't miss a game, but there was no approach for his services until a day in April 1949 when he was summoned to the Grand Hotel, Belfast, to be introduced to Angus Seed.

Despite playing so well against Rotherham United in the County Cup semi-final, he was unable to play at West Bromwich on the following Saturday because he'd been signed after the transfer-deadline day and the hosts were pushing for promotion. However, a week later, on the last Saturday of the season, he made his debut in the Second Division against Chesterfield.

At the start of the 1949/50 season he was first-choice right half and within two months he won his first international cap, against Scotland at Belfast. Yet it was a debut to forget, for the Irish were humiliated by an 8 – 2 scoreline. Danny was one of several who were omitted for the next game, but he was back in the side before the end of the season and retained a place throughout the following 10 years.

Danny's first full season at Oakwell had been a good one for him. He had established himself in the Barnsley team, he'd taken on the challenge of the Second Division and played twice for his country. However, 18 months later, in November 1950, the independent streak in his nature which was to come to the fore periodically during his career manifested itself.

The team had started the season well enough but a bad spell in November prompted Seed to order special training in the afternoons. Yet when the players reported at the ground they were not required to train. All Seed wanted was to keep them away from the cafes and billiard halls in the town. Some were keen cue-men and spent many an afternoon in a hall off Regent Street. As a result, when things were going badly for the team, Seed would get letters from irate fans complaining that the players spent too much time on the snooker tables. Consequently, when things weren't going well the players were required to spend afternoons at the ground. However, Seed believed extra training would leave the players short of energy on Saturdays. So, ironically, away from the prying eyes of the letter writers . . . they played snooker!

But, not being much of a snooker player, Danny thought he could use his time more profitably, practising with a football. Seed didn't like the idea. 'You'll take too much out of yourself,' he said. Danny persisted. 'Let me try it and see, and if I do I'll be the first to want to stop.' Nevertheless, Seed still refused but over the following fortnight Danny kept at him. Eventually, with obvious reluctance, he gave in. For the following few weeks, after completing the requisite number of laps of the pitch, Danny was allowed to practice with a football. But the privilege soon ended. In January the team lost a Cup-tie to a Third Division side. Extra training was ordered; the players gravitated towards the snooker room but Seed put his foot down when Danny mentioned his own preference.

'I don't believe in it. If you don't see the ball during the week you'll be more keen to get it on Saturdays.'

Danny was amazed.

'But if I don't get some practice I won't know what to do with it when I get it on Saturdays. I want time to practice with a ball.'

'I'm the manager here and you'll do as you're told.'

'That seems most unreasonable to me. I want to improve my game and surely that should be considered?'

'The trouble with you is that you think this club is not good enough for you.'

Amazement turned to annoyance:

'You're right. If you deny ball practice it's not good enough for anyone. I'll have a transfer to a club where I *can* practice!'

The outcome was that on 15th March 1951, for a fee of £15,000, Danny was transferred to Aston Villa. Yet something had preyed on his mind during the journey to Birmingham. While with the Villa chairman and manager, and before putting his signature to the contract, he said, 'There's something I want to clear up before I sign for you.' The officials recoiled: later, Danny realized that they thought he was about to ask for an under-the-counter payment. 'I want your word that I can train with a ball as much as I like when I have finished whatever other training you expect of me.' The two men seemed unable to believe their ears. Then the manager grinned. 'Sure, son, you can have the ball as much as you like.'

Danny's introduction to the First Division was against Burnley, with his new team at the foot of the table. His joining them on St Patrick's day must have been a good omen; they won 3 – 2 and at the season's end were well clear of relegation. He remained with Villa until December 1954, eventually asking to be transferred because there seemed to be no ambition within the club. He hoped to join Arsenal but, in the event, a higher bid was received from Tottenham Hotspur.

After three months with Spurs he was appointed captain – a role which, in the following year, caused a significant hiccup in what were 10 enjoyable years at the club. In March 1956 Spurs lost an FA Cup semi-final at Villa Park. With 10 minutes still to go and the team trailing 1– 0, Danny made a positional change which put an extra player into the attack. It didn't have the desired effect, and in the dressing room he was reprimanded by the manager who took exception to what he'd done A few weeks later, in an identical situation against Huddersfield Town, he again put an extra player into attack. Further recriminations followed, a consequence of which was that Danny gave up the captaincy because he wasn't allowed to exercise authority on the pitch.

He was reappointed captain in March 1959 by new manager Bill Nicholson. Soon afterwards Dave Mackay joined the club and with Nicholson in charge, Mackay stopping the opposition and Danny directing the team's play, Spurs went from strength to strength. In the next season they finished third in the First Division. A year later they reached the pinnacle of English football by winning the League championship and FA Cup. And they did it in style, finishing eight points ahead of the runners-up in the League and winning by two clear goals in the Cup final.

Under Danny's captaincy Spurs had become the first this century to win both League and Cup. Deservedly, and for the second time, he was voted the Football Writers Association's Footballer of the Year. He stayed with the club for a further three years, retaining a first team place until his retirement from the game in 1964 at the age of 38.

Soon after arriving in London he had begun writing Saturday evening pieces for the *Evening News*. Later, while still with Spurs and with their permission, he had a weekly column in the *Sunday Express*. As could have been expected, his thoughts were not always in line with those of the game's administrators. Consequently the Football League requested Spurs to forbid further writings; the club sought Danny's co-operation but he simply referred to their earlier permission and refused to be gagged.

On retiring from football he extended his press involvements by way of match reports and assignments in North America and the Middle East. During that time he spent three years in charge of the Northern Ireland side and nine months as caretaker manager of Chelsea.

He also became an accomplished broadcaster, his natural charm and conversation skills ideally suiting the role. Yet his employment by the BBC was perhaps surprising in the light of a previous encounter with them. In February 1961 it was intended that he be a victim of *This is Your Life*. The presenter, Eamon Andrews, collected him from White Hart Lane and accompanied him to Broadcasting House, ostensibly to take part in *Grandstand*. However, on their arrival, Andrews, as was his practise, produced a microphone and a large red book and said, 'Danny Blanchflower, this is your life.' Danny promptly turned on his heel, saying, 'Not for you it isn't,' and walked out of the building. It was the first time in the programme's five-year existence that anyone had reacted in that way, but Danny's view was that his life was his own affair and not for general publication. Newspaper reports of the incident prompted letters from 85 people – 83 of whom congratulated him on the stand he'd taken against what they regarded as an intrusive and embarrassing programme.

After that, it said as much for Danny's personality as for his high standing in football that the BBC wanted to employ him. But, as his brother Jackie was prone to say, 'Our Danny didn't just kiss the Blarney Stone – he swallowed the bloody thing!' He went on to have long spells as presenter of *Sportsnight* and *Junior Sportsview*, and for Yorkshire Television he hosted *Midweek Sports Special.*

Danny retired from journalism and broadcasting several years ago. His involvements are now with Spellthorne FC – a South Thames League side at Staines where he lives – and playing golf at the prestigious Wentworth course, often with well known people from Show Business. He plays off a handicap of 14 which has been down to 10 and he learned the rudiments of the game from Steve Griffiths, the man whose initial assessment of his footballing abilities proved totally correct.

Danny Blanchflower was purely an attacking wing half. He was an imaginative player who popped up all over the pitch, even on the left wing, but he couldn't tackle and wouldn't defend. Indeed, Angus Seed once said that he'd hate to be a full back playing behind him. Yet his positioning was so good that when the ball was cleared from defence it seemed always to go to him. His class was apparent right from the outset and his thinking on how the game should be played was years ahead of views then held at Barnsley. He was always destined for a bigger stage than Oakwell and the club's supporters were fortunate in having two seasons of Robert Dennis Blanchflower before he went on to grace major stadia throughout the world.

Cecil McCormack: The Classiest of Them All

Cecil McCormack's stay at Oakwell was of fairly short duration and ended in 1951. However, he created such good impressions among the supporters that, nearly 40 years on, he is spoken about with pleasure and admiration whenever men's conversation touches on the best players the club has had.

He was a centre forward of consummate skill and created the club's post-war scoring record in his one and only completed Oakwell season. Not the typical big, robust number 9 of his time, he was slight of build and less than average height – and his goals came from a combination of skill, anticipation and quicksilver finishing. Indeed, his ball control was quite superb and he would beat defenders with a deft feint or a body swerve performed with lightning precision, and then put the ball into the net in masterly fashion.

A North-Easterner, he was born above a newsagent's shop in Scottswood Road, Newcastle-upon-Tyne and won schoolboy honours with the city's boys' football team. He joined Gateshead as a 16-year-old in 1938 and became a professional in the following year, playing his first game in the reserves in 1941. It took place at Sunderland and he scored a hat-trick. That put him into the first team and he was top scorer in each of the following four seasons until joining the Royal Air Force in 1945.

Over the following two years he played for the RAF representative side and as a guest of Newcastle United, Aldershot and Manchester City. Stationed in the south of England, opportunities to play for his own club were infrequent but on one occasion he travelled 300 miles to a game at Bradford City. The train's late arrival left him 10 minutes in which to reach the ground and perhaps instructions to the taxi driver were not sufficiently specific for, to his dismay, he was taken not to Valley Parade but to the other ground at Park Avenue. By the time he got to where the game was being played it had been in progress for 10 minutes; Gateshead had travelled without a reserve which allowed him to make a belated entry onto the pitch and score the winning goal in true *Boy's Own* fashion.

In April 1947, soon after demobilization from the RAF, he was transferred to Middlesbrough. With them he made 37 appearances in the First Division and, on average, scored in almost every other game in which he played – but his wife, Connie, whom he had met while stationed in the South, could not settle on Wearside. He therefore asked to be transferred to a club in London or the Home Counties, but after a few weeks he was told the only offers had been from Blackburn Rovers and Burnley. Consequently he took matters into his own hands and joined Chelmsford City. And as they were outside the jurisdiction of the Football League he was able to move there without either the approval or agreement of Middlesbrough. But it was eventually disadvantageous to Barnsley, who had tried unsuccessfully to obtain him in 1948. On his move to Chelmsford, Middlesbrough had retained his registration with the League, and both they and Chelmsford required a transfer fee when he joined Barnsley. That occurred in July 1950. The move into Essex had fulfilled a temporary need and paid him handsomely, for his weekly wage of £30 was more than double the maximum available within the Football League. But he soon missed the big crowds in front of which he enjoyed playing and was glad of an opportunity to return to mainstream football.

His debut was at Oakwell on 19th August when the Reds lost 2 – 1 to Southampton. The afternoon provided no indication of the splendid season he was about to have, but he scored twice in each of the remaining three games of the opening month and it was soon apparent that the new centre forward was a very special player.

The high-point of his career came in September when Luton Town visited Oakwell. They were no pushovers and centre half Sid Owen became an English international, but Cecil completely demoralised him and scored five times in the Reds' 6 – 1 victory. The *Barnsley Chronicle* said the match would go down in history as McCormack's Great Day, describing him as 'Five-goal Mac, the Will o' the Wisp who bewildered, baffled and bemused Luton Town.' His third goal, in the 55th minute, was quite spectacular. It followed a 50-yard dash by Jimmy Baxter, Cecil fastening onto the latter's perfect through pass and outwitting Owen and another defender before shooting at a difficult angle past the advancing 'keeper.

Midway through the season he made a sentimental return to Ayresome Park, Middlesbrough, where Barnsley played a friendly game. He ran onto the pitch to generous applause from the spectators who quickly saw why he was top scorer in the Second Division. Time after time he baffled the home defence with delightful body swerves and bursts of speed, and he scored Barnsley's goal in typically slick style.

At the season's end his 33 League goals created a club record which stands to this day and were scored in only 37 appearances, and his total in first team games was a quite remarkable 46.

His departure was a frustrating experience for the supporters. It took place in November 1951 – a mere six months after being the highest goal scorer in the top two divisions of the League. He had already netted 10 times in the 13 games of the new season and the venue of his last goals was perhaps significant in so far as where the approach for his services originated. Within a matter of days of scoring twice at Nottingham Forest on 17th November an offer of

£20,000 was received from Notts County. Historically the instances of Barnsley Football Club refusing good money for players are few and far between – and this was not to be one of them. In fairness, it must be said that the transfer fee was the highest the club had ever received and the player was certainly not averse to the move. Nevertheless, the supporters were stunned and bitterly disappointed at the unexpected departure of a man who had endeared himself to them in such an exciting and positive manner.

Notts County's centre forward was Tommy Lawton, one of the most famous leaders the game has known, who was moved to inside left to accommodate Cecil. Almost exactly on the first anniversary of his departure he returned to Oakwell and his finishing was of the same clinical effectiveness which the crowd had previously cheered so loudly. He was kept in a tight grip by centre half Matt McNeil and escaped only twice – in the third minute when he beat his marker with a delightful body-swerve before putting a scorching left-foot drive past Harry Hough, and in the second half when he slipped the ball to a team-mate who scored to give the visitors their first win at Oakwell for 30 years. He remained with Notts County until the summer of 1956 and then had a season in the Midland League with King's Lynn, at the end of which he emigrated with his family to Canada.

He had signed a contract to play for a Toronto team, Wide Eagles, who lost no time in using him. He arrived in the city on a Sunday morning in September 1957, having travelled directly from England, and played in the afternoon in a temperature of 95 degrees. He remained with the Wide Eagles until he was 40, and four years earlier, he'd played for a Canadian All-Star team against Mexico. The Mexicans were touring North America in preparation for the 1958 World Cup competition and in all their games conceded only one goal ... which was scored by Cecil McCormack.

As a young man he served an apprenticeship in the engineering industry with Vickers Armstrong at Newcastle-upon-Tyne. On arriving in Toronto he resumed in the trade and worked as a fitter for De Havilland and the city council until reaching retirement age.

Cecil was widowed in 1984 and now lives alone in an apartment in the Toronto suburb of Scarborough which the family occupied when they first arrived in the city. They suffered a grievous loss in the death of the eldest son, Brian, when only 16 years old, but the five surviving children keep a constant and watchful eye on dad. His eldest grandson is six-year-old Bryan. The boy is showing an aptitude for football and is lucky to have such an expert as his grandfather to teach him the finer points of the game. But his first lesson, when he was three, might well have been his last. The ball accidentally struck him in the face, causing a little blood and a lot of tears and earning a severe rebuke for grandfather from an irate daughter-parent!

He learned to play golf at The Limes course in Barnsley and still enjoys the game. The legs which carried him so gracefully through opposing defences are now reacting to the sometimes savage treatment they received, and walking the length of the course is something they now prefer not to do. Consequently he uses a cart, and despite his handicap being a modest 18 he can claim with some pride to have once holed-in-one.

Cecil McCormack was a natural goal scorer – his reflexes were immediate and he needed only half a chance to tuck the ball almost nonchalantly into the net. John Steele, Oakwell's long-serving coach, manager, secretary and director has cast an expert eye over every Barnsley centre forward of the last 50 years and is in no doubt that Cecil was the classiest of them all. His team-mates reckoned his pre-match attitude was a good indicator to the kind of game he was going to have; certainly he must have been bubbling on 9th September 1950 when Luton Town were at the receiving end of a display of speed, craft and devastating shooting which can rarely have been surpassed in our national game. It was an historic occasion in Oakwell's long history and will surely remain for ever in the memories of the fortunate 21,964 spectators who were present to see it.

Pat Kelly: Excellent at Everything!

Pat Kelly had Irish ancestry but was born in South Africa and, as a young man, had exceptional athletic skills. His father supervised a physical education school and Pat's involvement in it from childhood helped towards him becoming an outstanding gymnast and well above average at all games. He won cups for swimming and diving, and he played rugby, cricket, hockey, golf and tennis. In fact, it was while on his way to tennis that he was persuaded to have his first game of soccer; as goalkeeper he acquitted himself so ably that he retained a place in the side and within three months won representative honours with the province of Natal.

Indeed, he was one of a multi-talented family. His father was an accomplished artist, his mother was a gold medalist in the National Eisteddfod of South Africa, and younger brother Sean is well known on the Johannesburg stage and appeared in films in the 1950s with Richard Burton, Curt Jurgens and Anita Ekberg.

It was while Pat was playing for Natal that Aberdeen FC saw his potential during their tour of South Africa in 1937. He signed professional forms and returned with them to the UK. The party travelled in the liner Stirling Castle, and while it was in Madeira he accepted a wager from two of his new colleagues to dive from the top deck into the harbour. The stake was five pounds, and after he'd plunged into the water the others reneged – no doubt fearful of the consequences if management discovered their part in what was, to say the least, a reckless escapade.

His debut in the Aberdeen side was during the 1938/39 season and in wartime football he played for St Mirren, Dumbarton, Hamilton Academicals and Arsenal. As a boy more than 5,000 miles from north London, Arsenal had been his favourite team and photographs of their players adorned his bedroom wall. Therefore the short spell at Highbury was nothing less than a dream come true.

The meeting with Edith, the Aberdeen girl who became his wife, stemmed from a blind date and foursome arranged by club-mate Herbie Currah. And as Herbie was one who refused to pay up after the death-defying dive into the harbour at Madeira, it proved Pat had a generous and forgiving nature. He and 17-year-old Edith were married on 30th September 1939, by which time he was serving in the Royal Air Force, having volunteered and been accepted into the service two days after the declaration of war. Thereafter, throughout the following five-and-a-half years, Edith travelled the length and breadth of the land in order to be with her husband.

At Oakwell the 1946/47 season began in tremendous fashion. By the first week in October the team had a three-point lead at the top of the Second Division, but two consecutive defeats in which nine goals were conceded spurred the manager into obtaining a new goalkeeper. He chose Pat, and the Kellys, with one-year-old Tim, moved to a club house in Prince Arthur Street where next-door neighbours were the Steele and Griffiths families. But the man from Aberdeen didn't halt the sequence of disappointing results. The team were defeated in each of the five games following his introduction, during which time he and others lost their places. He was out until May when he returned for the season's final month, and he then held the goalkeeper's position for the next four years.

His gymnastic expertise was always in evidence and the crowd loved it – even forgiving the occasional errors which occur whenever prudence is overtaken by showmanship. Nevertheless, some of his displays – including a 3 – 1 success against Leicester City when he made a splendid save from future England manager Don Revie's penalty-kick – compare with the best Oakwell has ever seen.

On 1st October 1949 he played for Northern Ireland against Scotland, but an event he had looked forward to as a high-point in his career turned into an absolute nightmare. He picked the ball out of the net eight times, but the *Daily Mirror* said he shouldn't blame himself for the defeat because Scotland were so superior that they would have won even if the Irish had had *two* goalkeepers!

Pat was inconsolable, and several months elapsed before he fully recovered from the trauma of that heartbreaking afternoon. But recover he did. In the following September he was cheered to the echo time and again during the Reds' thrilling draw at Leeds United. And a few weeks later, in the final minutes of a draw with Manchester City, he crowned a magnificent display by hurling himself through the air to beat away a succession of fierce drives. Reporting the game in the *Sheffield Telegraph*, W J Heald said if Pat ever gave a better display he'd give a lot to see it . . . yet he saw it in the very next game. Then, in his report on a 2 – 1 success at Leicester City, Heald waxed lyrical on Pat's acrobatic leaps, swallow dives and spectacular saves, and said his display was not only magnificent but truly amazing!

In February 1952 he was transferred to Crewe Alexandra and held a first team place until the end of the following season when he retired from the game at the age of 35.

Pat was a man who needed to be continually occupied, and on demobilization in 1945 he had combined football with work for the Aberdeen Electricity Company. In Barnsley he put his RAF training as a radio operator to good use by opening a radio and television repair shop in Peel Street, and on moving to Crewe he augmented his football income by working as a Council electrician. When he retired from football the family returned to Aberdeen where he was employed as a radio and television engineer, and in November 1958 they emigrated to Australia.

After staying temporarily with sponsors in Sydney they moved within New South Wales to Murwillumbah on the Gold Coast, where Pat obtained employment as foreman technician with one of the largest television retailers in the country. Soon afterwards he formed his own repair company and retained it throughout his remaining years in Australia.

The need to be totally occupied was as great as it had been in Britain and, over the next 10 years, spare time was almost entirely devoted to building two homes for his family. Both were at Murwillumbah – the first on Pacific Highway and the other on the inland side of town overlooking the Tweed River. He was so versatile that every aspect of the work was carried out by himself and Edith – and he had a full-time job as well. Through all the years it took to bring the houses to completion they would rise each day before dawn and work until it was time to earn his living. In the evenings their tasks continued under floodlights until the early hours. They felt the results were worth all their efforts: the second home was even more splendid than the first, being a ranch-style house with swimming pool and more than an acre of land in completely unspoilt countryside. Whilst the work was in progress the only respite they allowed themselves was to spend Sunday afternoons at the nearby Cabarita beach. Even that time wasn't completely their own, for on three Sundays out of four Pat had a voluntary duty as surf life-guard.

At the end of 1978 he and Edith disposed of home and business and returned to Aberdeen, while Tim and his family remained in Australia. In 1983 they moved to Rochdale to be near Edith's sister, but two years later Pat became seriously ill. The problem was a damaged blood vessel at the base of the skull and medical opinion was that it was of such long standing that it was almost certainly an old football injury. Treatment entailed several periods of hospitalization and he died on 7th September 1985.

It had been Pat's wish that his ashes be scattered on the sea off Cabarita. Consequently, in the following year Edith travelled to Australia and at sunrise on 26th November, Tim and his son, Matthew, in an aeroplane piloted by a friend, flew low over Cabarita Bay and Tim complied with his father's wish while Edith watched from a headland. Adding to the poignancy of the occasion, the date was the 48th anniversary of Pat and Edith first meeting.

Pat Kelly's remarkable abilities were not confined to games and athletics, for he could turn his hand to almost any practical task with a degree of expertise normally associated with those who make a living in that particular line of work. As if that wasn't enough excellence for any man to possess, he was also a perfect physical specimen – and although it is not uncommon for athletes to be able to walk on their hands, he could *run* on his! During his stay with Arsenal in 1942 their manager, George Allison, was quoted in the London press as saying he was good enough to play for any team in the world, and one has to come forward 40 years and move up a division to world-class Liverpool and a young Bruce Grobbelaar – coincidentally, a South African, to find another Football League goalkeeper with the same individual, spectacular style as Barnsley's Pat Kelly.

Gordon Pallister: Hero to the Stars

Gordon Pallister has had a direct and continuing involvement in Oakwell affairs throughout most of the last 50 years – first as player and captain, then as a member of the board of directors. He joined the club in 1938 to become part of one of the best teams the club has had in modern times – that which won promotion into the Second Division in 1939 – and 10 years later he captained the side which is generally accepted as Oakwell's finest, containing some of the greatest players ever to don the red shirt of Barnsley.

A Durham boy, he played school football at county level before joining Willington Juniors, a club near Bishop Auckland. He was one of six team-mates who joined professional clubs and in the summer of 1935 he had trials with Bradford City. Then an inside left, he scored for the reserves against the first team – whose goalkeeper was George Swindin, later to be again an opponent in an infamous FA Cup-tie at Highbury in 1952.

He became a professional with the club later in the year, and just couldn't believe the terms he was offered. He was a 17-year-old footballer – and his wage of £3.10s was what his father received at the end of an arduous six-day working week! His first team debut was on New Year's Day 1937 as a left full back, in which position he was to play for the remainder of his career, and he won a regular place in the side at the start of the following season.

As an ambitious young man he was encouraged by newspaper reports that his stylish play would soon attract offers from the leading clubs in the game. He was, therefore, initially unimpressed by manager Angus Seed's suggestion that he be transferred to Barnsley. However, the manager was able to persuade him that he would be joining a club destined for early promotion, and that proved to be the case.

Yet opportunity to play at the higher level was abruptly curtailed. His initiation to the Second Division was against Coventry City on 2nd September 1939 – the day preceding the beginning of the Second World War – and the normal Football League programme was then abandoned for the following seven years.

Almost immediately he joined the Royal Air Force, served as a PT instructor and attained the rank of Flight Sergeant. During the following four seasons he rarely appeared at Oakwell, playing instead for Carlisle United and, occasionally, for Darlington and Nottingham Forest. From August 1943 he became more available for Barnsley, playing 101 games prior to the termination of the war-time leagues in 1946.

The 1945/46 season saw a resumption of the FA Cup competition. At the early stages there were two legs, the first leg of the third round at Newcastle attracting 60,384 spectators. Trailing 2 – 1, Barnsley were awarded a penalty and captain Joe Wilson who, like Gordon, was a North-Easterner, was expected to take it. Tension was at its height and a hush had descended on the ground when the captain said to the left back, 'Go on, stick it in.' Gordon promptly did so, but the game ended 4 – 2 in the home side's favour.

Newcastle seemed to think they only had to turn up at Oakwell in order to get into the next round. But the Reds tore into them from the start and, despite Gordon having another opportunity to score from the penalty-spot which brought the only groan of the afternoon from the near-30,000 crowd, their 3 – 0 success provided a victorious 5 – 4 aggregate and one of the best Cup-ties Oakwell has ever seen.

In the following round a superb display of attacking football beat Rotherham United 3 – 0. But in the second leg at Millmoor Gordon was injured after only four minutes and spent the remainder of the game hobbling in great pain on the right wing. Playing against virtually 10 men, the home side continually pounded the Reds' defence to establish a 2 – 0 lead and there seemed every likelihood of them scoring again to equalize the aggregate score. However, two minutes from time with almost every player in the Barnsley half, the ball was booted out of defence to the unmarked Gordon, who limped towards the Rotherham goal and beat the 'keeper with a carefully placed shot to put the result beyond doubt.

In October 1950, at the age of 33, he was chosen to play for the Football League against the Irish League. He heard of his selection on a BBC news bulletin and no-one was more surprised than he. Yet he was then playing better than at any time previously and had every intention of continuing for a further five years. But that was not to be, for early in 1952 he sustained a slipped disc which brought his career to an end in the following summer.

He had always hoped to enter club management and, in the systematic way which is typical of his approach to all things, had prepared himself well for the task. To his skills as a PT instructor he had added qualifications in physiotherapy and coaching, but in 1953 his attempt to become manager of the club he had served for almost 15 years was unsuccessful. He was one of the four applicants whom the board interviewed but, in the event, the job went to Tim Ward. Soon afterwards he was in line for appointment at Bradford City, but his suspect back disqualified him when their directors began to favour a player-manager appointment.

He decided against seeking posts further afield because in 1949 he and his wife Jean, with an eye to the future, had purchased the old-established Billy Wright's Temperance Bar in Regent Street South. Its draught sarsaparilla was as renowned in the town as the beer brewed at premises adjacent to the local football ground and, under the name of the new owners, the premises continued as a focal point for the town's young people and were open 12 hours a day and seven days a week. The Pallisters had the business for 10 years, then purchased a half share in a local company, Beckett Brothers, manufacturers and distributors of mineral waters. Later they became principal shareholders and retained the business for 14 years, considering the subsequent sale to Clover Dairies to be apt reward for many years of joint endeavour. It enabled them to retire in their mid-fifties and provides financial independence for the remainder of their lives.

Gordon was elected to the board at Oakwell in August 1954. Although it was not uncommon for former pros to become directors, it was exceptional for it to happen so quickly after a man had ceased to play and while the team still consisted mainly of his former playing colleagues. He served continuously until 1984, and then became a life vice-president.

He was a club cricketer from schooldays in Durham and, although a naturally left-footed footballer, he was a right-handed cricketer – a forceful middle-order batsman and a fast bowler – and joined Barnsley Cricket Club on demobilization from the RAF. He had two seasons with the club, and three young members who were to become internationally known in different fields – Dickie Bird, Geoff Boycott and Michael Parkinson – were among the dozen or so youngsters who heaped hero-worship on the handsome, hefty six-footer who was one of their favourites at Oakwell and who was prepared to spend all evening bowling to them at the Shaw Lane nets. From there he moved into Sunday League cricket and spent the following 18 seasons with Stainborough CC.

His other sporting interest is golf, and he has now been at Silkstone Golf Club longer than any of the other playing members. During 40 years there he has won almost every trophy within the club – some more than once – and has holed-in-one on four occasions.

Gordon Pallister was a good 'reader' of the game, and when he launched those long legs into a sliding tackle they were clinical in their effectiveness. On joining Barnsley in 1938 there was little doubt he was destined for much higher things – if not with this club, then with another. The fact that the Second World War compelled him to spend his best years with the Reds was very much to their advantage; he totalled 322 games for them and had that extra touch of class which would win him a place at full back in Oakwell's best-ever team.

Jimmy Baxter: 'But He's All Heart, Mr Chairman!'

Jimmy Baxter features prominently in Barnsley's early post-war soccer history, yet his beginnings were anything but auspicious. His debut as a small, frail-looking 19-year-old, within days of joining the club from Dunfermline, was on the left side of defence against Preston North End who had the great Tom Finney at outside right. He was already experiencing the misery of homesickness and, after the 5 – 1 drubbing, decided that if Finney's skills were an example of what he would have to cope with in England he wouldn't make the grade, and he promptly returned home. Six weeks later the manager escorted him back to Oakwell and he went on to play 269 games for the club. Coincidentally, he later had seven seasons as a First Division team-mate of Tom Finney and partnered him in attack when Preston were runners-up in the League championship and Wembley finalists in the 1954 FA Cup competition.

He is a native of Dunfermline and joined the town's Scottish League club as a 16-year-old amateur in 1942. A year later he became a professional and played regularly in the first team in the war-time league at wing half behind the Scottish international duo, Jimmy Logie and Billy Liddell. He also played as a guest of Dundee and the club wanted to sign him, yet hesitated at the asking price of £3,000. Manager Angus Seed paid that amount in August 1945 to complete Dunfermline's most valuable transfer and the player went straight into the team for the opening game of the season against Preston North End at Oakwell.

After his unauthorized and hasty return to Scotland, Jimmy sent a series of telegrams to Seed describing injuries which he pretended to have sustained at work. And by using assumed names he played for different teams each weekend – a subterfuge which was possible within the regular movement of players in war-time – but all was revealed when the same referee was in charge of successive games in which he played. The outcome was that the manager travelled to the Baxter home and brought him back to Barnsley, and while Jimmy settled in the town Seed accommodated him for three months at his own home – the White Hart Hotel in Peel Square. The settling-in process was helped by resuming his previous employment in the mining industry and he worked at Wharncliffe Woodmoor Colliery until 1946.

Initially he was at left half before moving to inside left to partner Johnny Kelly. Principally that was brought about because Kelly was such an individualist that others weren't all that keen on partnering him. Several had been tried in the position but when it was Jimmy's turn the two of them were immediately compatible and their pairing became one of the most fruitful and enjoyable events in post-war Barnsley football.

In his opening season he had a major part in what is undoubtedly one of the finest games Oakwell has ever seen. The FA Cup's third round brought Newcastle United to the town with a 4 – 2 advantage from the first leg, but Barnsley played brilliantly to establish a 2 – 0 lead and the near-30,000 crowd went almost delirious with delight when Jimmy scored the third and winning goal.

In 1947 he scored a vital goal in the FA Cup at Huddersfield Town. The Reds' trainer, Tom Wilson, had previously been the Huddersfield trainer and, in a tactical talk before the game, told the players that their goalkeeper, Bob Hesford, had a tendency to stand on the 18-yard line when his team were attacking the other goal. The trainer emphasized that if the ball could be got out of defence quickly the receiving forward should look for an opportunity to 'lob' the 'keeper. It worked exactly as Wilson had anticipated. In the 68th minute, with the score 3 – 3, Jimmy received the ball well outside the Huddersfield penalty-area and, as Hesford desperately tried to regain his line, he flighted it beautifully over him for a dramatic winning goal.

In July 1952 he was transferred to Preston North End for a fee of £16,000. The club had wanted him in the previous year and he had refused the move, but 12 months later most of those with whom he had shared the good post-war years had departed Oakwell, so he decided the time was right.

Angus Seed took him to Deepdale to complete the formalities with the Preston chairman, Nick Buck, who couldn't come to terms with Jimmy's small stature. Several times the player was asked to stand for the chairman to look him up and down and he kept repeating, 'This bloke's not very big, is he?' Seed's response was to tap his own chest and say, 'But he's all heart, Mr Chairman, and he'll play all day for you!' Buck was so uncertain about proceeding with the transfer that, in Jimmy's presence, he held several telephone conversations in which he discussed the player's build with other directors before eventually producing the appropriate forms for signature.

The early impressions of Tom Finney were confirmed and enhanced during the following seven seasons. He wasn't only the best winger Jimmy ever saw but also the best centre forward, and the fact that he was a Preston player brought invitations to the club to undertake summer tours throughout the world. Jimmy played several times in the Rand Stadium in Johannesburg and he particularly enjoyed games against Johannesburg Select XIs. They attracted attendances of 50,000 and the segregated Africans were loud and boisterous in their support of the visitors. Some travelled hundreds of miles to see them and at the final whistle the players had what could be the frightening experience of seeing hordes of black men swarming across the pitch towards them – then found themselves being carried shoulder-high amid scenes of great joy to the dressing room. Hundreds would wait outside for the team to reappear, then run alongside the coach, still cheering, until it was well outside the city.

In 1958, in a game against Manchester City, he sustained a torn leg muscle. There were no substitutes in those days and the injury was aggravated by him continuing on the pitch, and then by returning to the side too soon. Despite the best possible treatment he didn't fully recover, and 12 months later Preston were happy to transfer him back to Barnsley.

Manager Tim Ward was aware of the injured leg, but perhaps didn't realize just how bad it was. Jimmy was appointed captain, but was insufficiently fit to play every week and was released at the end of the season. But he loved football too much to give in easily, and over the next four years he had short spells with Morecambe in the Lancashire Combination and Wombwell in the Yorkshire League before finally retiring from the game.

On returning to Barnsley in 1959 he bought a newsagency in Sackville Street and had that for three years until the seven-day involvement and exceptionally early starts decided him to find other means of livelihood. He became an agent for the United Friendly Insurance Company and remained with them for four years and, from 1967, he was employed by Shaw Carpets Ltd at Darton as a printing machine operator until taking early retirement in 1989.

Jimmy's career was undoubtedly handicapped by his lack of height and weight – he was 5′ 7″ and nine and a half stones – and, for that reason, Angus Seed had had distinct reservations about acquiring him in the first place. When he arrived at Oakwell his new colleagues expressed surprise among themselves that the manager had signed 'that poor little Scots kid' and were appalled when they learned he was intended for the first team. But their views changed immediately they saw him with a football. He oozed class and skill, and absence of bulk was compensated by an abundance of spirit and courage. An example of this was seen in the first post-war season at Millwall when he beat their centre forward, Jim Jinks – a 6′ 2″ mountain of a man – with a delightful display of skill and was promptly hooked to the ground. In a flash he was on his feet and glaring up at the giant and, to the great amusement of nearby team-mates, shouted angrily into his face, 'That attitude will get you nowhere, *Sir*!'

The happy association with Preston North End and Tom Finney was renewed briefly in November 1988 when Tom was the subject of *This is Your Life*. Recalling days from more than 30 years ago when Jimmy would begin training with the others but always managed to be in the bath, smoking, when they finished, the programme reproduced that scene at Deepdale. The viewing millions saw the delight of Tom and former team-mates as the camera focused on Jimmy, chubbier but with the same lop-sided grin, nonchalantly puffing away in the bath exactly as he had done almost daily throughout seven seasons in the 1950s.

As a boy in Dunfermline he spent countless hours passing a ball against a wall of the shop at the end of the terrace in which he lived – and the shopkeeper demanded from his mother an almost equal number of shillings in payment for bottles which had been shaken from shelves by the constant pounding at the other side of the wall. But it was a small price to pay for skills which developed from a boyhood pastime. His use of the ball was sheer artistry. Colleagues always received it at exactly the right moment and, whenever they wanted to find him, he was always in space – a true indication of a quality player. It was surprising his move into the First Division was so long in coming, but the reason can only be that already mentioned. Similarly, had fortune been kinder, he would have been an automatic choice for the Scottish national side for many years. Nevertheless, in the context of football at Oakwell, Jimmy Baxter stands ten feet tall. The perfection of his distribution when, time after time, with a pass of almost mathematical precision he would give a winger what seemed like acres of space on the flank or send the centre forward on a clear-cut path to goal has not been seen at the ground since his departure in 1952, and his name will remain for all time on the roll of the club's greatest players.

Tommy Taylor: The Greatest

Tommy Taylor's best footballing years were spent in the First Division with Manchester United and as a member of the English international side – levels at which those who saw his earlier displays with Barnsley were in no doubt he would attain. In five years at Old Trafford he won two League championship medals, played in an FA Cup final and European competitions and represented England on 19 occasions. He was well established in the international side and his 14 goals included two hat-tricks. Yet at 26 years of age, with much still to achieve in both life and his chosen career, he was one of eight team-mates who died as a result of a disaster on a slush-covered runway at Munich Airport on 6th February 1958 – one of the saddest days British sport has ever known.

Tommy was born in Barnsley at number 4 Quarry Street, Smithies, on 29th January 1932. He attended Raley Secondary Modern School and, surprisingly for one who was to make such impact on the professional game, as a schoolboy footballer he was somewhat lacking in enthusiasm. In his last school year he played for Raley and Barnsley Boys but was reluctant to participate outside school hours. As soon as lessons ended he wanted to be off home with his pals from Smithies, and after twice arriving without boots on days when he had been selected for inter-school matches he was never again chosen for either the school or town teams.

The disinterest continued after leaving school. He obtained work on the pit top at Wharncliffe Woodmoor Colliery and two years elapsed before he again had any football involvement. Then he began to have occasional games with Smithies United – a team based at the Woodman Inn where his aunt, Esther Raynor, was licensee. Very quickly he came to the notice of a Barnsley scout and he accepted a job on the Oakwell ground staff. And for a 16-year-old destined to become the best centre forward in England, Smithies United were paid . . . three pounds!

He was then a rather skinny lad and, despite non-stop activity on training ground and playing pitch, was still on the puny side when called for National Service. But two years in the Royal Artillery changed that. He entered the army a boy and left it a man – having put on a couple of stones, grown two inches in height and gained immense strength. In-between-times he served mainly in

North Wales and played football for Northern Command and his regimental side in Division One of the Welsh League.

It was while in the army that he was introduced into the Barnsley first team. His debut was in October 1950 at inside right alongside the quicksilver Cecil McCormack who did the hat-trick against Grimsby Town. As if to show he'd noted exactly how it should be done, in Tommy's next game he too scored a hat-trick – in a 7 – 0 victory over Queen's Park Rangers.

Her Majesty's requirements limited him to 16 appearances in two years but he became a full-time professional in May 1952 on completion of National Service.

He was at centre forward at the opening of the following season – and representatives of the country's leading clubs were present at every game in which he played. He opened his scoring in early September in a 3 – 1 win over Swansea Town and got two more in a 5 – 1 drubbing of Hull City. In January he had a leading role against Brighton in what was perhaps the greatest FA Cup fight-back that Oakwell has ever seen; after half-an-hour the Reds trailed 3 – 0 but a remarkable second-half resurgence saw Tommy score twice – including the winner three minutes before the final whistle.

By then the club was receiving regular offers for his transfer. To this day Cecil McCormack suffers pangs of remorse from telling him, a year before the eventual departure, that Manchester United was the team he should try to join. Yet others were urging him to stay. Among them were the coaches – men concerned more with performance and results than politics and finance – but the chairman sent for them and said he knew what they were doing and they had better alter their attitude because there was dire need of the big fee to be had from the player's transfer. To those inside the club Tommy's own view was well known. He loved everything about the place: to the coaches he was a willing listener and eager learner – he'd have slept there if they'd let him and often had to be *sent* home, hours after training had finished. And he wanted to stay where he was. But constant newspaper speculation made him concerned about what his future was to be and he sought out the chairman immediately after what proved to be his last game at Oakwell – a 1 – 1 draw with Lincoln City on 14th February 1953. Together they walked slowly along the corridor beneath the main stand, to stop outside the room where the afternoon's gate receipts were being counted. Tommy, with head down and obviously upset said, 'I don't want to go, Mister Richards.' The chairman, brusque and to the point, replied, 'You've got to go Tommy, and that's the end of it.' And Tommy went, on 4th March, for a club record fee of £29,999.

It had been Manchester United's intention to pay £30,000 but their manager, Matt Busby, did not wish to burden the player with a price-tag of that magnitude so he gave the odd pound to Lily Wilby who had served tea in the board room during the transfer discussions. Well intended though Busby's action was, in the event it attracted more publicity onto Tommy than if the fee had been what the club had originally decided to pay. The cheque was the biggest that Manchester United had handed over but the transaction proved to be one of the best they ever made.

The 21-year-old's unworldliness was apparent when he reported at the world-famous Old Trafford ground carrying his boots in a brown paper bag. Yet, footballwise, he was an instant success. His debut was three days after his arrival and his splendidly headed goal opened the scoring in a 5 – 2 victory over Preston North End. And his impact on the First Division was such that within 10 weeks he became an English international. His years with the club included scoring in the 1957 FA Cup final when his team lost by the merest margin to Aston Villa after a sixth-minute injury to goalkeeper Ray Wood who was later to become an Oakwell player, and League championships in 1956 and 1957. In the first of those years it was his winning goal against Blackpool on 7th April which secured the title, and a week earlier in a victory at Huddersfield Town he scored with a tremendous header from *outside* the penalty-area!

In 1957 the European Cup holders, Real Madrid, offered £70,000 for him. His club rejected it out of hand but, had the deal gone through, Tommy would have received a signing-on fee of £20,000 at a time when the maximum wage in the First Division was £15 per week.

The winning of the League championships provided entry into the European Cup in 1957 and 1958 and, ironically, it was the domestic success which eventually brought about the ill-fated visit to Munich Airport.

Exactly a year earlier, in February 1957, Manchester United played Atletico Bilbao in the European Cup quarter-finals. They trailed by two goals from the first leg in Spain and the second game was played at Maine Road before 65,000 enthralled spectators. On a night packed with thrills and excitement Tommy scored the second of his side's three goals and they achieved a memorable 6 – 5 aggregate victory. The much-travelled George Follows of the *Daily Herald* reported that it was the greatest football match he had ever seen, cheered by the greatest crowd he had ever heard, and starred the greatest centre forward he had ever seen – and he reckoned that Tommy Taylor had proved himself to be the greatest centre forward in the world. A year later, almost to the day, Follows himself was to die in the crash which destroyed one of the best club sides football has ever known.

The tragedy followed closely upon a 3 – 3 draw with Red Star Belgrade which put Manchester United into the semi-finals for the second consecutive year. Belgrade newspapers were rather scathing about what they saw as overly vigorous play by the visitors, but one of them, *Politika*, made specific reference to Tommy in the terms: 'He knows what he wants and is as adroit and dangerous as a devil.'

It was the last game that superb team were to play. On the homeward journey on 6th February at 3.03pm local time the BEA Elizabethan 609 ZU carrying the Manchester United party and accompanying press representatives made a third and fatal attempt to take off from Munich Airport. It appears the 'plane barely left the ground. It careered off the runway and crashed through the perimeter fence and into a house, and wreckage was strewn over a wide area.

Many heroic deeds at the scene included action by some of the team but, in the final analysis, eight players, three members of the staff, eight journalists, two crew members and two other passengers died either at the scene or later in hospital. Tommy Taylor was one who perished in the aeroplane.

His remains were interred at Monk Bretton Cemetery ten days later. As the cortege passed the Burton Road Junior School which he had attended the pupils were lining the pavement and the football team wore their playing kit. Hundreds of people were at the Parish Church to pay their respects. The coffin was borne by friends from schooldays; representatives of Manchester United were in attendance and players and staff from Oakwell formed a guard of honour at the church.

Much as Tommy was mourned by his many friends inside and outside football, as always it was the family who suffered the most grievous loss. Three brothers and two sisters had lost a much loved brother and their grief was shared by Carol Phillips, a Sale girl, who had become engaged to Tommy at Christmas – a mere seven weeks earlier. His mother, Violet, never recovered from the trauma associated with his death. Twelve months previously she had undergone major surgery but seemed on the way to a complete recovery. She was totally devastated by the circumstances of Tommy's passing and the illness which seemed to have been overcome again took over. She went steadily downhill and died soon after her second youngest son.

Tommy had a happy – almost cheeky – attitude to life, was easily given to laughter and able to get on with almost everyone with whom he came into contact. While he was at Oakwell every big club wanted him, for, even then, he was one of the best centre forwards in the country. And having established himself in the England team he would have stayed there for years, there was just no-one to compete with him. It was an indication of his quality that he played for the national side – as he did for each of his clubs – at both centre forward and inside forward. His style was based on great physical strength, rapid acceleration and tremendous power in the air. At corner-kicks he would position himself on the corner of the penalty-area and begin his run as the ball was kicked. Centre halves were torn between a need to watch the ball and an awareness of this powerhouse charging goalwards, totally committed to putting the ball into the net. In 166 First Division games he scored 112 goals, and in a career which was tragically curtailed he totalled 156 goals for Barnsley, Manchester United and England.

At every level at which he played he was with some who were among the best ever to represent club and country. His early games with Barnsley were in teams containing Blanchflower, McCormack and Johnny Kelly; at Old Trafford he played alongside Carey, Rowley and Duncan Edwards, and he was in England sides with such immortals as Nat Lofthouse, Tom Finney and Stanley Matthews. And it was appropriate that that should be so, for Tommy Taylor, from Quarry Street, Smithies, ranks alongside the finest footballers his country has ever produced.

Eddie McMorran: The Gentle Irish Tank

Eddie McMorran was a six-foot, thirteen stone international centre forward whose gentle hobby of breeding budgerigars was completely out of keeping with the tough, all-action style which he displayed on the football pitch. His professional career began in Northern Ireland with Belfast Celtic and after playing in the First Division with Manchester City he was with Leeds United immediately prior to joining Barnsley in 1950. Already having had international recognition, while at Oakwell he was chosen for his country on a further nine occasions – more times than anyone else in club history.

A native of Larne, he won schoolboy international honours in the mid-1930s and on leaving school he worked as a railway fireman. Finding the job limited his opportunities for football, he became a blacksmith at Ballyclare Paper Mill and played in the Mill team. From there he joined Linfield as an amateur and then moved to his home town club before becoming a professional with Belfast Celtic in 1945. Over the following two years he scored 57 goals, won Irish League representative honours and a League championship medal, and played the first of 15 games for Northern Ireland.

In 1947 he was transferred to Manchester City and there learned the importance of making an early start on journeys to grounds at which he was due to play. En route to Maine Road for an evening game against Derby County, he got caught in the rush-hour traffic and found it impossible to get a bus to the ground. He started to walk there, then, realizing he wasn't going to arrive in time, purloined a bicycle which was unattended against a wall. He reached his destination with 10 minutes to spare, and an evening which began with worry and uncertainty ended with the pleasure of scoring the winning goal.

In January 1949 he was transferred to Leeds United and moved to Oakwell 18 months later in readiness for the start of the new season. He was soon among the goals. Within a fortnight he had scored in a 4 – 2 defeat of Hull City and in a 2 – 0 success at Bramall Lane and his displays were such that, after an interval of four years, he was recalled to the international side and scored against England at Belfast. He held a regular place in the Irish team for the following three years and continued with occasional appearances until he was nearly 34.

For the first 14 months at Oakwell he played at inside right, reverting to his more usual centre forward position on Cecil McCormack's departure in 1951.

In March 1953 he was transferred to Doncaster Rovers – the deciding factor in the move being that their manager, former Irish international Peter Doherty, had been his boyhood hero. The move to Doncaster took place on the day that team-mate Tommy Taylor joined Manchester United and it is unlikely that another club has ever transferred two centre forwards – one an international and the other shortly to become one – on the same day. He remained at Doncaster for four years, during which time, due to Barnsley's relegation in 1953, there was little contact between the two teams. Nevertheless, when they met in October 1956 he gave a vivid reminder of his capabilities by scoring in the fourth minute in what became a 5 – 2 rout of the Reds.

His last senior club was Crewe Alexandra. He joined them in November 1957 and stayed for the remainder of the season. Then followed two seasons with Frickley Colliery in the Midland League before he moved into local football to spend a final season as player-coach with Dodworth Miners' Welfare.

An interest in birds stemmed from boyhood in Ireland when he lived among a pigeon-racing fraternity. In Barnsley he turned his attention to budgerigars, specializing in the light green variety which he bred in an aviary at the rear of his home in Derby Street. His stock was in the region of 100 birds and people came from all over the country to buy them. Success as a breeder of champions elevated him to the County Cage Birds judging panel – an office he held for several years until family circumstances compelled him to terminate the hobby.

He was a compulsive practical joker. Within a few weeks of him joining Leeds United a rumour circulated in the city that the club was to sign a Chinese player. As soon as Eddie heard it he arrived for training wearing Chinese national costume and a pigtail, and delighted his team-mates with some choice Confucious sayings delivered in a rich Irish brogue. When the local press learned of the prank he was persuaded to dress up again for photographs, but the joke misfired when the newspaper was inundated with letters from irate supporters who accused him of ridiculing the club. Another of his jokes was the use of a latex mask which he had obtained during an Irish tour of the United States, long before TV's *Spitting Image* brought that kind of disguise to the public notice in Great Britain. One can well imagine the consternation created in a railway station toilet in Birmingham while Doncaster Rovers were awaiting a connection to the West Country, when other users of the men's room found themselves standing in line with a hefty, six-foot Frankenstein – complete with bolt through his neck!

A further example of his extrovert nature was seen in a hotel restaurant during a holiday at Blackpool with his wife, Muriel, when a waiter was dilatory in responding to Eddie's request for more bread with his meal. Tiring of waiting, he sang loudly, 'More bread ... More bread ... More bread ...' He sang throughout the 30 seconds the waiter took to respond and, not surprisingly, they were the most embarrassing 30 seconds of Muriel's life. Yet there were occasions when he was very self-conscious. He had a beautiful tenor voice, but at family gatherings he was so bashful that he would only sing if the lights were turned low so those present wouldn't see him blushing.

Eddie and Muriel married in 1954, but Muriel had ill-health throughout most of the years which followed. After a season at Doncaster the manager insisted Eddie lived in the town and the newly-weds were provided with a club house, but after Muriel had been there only a few weeks she contracted pneumonia. Eddie brought her back to Barnsley to be cared for by her mother, but the illness complicated her long-standing bronchiectasis. Thereafter she had frequent spells in hospital and lengthy confinements at home, and she died in September 1973 when 42 years old. Eddie was completely devastated. Muriel's illness had taken toll of his own health and he had been unwell for some time prior to her death. Stomach ulcers were diagnosed but his general condition was such that the doctors felt unable to resort to surgery. He had to give up his job as a cranedriver at BSC's Stocksbridge Works and he was hospitalized on four occasions before leaving Barnsley in 1981 to live in Larne. Even so he retained an appearance of well being: he had always looked after himself and carried no excess weight, his complexion still had the glow of earlier years and the black wavy hair had only a touch of grey at the temples. But appearances can be deceptive and only close relatives knew how ill he really was. He died in Larne in January 1984 at the age of 60, and Muriel's family are in no doubt that his demise was brought about by a heart which had been broken 10 years earlier.

Eddie's home in Barnsley was only a few hundred yards from the town centre where he was a familiar figure in his post-playing years – always with a friendly acknowledgement for those who recognized him from his time at Oakwell. As a player his strong, bustling style, with elbows working like pistons, made him extremely difficult to dispossess and when making for goal he was as likely to go right over an opponent as round him! He had a body swerve which could send three opponents in different directions at the same time and he was particularly effective on heavy grounds, the way he ploughed through defenders prompting the supporters to nickname him 'Tank'. Indeed, a *Sheffield Telegraph* report on a success against Everton – in which he scored the only goal – referred to him as 'that raw-boned Irish mudlarking expert' and said he set the whole field an example of how soccer should be played on a wet day. Frank Swift, who was to perish at Munich Airport 12 years later along with Eddie's former team-mate, Tommy Taylor, was England's goalkeeper when the big Irishman made his international debut and is on record as saying he was the toughest opponent he ever had to deal with. Such sentiment would doubtless be echoed by many in the Second Division, for Eddie McMorran was the kind of player always likely to be a match-winner and, overall, a grand man to have in your side.

Johnny Kelly: A Prince Among Wingers

Johnny Kelly is an extraordinary man. He was a winger who could demoralize the best full backs in the land and is the only one of Barnsley Football Club's innumerable Scottish players to win full international honours. As he approaches his seventieth birthday he continues to participate in his second sporting love, distance running. He competes regularly in road races in Scotland and in Barnsley and he still plays football – and it has been suggested that in a single afternoon at Oakwell in 1949 he changed the whole future pattern of the national game.

He is a native of the Clydeside town of Barrhead and, after working on a building site and in a bleach factory and playing football for Glasgow junior team Arthurlie, be became a professional with Celtic in 1938. In that year he won junior international honours for Scotland against England and played regularly in the Celtic team at outside right during the first two war-time seasons. A hand injury sustained in previous employment disqualified him from military service and throughout the war he worked as a lorry driver. Initially, he delivered provisions to merchant vessels and warships on the Clyde coast and later he worked within the engineering industry, delivering war materials to factories and shipyards throughout western Scotland.

In 1941 he joined Morton and for four seasons their left wing consisted of Johnny and Billy Steel – the man who in 1947 became British football's costliest player on his transfer to Derby County. And the two joined forces again in 1949 as members of the Scottish international team.

Johnny's transfer to Barnsley was in December 1945 and manager Angus Seed, knowing he had previously played in right and left wing positions, asked him his preference. The player's reply was in keeping with the happy disposition he has to this day: 'I'm not really bothered boss, I can play badly on either wing.' But bad games were to be a rarity and it was immediately apparent he was another of Seed's masterly signings. Always at outside left, he was a superb winger – a man who could beat a full back with the merest flick of the hips and create absolute havoc in opposing defences. In his opening season the fourth round of the FA Cup brought Rotherham United and more than 37,000 spectators to Oakwell. The visitors were having the most successful season in their history but it was unlikely they'd previously met a winger like Johnny

Kelly, for he led them a merry dance and beat them almost on his own, scoring the first goal in a decisive 3 – 0 victory. A few weeks later he was the mainspring of a brilliant attacking display in a 3 – 0 success over Sheffield Wednesday at Hillsborough, and it was then on to Goodison Park where he was again among the scorers in a 4 – 0 victory over Everton.

By 1949 he was one of the most sought-after players in the country, but the maximum wage then in operation meant he would not benefit financially by being transferred. Similarly, the club was not in need of the large fee he would have commanded and refused an offer, among others, of £20,000 from Newcastle United. In January of that year Blackpool came to Oakwell – a Blackpool of Matthews, Mortensen and England skipper Harry Johnston. The spectators were therefore able to see on the same pitch two of perhaps the best three wingers in the country, and the Barnsley player lost nothing by comparison with the legendary Stanley Matthews. The visitors won by a single goal, but time after time Johnny swept downfield to harass their defence. When Blackpool countered he was back to negate the threat of the England winger, and Matthews paid him the compliment of similar attention.

But the game in which he received widest acclaim had taken place a few weeks earlier, on 9th October 1948, when the visitors were Southampton. Their right back was Alf Ramsay, a man on the brink of a long international career and destined to become manager of England's World Cup-winning team of 1966. He was undoubtedly one of the best full backs in the world – yet Johnny Kelly destroyed him. At one stage he demonstrated his complete mastery by beating him, waiting with foot on ball for him to recover, then beating him again. The supporters revelled in the sight of Johnny ruining the reputation of such a renowned defender and shrieked their derision, and Ramsay could not have had another such dispiriting afternoon throughout all his years in football.

Referring to that game in his book *Football Daft*, author Michael Parkinson suggests it had a radical effect on Ramsay's thinking and, eventually, on the whole future of football. He says he believes that while the Southampton player sat in the Oakwell dressing room, scraping mud from his boots and his reputation, he thought of his revenge on wingers – and decided on the destruction of the whole tricky race. And years later, as manager of the England team, he created a football formation – to be copied throughout the game – in which there was no place for wingers.

It may be that Parkinson's suggestion was made tongue-in-cheek but, be that as it may, no-one will ever know Ramsay's innermost thoughts as he reflected on the afternoon's happenings. But there is no doubt that he had had the kind of experience that no man, in whatever field his working life was spent, would ever forget or want to repeat. And perhaps the almost total disappearance of traditional wingers *can* be attributed to the exceptional skills of a Barnsley outside left, as displayed at Oakwell on a Saturday afternoon 40 years ago.

Although the club consistently refused to transfer Johnny, there was an approach made directly to him in June 1950 in which it was powerless to intervene. The offer came from a club outside the jurisdiction of the Football League and FIFA – the Millionarios in Bogota, Columbia. And it was at a time when the normally good relationship with his club was, in both a personal and financial context, somewhat strained.

When he came to the town in 1945 his wife and children remained at the family home in Barrhead, and he felt the club had never been particularly helpful in allowing him to spend time with them. Also, the two parties were in disagreement regarding his entitlement to a benefit; he maintained it was then due, but the club said service prior to August 1946 did not count. It was stalemate until the approach from Bogota. The highest wage he ever received at Oakwell was £14 per week, but the Millionarios offered him £125 each month plus bonuses and a signing-on fee of £3,000. He knew he could earn only a fraction of that amount during the remainder of his career in England, yet he had no intention of going to Bogota. But the Barnsley directors didn't know that and did all they reasonably could to influence him to stay – granting an immediate and maximum benefit and allowing a five-day expenses-paid visit to Barrhead each month. Needless to say, Johnny was pleased to accept.

Ironically, in view of the enjoyment he had had at the expense of Southampton, it was their ground which saw the beginning of the end of his career – on an icy pitch in December 1950. It resulted from a tackle by their right full back, but it must be emphasized that he was not Alf Ramsay! The two ended up in an untidy heap on the slippery surface and Johnny's right knee was so badly damaged that it required four operations and he was out of the game for 12 months. He returned to the side in the spring of 1952 but it was then apparent his best years were behind him and after one more season he was transferred to Falkirk.

However, some of the Falkirk supporters were not at all keen to have him and voiced opinions that the club should have obtained a younger player. Perhaps the rather sparse hair suggested he was older than his actual age of 32, but he had been noticeably 'thin on top' when he joined Barnsley as a 23-year-old. Nevertheless, the manager had confidence in him and knocked a couple of years off his age to try to placate the fans. Johnny was determined to justify a place in the team, and after a 4 – 0 win over St Mirren he was voted Man of the Match and received good notices and the supporters' cheers for the remainder of the season.

Thereafter he had a second spell with Morton and seasons with Halifax Town and Portadown in the Irish League, and he remained in the senior game until 38 years old. He was also player-coach with junior side Dalry Thistle and the Armitage-Shanks porcelain works' team, and his long coaching involvement with Barrhead Boys Club was the subject of a 1975 documentary programme on Scottish television.

While at Barnsley he used his pre-war work experience to start in business as the manufacturer of Kelzone bleach – advertised in the Oakwell programme as 'The 100-per-cent bleach cleanser and purifier – a boon to the housewife and honest value for money'. It was made in an outbuilding at the Mason's Arms at Worsbrough Dale and he was also the salesman and distributor. And through the good offices of Oakwell director Horace Pickering, a former secretary of the Barnsley British Co-operative Society, he was able to include the Society among regular outlets for his product. The post-playing years of his working life were spent in his home town. Initially he and brother Tommy were in partnership as coal merchants and he later bought a half share in a bookmaking business. His last working years were as a lorry driver in the building trade and chemical industry, and he reached retirement age in 1986.

Distance running has been part of his personal training schedule from teenage to the present day, and in recent years he has combined it with fund raising for charitable purposes. For the last five years he has participated in the annual Barnsley Six road race, and the frequent shouts of 'Good old Johnny' and 'Up the Reds' from the thousands lining the route show the affection there is still for him within the town. For more than 30 years he has played in charity football matches for the Old Crocks – a team of former Celtic and Rangers players – and a measure of his love of football is that he gets the same feeling of excitement before a game with the Crocks as he got when preparing to run onto the pitch in front of a full-house at Hampden Park or White Hart Lane.

Barnsley's most eminent citizen, Lord Mason of Barnsley, who was the town's Member of Parliament for many years and is an almost life-long supporter of the Reds, sponsors an annual competition in the match programme on an aspect of Oakwell history. In 1985 the subject was 'The Best Footballer to play for Barnsley' and entrants were required to give reasons for their nominations. Entries were received from every age-group within the club's support and the judges – the sponsor and the sports editor of the *Barnsley Chronicle* – decided the winner was Mr Harry Marshall of Queen's Drive, Barnsley, who bestowed the accolade on Johnny Kelly.

Johnny's most treasured possessions are a Scottish cap embroidered with his two appearances for the national side – against Wales and Ireland – in 1949, and an engraved silver cup presented by the directors, staff and players at Oakwell in recognition of his international selection. He had the ability to put opposing defences in complete disarray and his skill in controlling the ball at speed was quite superb. But for his style being totally individualistic he would surely have played for his country on many more occasions, yet in an era rich in quality wingers he was undoubtedly a Prince among them. There are now dozens of middle-aged men in Barnsley who have fond forty-year-old memories of Sunday afternoon kick-arounds in Locke Park with a far-from-home Scottish international footballer who loved the game so much he would play it with hero-worshipping schoolboys. And fortunate indeed were those supporters who flocked to Oakwell in the 1940s to admire and applaud the unique footballing skills of the great John Carmichael Kelly.

Arthur Glover: So Near, Yet So ... Unavailable

Pogmoor-born Arthur Glover attended St Mary's School and while there he played football for Barnsley and Yorkshire Boys and also represented the Rest of England Boys against the national side. On leaving school he joined Regent Street Congregational Church FC – known locally as Regent Street Congs – one of the best men's amateur teams in the area. And as a 15-year-old he was by far the youngest of their players.

While with the Congs in March 1933 he played in a trial game for Wolverhampton Wanderers. After only a few minutes he was concussed, but a douching with the magic sponge enabled him to resume almost at once, only to again lose consciousness immediately after the final whistle. He revived in the office of manager Major Frank Buckley and, despite the stunned state in which he had been for most of the game, was offered a place on the ground staff. However, his mother had died some years earlier and he was being cared for by his maternal grandmother, who roundly scolded the scout who accompanied him from the Midlands to suggest he joined Wolves. 'How would you like *your* son to leave home at 15 to live in a strange town? He definitely won't!'

Arthur was then a scales and weighing machine apprentice with T G Garner & Sons Ltd in The Arcade. Mr Tommy Garner was a Barnsley supporter and friendly with chairman George Tomlinson, and on learning that his young employee had had the chance to join Wolves, he promptly arranged for him to become an amateur at Oakwell. Two years later Arthur was a professional and made his debut in the first team during the 1937/38 season.

In January 1940 he joined the army and was posted to 6th (Training) Battalion RASC. Stationed initially in South-East England, in the first war-time season he assisted Herne Bay to win the Kent Cup. The battalion could field a team of former professional players, and when it moved to Sheffield he expected to have plenty of opportunities to play at Oakwell. What he had not anticipated was the soccer-mad Commanding Officer ordering the former professionals to perform duty on every Saturday afternoon throughout the season – by representing the RASC in the Sheffield Association League. Being in Sheffield enabled him to spend most Saturday evenings and Sundays at home, but despite being little more than a dozen miles from Oakwell he was prevented from playing football there.

His final war-time season was in the South-West, where he was a guest of Yeovil Town. There was then some advantage in being unable to play for Barnsley – for his own club adhered rigidly to the £1 10s. match fee, whereas at Yeovil he was paid £5.

He won a regular place in Barnsley's Second Divison side in the first post-war season and retained it for five years. He played less regularly during 1951/52 and, by then, was being used as player-coach in the reserves. But in the following season an injury in a Central League game brought his career to an end.

He then obtained employment at Barugh Green Coke Ovens and accepted manager Tim Ward's invitation to coach the Barnsley 'A' team in the Yorkshire League. It was a responsibility he enjoyed, but found it impinged too much on work commitments for him to continue for more than one season. He had been a one-club footballer for almost two decades, but his post-playing occupations were usually of fairly brief duration. He remained at the Coke Ovens for a year, then worked for two years at North Gawber Colliery. From there he moved to the BXL factory at Darton before joining the Barnsley Co-op Traffic Department, and his next job was as a driver with Barnsley Borough Council. He eventually settled at the Brook Motors factory at Barugh Green and remained there for the last seven years of his working life. The frequent job-changes always provided improved pay, a consequence of which was that in 1980 he was able to retire at the age of 62.

As a teenager he was a keen boxer and trained at Charlie Glover's gym in Shambles Street, and he had two fights as a professional. One was in Belfast, and the programme was so far behind schedule that he was required to 'take a count' in an early round so that his party could catch their connection back to Liverpool. His father had also been a professional boxer, but Arthur realized the sport was incompatible with the career he hoped to have in football and he took no further part in it after becoming a professional player at Oakwell. In the last pre-war season boxing featured in the club's training programme as a means of improving balance, reaction and self-control. All those taking part were fit, energetic young men with varying degrees of aggression – yet, not surprisingly, not one of them was keen to tangle with the ex-pro!

In school days he had also represented Barnsley Boys at cricket, later playing for Gawber CC until joining the army in 1940. He was a wicketkeeper-batsman and a renowned big-hitter and, after the war, played in turn for Pogmoor, Cawthorne, and the Barnsley Co-op team until retiring from the game in 1972.

His sport is now cycling. He rides 10 miles on several occasions each week, and rides 30 miles in the Penistone area each Sunday morning in company with his brother. The other is the younger by several years and usually takes the lead; Arthur's only reservation about accompanying him is that he always seems to want to ride up hills!

The name of Arthur Glover is not one which comes quickly to mind when one considers Oakwell's exciting team of the late 1940s. More readily recalled are Jimmy Baxter and John Kelly, the classy Danny Blanchflower, dashing

Gavin Smith and George Robledo. But Arthur's dour defensive style was as vital to the team's overall play as the individual skills of some of the more renowned members of that excellent side. Over the years he was chosen for all the outfield defensive positions and even had emergency stints in goal. And the fact that he was a Barnsley player for 18 consecutive seasons – longer than any other man in the club's modern history – is an indication of the high regard in which he was held.

Sid Normanton: A Fearsome Opponent

In the Barnsley area there is a commonly held belief that Sid Normanton's nickname 'Skinner' was bestowed upon him because he 'skinned' opponents on the football pitch. The theory is appealing but quite without foundation, for he received the name as a child – long before he had an interest in the game which was to provide his livelihood. Yet it contained an element of prophecy, for when he became a footballer he was known throughout the Second Division as a man who, while not actually skinning the opposition, was robust and unflinching in the tackle and relished a bruising encounter.

He has lived all his life in the Lundwood area of the town where he attended Littleworth School and played football for the local youth club. At 14 he began work underground at Wharncliffe Woodmoor Colliery and remained in that employment until becoming a professional at Oakwell. At 17 he joined the Barnsley Main Colliery side whose trainer had an unusual item among his equipment – a long handled net which he used with great regularity to fish the ball out of the River Dearne which flowed alongside the pitch.

In those days Sid was a centre forward and in April 1945 he scored twice when Barnsley Main beat Shipcroft United in a local Cup final. His Saturday evenings were usually spent at dances at Barnsley Baths or Howards' Gym in Dodworth Road, and on the night of the victory over Shipcroft Barnsley manager Angus Seed visited the family home with a scout who had watched the game in the afternoon. Seed knew other clubs had been represented and he was anxious to speak to Sid, and when the head of the house said he didn't know where his son was he replied, 'Come on, there's twenty pounds for you if you'll tell me where he is.' Sid senior's response was, 'You can offer me a hundred pounds but I still don't know where he is!'

Seed returned next morning with an offer of part-time terms but he had been unaware that Sid was registered as an amateur with Leeds United. There was some delay while that arrangement was cancelled, and the player became a professional at Oakwell in September 1945. Early games were at centre forward in the 'A' team, but in an emergency he played at right half in the Central League at Liverpool. Thereafter, apart from occasional games at inside forward, he was always in one of the wing half positions and he made his Second Division debut in November 1947 in a 2 – 0 win over Doncaster Rovers.

Close marking and hard tackling were the main features of his play and were much in evidence during the opening stages of the Reds' FA Cup-tie at Highbury in 1952. At left half, he was the rock on which almost all Arsenal's attacks foundered as he completely obliterated the threat of Jimmy Logie, the home team's international inside right and main schemer. Ten minutes before the interval and with neither team having scored, he and Arsenal's Alex Forbes went together for a 50–50 ball. And whereas Sid had every intention of winning it, Forbes' boot went over the top and tore the ligaments of his right knee. Skipper Gordon Pallister was almost within touching distance and, pointing at the offending player, shouted angrily to the referee, 'Aren't you going to send him off – he might have broken this lad's leg!' The reply was, 'Shut up or I'll send *you* off!' The incident brought not even a word of caution from the referee but caused Sid to be stretchered from the pitch and he was out of action for the remainder of the season.

The injury was of such severity that he never fully recovered and it would have been to his financial advantage to have quit at that stage and sought compensation from the Football League. But he loved playing too much to do that, and after lots of perseverance he returned to the team in August for the start of the new season. It proved, however, a disastrous campaign. There was the acute sadness of Angus Seed's death in January, to be quickly followed by the only real bright spot of the season when Brighton came to Oakwell in the third round of the FA Cup. On that day Sid was at left half in the team which trailed 3 – 0 at half-time but made what is perhaps the Reds' best-ever FA Cup recovery to win 4 – 3. Despite the magnificence of that revival, only five League games were won and the team suffered the almost inevitable consequence of relegation into the Third Division.

Seed's successor was Tim Ward. He too had been a wing half, but of rather different style to Sid and soon after the start of his first season in charge, that of 1953/54, Sid had an unusual experience at his hands. In one of the Tuesday morning practice games Sid's opponent was outside left Johnny Kelly and the referee was Tim Ward. So far as Sid was concerned a game of football required total commitment, irrespective of whether it was a practice or the real thing – but that attitude was not, apparently, shared by the manager. Kelly and Sid had had encounters in training almost weekly for the previous several years and, with the proviso that one didn't intentionally harm one's team-mates, each expressed his different style to the full. Yet to the amazement and great amusement of all the other players, when Sid grounded Kelly for the third time with a heavy but scrupulously fair tackle the referee-manager ordered him from the pitch!

The effects of the Highbury injury restricted him to 10 appearances during 1953/54 and that was to be his last Oakwell season. In July he joined Halifax Town but again he was handicapped by the damaged knee, which brought his career to an end in the summer of 1955 when he was 28 years old.

For the following six years he was employed as a driver at the Barnsley British Co-operative Society's warehouse in Perseverence Street. During that time he had no football involvement of any kind but kept himself fit by daily exercises and cross-country running. In 1961 he was offered the post of player-manager of Grimethorpe Athletic – the Grimethorpe Colliery side. The job also provided employment at the colliery and he worked there and later at Barnsley Main as a driver until taking early retirement in 1985. He was with Grimethorpe Athletic for four seasons, during which time the team's winning of the Sheffield Association League championship was the first such success the club had had in its long existence.

Principally his retirement activities are watching junior football and gardening. Each summer his attractive garden at Cundy Cross is dominated by a magnificent display of sunflowers. He has grown them to a height of 12 feet with as many as 28 dinner plate-size blooms on a single stem.

His seasons at Oakwell gave him a life on the national sporting scene and a familiarity with luxury travel and quality hotels which few boys from Lundwood ever experience. And 20 years after his retirement from the game he received renewed acclaim when author and TV personality Michael Parkinson revealed that Skinner Normanton had been his boyhood hero.

Fate dealt harshly with Sid at Highbury in 1952 but, as though to try to compensate for the untimely ending of his playing career, the intervening years have been kind to him. He still has the same fair crinkly hair and his features are unmistakably those of the young man who was a Barnsley footballer 40 years ago. He was no heavyweight, being 5′ 8½″ and 11½ stones, but he was as hard as nails and utterly fearless. The ferocity of his tackle was renowned throughout the Second Division and it was certainly preferable to have him in your side rather than among the opposition. But a measure of the genuine way in which he played the game is that not one of the hundreds of men who, over the years, were at the receiving end of his special attention ever had to leave the field of play as a result of it.

Gavin Smith: The Lightning Strike

Gavin Smith joined the Oakwell staff in February 1939 as an addition to the squad which was making a determined push for promotion into the Second Division. He was already an established professional, having had almost four seasons with Dumbarton who had rebuffed the Reds' earlier approach at the turn of the year and refused to release him until they were out of the Scottish Cup. By the time that happened Barnsley had gained a 12-point lead at the top of Division Three (North) and Gavin didn't have an opportunity to play in the side during what became the championship season. Nor did he take part in any of the three games which took place at the higher level prior to the commencement of the Second World War on 3rd September 1939. But he won a place immediately the regional leagues began and retained the outside right position for 13 consecutive seasons. The 233 games he played in war-time competitions is the highest total of any Barnsley player, and when League football resumed in 1946 he went on to play a further 271 times.

He joined Dumbarton as an 18-year-old and went straight into the first team, and at the time of the move to Barnsley he had just completed an apprenticeship as a glassworks engineer. On the outbreak of war the players were required to join HM Forces or take what was classed as essential employment; Gavin joined the workforce at the Stairfoot glassworks which were owned by the Oakwell chairman, George Tomlinson, and he remained there until 1946.

He was an outside right throughout his career, but he was more than just a winger – he was a winger who scored a lot of goals. His first came at Christmas 1939 in a 4 – 1 defeat of Grimsby Town. A few days later he scored a hat-trick in a 4 – 0 success at Rotherham United and his opening season in the Barnsley first team ended with him being leading scorer. In fact, exceptionally for a winger, he was leading scorer in three of the seven war-time seasons.

In August 1940 he scored in a 6 – 2 thrashing of Doncaster Rovers and a fortnight later he scored twice when the Reds, with a splendid display of attacking football, destroyed Sheffield Wednesday 5 – 0. In the War Cup competition he scored in a first-leg victory at Chesterfield, and when the Oakwell ground was unfit for the second game the teams played again at Chesterfield and he got a hat-trick in the 5 – 2 success there.

Other war-time highlights were in front of a crowd of more than 28,000 on

Boxing Day 1944 when he scored the goal which beat Liverpool. And in the following season's FA Cup competition he streaked down the right wing to score the Reds' second goal and equalize the aggregate score in a tremendous game when Newcastle United were beaten 3 – 0.

During the war he played mid-week games for Bradford Park Avenue and Huddersfield Town. At Bradford he formed a right wing with the great Len Shackleton, and at that time Sunderland tried to secure him as partner for England's Raich Carter. Coincidentally, it was Carter as manager of Leeds United who, 10 years later, was one who tried unsuccessfully to obtain him from Oakwell.

During the 1952/53 season Gavin lost his place to the up-and-coming Arthur Kaye. He played only 14 times, and in March he was put on the transfer list. Then almost 36 and having served the club for 15 years, he was amazed to learn that a fee was expected for him. On taking this up with the chairman, he got the reply, 'You're worth some money, Gavin, and a thousand pounds is the least I'll accept.' The Uniteds of Leeds and Sheffield would have liked to have had him but weren't inclined to pay a fee for a player of his age, so it appeared his League career was over. And it would have been but for National Serviceman Private A Kaye failing to arrive from Aldershot on the evening of 28th August 1953 in readiness for the first home game of the season. On the following morning the manager re-signed Gavin, and spectators at Oakwell in the afternoon were surprised to see their old favourite take his former place on the right wing. He went on to play a further 11 times in what was an unexpected and final season with the club. The renowned pace was, to a great extent, still there: on 10th October in the last minute of a game at Halifax he raced down the wing to send in a shot which the 'keeper could only knock into the air, and Tommy Lumley was on hand to provide the team's first away win in almost a year.

During that season Gavin became the licensee of the Bush Inn at Kingstone – not the existing premises, but those which had stood on the same site at the junction of Park Road and Keresforth Hill Road since 1882. He remained there for 10 years and was the first licensee of the new premises, but he left the trade before they opened for business. He decided to leave because the work was so tying and his children were growing up without him seeing as much of them as he wished to do – but he had also put on three stones in weight and knew that couldn't be good for him. Customers were always wanting to buy him drinks and talk about football, and many a time he left the bar just to get away from that subject of conversation.

He took employment at St Helen's Hospital in the town. Initially he was a porter and enjoyed the involvement with people and the opportunity which it provided to be helpful. Later he worked as a driver and continued in that role at the new District General Hospital until his retirement in 1983. Part of his duties was to collect nursing staff from their homes at 5am – and, holidays apart, he didn't have a Sunday off for 18 years.

In 1961 Gavin and his son, Bobby, became the first father and son to have played in Barnsley's first team. Bobby made his debut in a League Cup-tie against Workington Town and had several games in the Third Division before moving into non-League football with Chelmsford City. He held a place in the side for 10 years, winning Southern League championship medals in 1968 and 1972.

Gavin Smith's greatest asset was his exceptional pace. Colleagues considered him the fastest player they ever saw, and defenders he passed had no hope of catching him. There were those who subdued him by taking an early opportunity to kick him over the touchline, but to do so they had to get close and that could be a difficult thing to do. Time and again his speed carried him down the opposing flank, and many goals which helped build the reputations of such Oakwell 'greats' as George Robledo and Cecil McCormack came from Gavin's crosses from the goal-line after electric bursts down the right wing. Speed also enhanced his own goal scoring. A *Sheffield Telegraph* report of a 4 – 3 success against Coventry City described how he raced 50 yards at amazing speed before steering the ball past the advancing 'keeper for the winning goal. And against Hull City in December 1951, on receiving from Eddie McMorran a pass which the same correspondent described as a winger's dream, he flashed towards goal like a thunderbolt and finished with a scorching drive into the roof of the net. It was said to be Oakwell's best goal of the season and the crowd rose as one man to applaud him. His fast approach was in sharp contrast to the ball-playing skills of fellow Scot Johnny Kelly at outside left, and their completely different styles provided a perfect balance in some of the finest forward lines the club has had.

Harry May: An Achiever

Season 1954/55, when Barnsley won promotion into the Second Division, was Harry May's third and final season at Oakwell. He was transferred shortly afterwards in the wake of a story which didn't reflect well on the club appearing in a national newspaper and chairman Joe Richards suspecting he had supplied details to a local reporter. The suspicions were ill-founded, but Harry wasn't bothered because he'd previously vowed not to spend more than two years at any club, and Barnsley was the only place where he stayed longer.

Unusually, by way of study and additional employment, he was a player who planned a post-football career. So successfully, in fact, that senior positions with multinational Corporations over 30 years have enabled him to achieve the kind of life-style which is available only to the very comfortably off.

Born in Glasgow, the sixth of a family of seven children, he was named after his father's cousin Harry who, at Ypres in 1915, won the first Scottish VC of the First World War.

On leaving Glasgow's East Bank Academy at 15, he obtained employment as a junior clerk with the New Zealand Shipping Company in the city. There he developed skills which were to be useful in years to come. Starting pay of £25 per annum was doubled after a year, but by then he was earning triple that amount from additional part-time work. Having had a morning and evening newspaper delivery round from being nine years old, he enlarged it by taking orders for groceries and delivering them with the newspapers – a practise which continued until his conscription into the Royal Navy as an 18-year-old in 1946.

After 18 months' naval service he returned to Glasgow to take up an appointment as manager of a Norwegian shipping company. Post-school football had been as an outside left with junior professional clubs in Ayrshire and Glasgow but on demobilization, at nearly six feet tall, 14 stones and hard with it, he became a full back with Thornie Wood United in the Lanarkshire League.

In August 1948 he joined Cardiff City but, as understudy to Welsh captain Alf Sherwood, he had only one first team outing in two seasons. Deciding to try his luck where there wasn't such high level of competition, he joined Swindon Town where he had a regular place throughout the following two seasons.

In 1952 he was in the Swindon team which reached the fifth round of the

FA Cup. During those games he had the pleasure of a standing ovation from the Cardiff supporters when Swindon held the First Division side to a goal-less draw before beating them 1 – 0 in the replay.

He was transferred to Barnsley in 1952 and began the season in the first team. However, the upheaval and uncertainties brought about by manager Seed's long illness and his death in February 1953 had a dispiriting effect on performances. A consequence was relegation into Division Three, Harry having played only 19 times.

At the season's end he told new manager Tim Ward that he was going to Glasgow and wouldn't be coming back. Nevertheless, he'd taken a liking to Ward and allowed himself to be persuaded to return. He held a regular place throughout the following two seasons – playing in all 46 games when Barnsley became Third Division (North) champions in 1955.

It was in August that a disagreement between club and players over the date on which summer wages came into effect was published in the *Daily Mirror*. The report by Spencer Hill, a local freelance journalist, was that things weren't well at Barnsley because players were being kept on the lower summer wages longer than should have been the case. This incensed chairman Richards. Harry and his pal Bob Brown had put the players' case to the board and the chairman, for whatever reason, suspected Harry of having supplied details to Spencer Hill.

The outcome was that he was made available for transfer and, within 24 hours, joined Southend United. Two years later he moved into non-League football as captain of Gloucester City and, as could have been expected, was there for two seasons. His playing career then ended, not for lack of opportunity but because, at 30, he'd decided that the time had come for him to do something more financially rewarding.

Already well versed in the ways of commerce, one of his achievements as a 20-year-old manager of a shipping company had been to arrange a one-year contract to transport 90,000 cases of whisky to Canada each week. At Southend he had worked in Shell International's customer liaison department; on reporting for training each day at Oakwell he'd already spent three hours delivering Co-op milk and each afternoon he worked in the export department of Suba-Seal in Peel Street. And two years at Swindon Town when he had a franchise from a London dealer to sell whisky to clubs and pubs throughout Wiltshire had given him first-hand experience of the rewards available to those with entrepreneurial skills.

Studying for a second career came easily to him. For 16 years he was a student at Gloucester Technical College, obtaining qualifications in engineering, law, international banking, French and German, and becoming an Associate Member of the Institute of Export. Practical experience was gained on the shop floor as a turner/fitter at the local Hawker-Siddely diesel engine factory. Fifteen months later he was the company's Senior Clerk in charge of an operation which sold engines and spare parts to almost every country in the world.

After five years with Hawker-Siddely he joined Bryce Burger – a Hawker-Siddely company – as Senior Export Clerk and in five years supervised a twentyfold increase in export sales. In 1961 Bryce Burger was taken over by Lucas Industries and Harry was promoted to the position of Commercial Manager (Overseas).

He is now Export Controller (Europe) of the Eaton Corporation of Cleveland, Ohio, which has factories in France, Germany and Spain making gear boxes and axles for every major vehicle manufacturer in Europe. In 1988 business in Harry's area of responsibility increased by 30 per-cent. That is what he does best. He is an achiever, constantly finding and developing new business, and to that end he guarantees to supply his company's spares anywhere in the world within 24 hours. There have been occasions when he has become involved in multilateral trading, ie., accepting payment in such items as jams and ball-bearings – and he's made a profit on selling those, too!

For the last 20 years Harry has lived in the Gloucestershire village of Frampton-on-Severn, and his home is in an idyllic setting. The garden borders a four-acre lake surrounded by mature greenery and containing approximately 4,000 carp, chub, roach and perch – many of specimen size. Kingfishers dart over the shallows and a heron visits for breakfast every morning. Yet an over-riding sadness is that he has no-one to share the delights of living at 'Lakeside'. For his wife, the former Daphne Elisabeth Walton of Hood Green, Barnsley, died suddenly and unexpectedly on 9th June 1980 when 46 years old.

Daphne had been a manager with Avon Cosmetics for 11 years, and Harry takes considerable pleasure from the way in which their daughters, Vivienne and Tina, have progressed within their own careers. Vivienne, the elder, is a Cambridge MA, a Bachelor of Medicine and a Fellow of the Royal College of Surgeons. Tina is an Honours graduate in Languages of Cardiff University and a professional jazz singer, listing Ronnie Scott's Club in London's West End and the Jazz Club of Paris among the many venues at which she has performed.

In addition to the time devoted to sport, work and study, Harry has always had a wide variety of interests. As a younger man he was a keen ballroom dancer and there was an occasion when he and a partner were placed fourth in the West of England finals. During two years with Swindon Town it became his custom on Wednesdays to catch the one o'clock 'Cheltenham Flyer' to London, take in the first house at the Palladium before going on to the Lyceum Ballroom in the Strand and arrive back in Swindon at 7.30am. Such activity was contrary to club rules but he didn't care – if the worst came to the worst he knew he was capable of making a living elsewhere. An accomplished pianist, he is involved with the Frampton Musical Society; he collects pictures, Waterford crystal and first edition books; he takes on the weekly challenge of the *Sunday Times* crossword and uses his engineering skills to completely renovate old cars of quality.

Harry May joined Barnsley as replacement for Gordon Pallister who had had to retire through injury. It was almost as though manager Seed wanted a Pallister-look-alike, for Harry had the same height and build, the same polished style and even a right foot that was used mainly for standing on. Not in the least concerned about the little use made of that particular limb, he dismissed team-mates' banter with, 'This *one* of mine is better than the *pair* which most of *you* have!' Lacking a good right foot he might have been, but confidence he has in abundance – an aspect of his personality which must have had great bearing on what he has achieved in business over the last 30 years.

Tommy Lumley: The First Midfielder

It didn't mean much to Charlton Athletic's Tommy Lumley when he learned that Barnsley wanted to sign him: he didn't really know where Barnsley was, nor was he aware that the two managers – Jimmy Seed of Charlton and Angus Seed of Barnsley – were brothers. Yet the transfer proved to be the best thing that happened within his career, for it provided him with two very successful playing seasons and membership of Barnsley's 1955 Third Division (North) championship side. For the club it was a fortuitous signing. On his arrival relegation seemed a real possibility and his seven goals in the season's remaining 10 games went a long way towards retaining a place in the Second Division.

As a pupil at Annfield Plain School in his native County Durham he was in the 14-year-old football team from the age of 11. The under-age involvement continued with Annfield Plain Juniors. Theirs was an under-18 side: Tommy had a place from being 14 which was held by footballing skills rather than physical prowess, for even on reaching manhood he was of less than average height and weighed well under 11 stones.

On leaving school he worked as a trainee grocer at Leadgate Co-operative Society. With its Saturday afternoon requirement the job put him out of organized football for almost two years. Then he became an order-seeker – someone who called on the Society's customers each week to obtain their grocery orders which were later delivered by horse-drawn dray. The new job didn't require him on Saturday afternoons and he joined Crookhall Juniors in the North-West Durham League. He had a couple of games as an amateur in Sunderland reserves and remained with Crookhall until March 1943 when he was conscripted into the Royal Navy.

A Portsmouth rating, ordinary seaman Lumley qualified as a Wireman – a shipboard electrician. As such he was involved in the D-Day invasion of occupied France. During the early hours of 6th June 1944, under cover of darkness and a naval bombardment of the enemy's shore defences, he was part of a 12-man crew of a landing craft which was one of a flotilla taking tanks across the English Channel. The part of the operation in which Tommy was involved entailed landing near Caen in Northern France. Coincidentally, his younger brother, Jimmy, was similarly involved with American forces who landed some 20 miles to the east.

Tommy remained on those duties for two weeks, following which he joined the crew of the Empress of Australia which was conveying troops to India. Once there he served on HMS Marve – a shore base in Bombay – where he worked on the maintenance of craft used by the Royal Marines.

Demobilization took place in March 1946. He obtained work as a joiner's assistant at Consett Iron Company and told Sunderland he was again available. They responded with an invitation to play in the reserves, following which he made a 30-mile bus and train journey to Roker Park only to find he wasn't in the final eleven. That turned him off Sunderland for ever and he joined Consett in the North-Eastern League. It was a league which had the reserve teams of the area's Football League clubs and after only three games Consett signed him as a part-time professional. In April 1948 they won the Durham County Cup when Tommy scored in a 4 – 1 win over Spennymoor on Sunderland's ground, and by the end of the year he was a professional with First Division Charlton Athletic.

Charlton paid £1,150 for him. It was a record fee for the North-Eastern League and enabled Consett to build a new stand at their Belle Vue Park ground. Yet the move worsened Tommy's own financial position. His part-time football pay and wage from joinery totalled more than he could be paid as a first year full-time professional and there was the additional expense of living away from home. Nevertheless it was a move he was glad to make and he arrived in London on 9th December – his 24th birthday.

Eighteen months earlier Charlton had won the FA Cup and more than half of that side were still in the team. In such august company, Tommy Lumley, newly out of non-League football, made his First Division debut against Sheffield United on 12th March 1949. His first goal came a fortnight later to win a game at Blackpool and on 10th September, in front of 45,000 spectators at The Valley, he did the hat-trick in a 6 – 3 victory over Newcastle United.

By this time he had a regular place in the team, but early in the next season he and his wife, Vera, lost their first child within two days of the birth. They were both completely distraught. Tommy's form was affected to the extent that he lost his place in the side and in the end he couldn't wait to get away. However, his club weren't of the same frame of mind and refused his application to be transferred. Consequently he played in the reserves for nearly two years with only occasional games in the first team – a situation which ended in the spring of 1952 after the brothers Seed discussed Angus's urgent need to strengthen his side.

The agreed fee was £4,500. Barnsley were in second-bottom position in the Second Division and Tommy went straight into the team against Cardiff City. That game and the next one were lost, but on his third appearance he began to make his presence felt by scoring twice in a 3 – 1 win at Leicester City. Indeed, his second goal was a splendid affair: he ran through the home defence from just inside the Leicester half, beating two defenders by sheer speed before slamming the ball into the net. At this stage points were priceless and in the team's last home game – against Doncaster Rovers – he equalized three minutes before the final whistle. In a frenzied end to the season he provided a 1 – 0 interval lead at Goodison Park, and although the home side brought the scores level his goal was sufficient to ensure Second Division survival.

In the following season, on 15th November 1952, he scored the winner at Southampton and three weeks later he had a leading part in a fine 2 – 0 win over West Ham. Of that performance the *Barnsley Chronicle* reported that he completely bewildered the visitors with uncanny ball control on an ice-bound surface, time and again putting their rearguard into a tangle with his defence-splitting passes. However, the team didn't win another game in the League in the remaining *five months* of the season, an almost inevitable consequence of which was relegation to the Third Division.

In the Northern Section his goal at Halifax on 10th October 1953 provided Barnsley with their first away win in nearly a year. In all he had 15 goals in a season which ended with the team in second-top position.

The championship came to Oakwell in the following year, 1955. Tommy wasn't as productive as previously but the goals he did get were at crucial times. In the opening game he scored a last-minute equalizer against Oldham Athletic and got winners at Tranmere and Darlington. In-between-times he pulled the team back from 2 – 1 down to win 3 – 2 in the FA Cup against non-League Wigan Athletic. Promotion was virtually secured on 30th April at Chester after his goal had put the Reds on course for a 2 – 0 success. In the following week the championship was theirs, the trophy being presented immediately after Chester had been beaten, again, on the Wednesday evening.

However, the occasion had a sequel which caused Tommy some embarrassment – both within the club and at home. After the presentation the players were invited into the board room for drinks. Tommy, almost teetotal, had eaten very moderately during the day and two whiskies made him so light-headed that he had to be helped into the dressing room where he laid down while the merrymaking continued along the corridor. Two hours later when the party was breaking up, Harry May found him still in the dressing room, asleep. Unable to rouse him, Harry hoisted him onto his shoulder, carried him outside to his car and drove him to the Lumley home in Victoria Crescent. Vera had retired for the night and on answering the knocking on the door she showed the extent of her sympathy for her husband's predicament by instructing that he be laid on the settee in the front room, then ushering Harry outside and promptly returning to bed.

In the Second Division Tommy held a place in the team until late December. Injury put him on the sidelines over the holiday and he returned for a third round FA Cup-tie against Blackburn Rovers. That was his last game for Barnsley. At the end of the season he enquired if he was to receive a benefit payment. On learning that he wasn't, he asked to be transferred.

In August 1956 he joined Darlington, receiving half of the £800 transfer fee as an accrued share of benefit. Yet to this day he regrets leaving Barnsley when he did. At Darlington he couldn't keep free of injury; he played only a handful of games and was not retained at the season's end.

He then put the clock back 10 years and re-joined Consett. Two seasons later he moved to North Shields, later playing for Horden Colliery Welfare and

Crawcrook Albion. In 1964 he relinquished professional status and spent three seasons with Consett Wednesday in a local mid-week league before retiring from the game at the age of 43.

On leaving Darlington and full-time football he returned to the Consett Iron Company where he'd worked following demobilization in 1946. Twenty years later after working in the Plate and Billet Mills and in the Planning Office he was made redundant. He then worked for Redpath-Dorman-Long at Consett. On becoming redundant again in 1984 he decided, at 60, that he could properly consider himself as being in retirement.

Tommy and Vera have now lived for more than 20 years in the Durham village of Medomsley. Their home on the edge of the village overlooks the Derwent Valley and on a clear day the view extends more than 40 miles to the Scottish Borders. Each has an active part in village life. Vera is involved with the local Methodist Church and is a leader of the Girls Brigade. For 10 years Tommy was a part-time youth leader at Consett YMCA. Now he takes weekly football classes at a church school in Medomsley and is with the team at matches. He also does a weekly stint as a driver for the WRVS Meals on Wheels.

Tommy Lumley's early years in football were as an attacking player and he was thus able to display his dribbling skills to best effect. However, at Barnsley he changed his style to become a link between defence and attack. He became the king-pin of the side. The excellence of his distribution set attacks in motion and team-mates passed to him in the sure knowledge that when the ball was returned it would be placed to perfection. He was, in effect, a midfielder – more than 10 years before such position became an accepted part of the British game.

Bob Brown: An Amazing Coincidence

At eight minutes past four on the afternoon of Saturday, 23rd January 1954, in a Third Division game against Darlington, Bob Brown was within an inch of securing a place in Oakwell's goal-scoring history. But having already scored four times, his 57th-minute penalty-kick crashed against the cross-bar, thus losing him an opportunity to rank alongside four men who had each scored five times in a single game. Nevertheless, his 25 goals in that season was an exceptional total for a player who wasn't a centre forward.

Bob had been a semi-professional with Scottish junior team Glasgow Perthshire before joining the Black Watch regiment in 1942. He was then 17 years old and served in North Africa and Italy before returning to the UK in 1946. His demobilization was delayed for two days as he was required for an Army Cup-tie against the Royal Engineers; the opposing goalkeeper being a Derby County player who was sufficiently impressed to arrange a trial for him at the Baseball Ground. He later signed for Derby and although retained for only one season and not getting into the first team, he joined his next three clubs on the strength of good impressions created there.

His move to Southend United in the summer of 1948 was on the recommendation of a Derby-based friend of the manager; two years later he joined Shrewsbury Town – managed by Sammy Crooks who had been a coach at Derby – at the start of what was the club's first season in the Football League and in 1953 he joined Barnsley, where manager Tim Ward had been the Derby County captain. The move to Oakwell came immediately after the club's relegation into the Third Division and Ward was so keen to get the player that he traced him to a holiday caravan at Skegness in order to obtain his signature.

He was an instant success – as early as 29th August putting the team on course for their first home success in 27 attempts with a fine opening goal in what became a 2 – 1 win against Bradford Park Avenue. The Reds ended the season as runners-up and Bob's contribution of goals was the second-highest the club had had in the post-war years.

The following campaign, that of 1954/55, brought the Northern Section championship to Oakwell. It was as good as won when Bob, with a goal three minutes from the end, secured a 2 – 0 win at Chester on 30th April. Four days later the Reds were champions in both name and deed. Then, in the final game,

Chester – again – were beaten and Bob's season finished on a personal high note with a hat-trick in a 4 – 2 victory.

During the following summer he and team-mate Harry May felt that the players should have been eligible for winter wages three weeks earlier than the date the club had decided upon, and they approached the board on behalf of the remainder of the staff. The difference of £3 between winter and summer wages may seem of little significance now, but in 1955 it was twenty per-cent of first team pay. The directors' original decision prevailed but, somehow, details were 'leaked' to the press – despite a rule that players should not discuss club affairs with reporters without the board's prior approval.

Although Bob had always been an inside left with an ability to play at centre forward, in the private practice games during August he was selected at outside left. When he was retained in the role for the first public practice he could not help but think that it had something to do with his part in what had eventually been published in local and national newspapers. Consequently he handed in a written request to be transferred.

The handful of spectators at the practice game must have soon become aware of his dislike of the outside left position because for the opening 15 minutes he seemed almost disinterested in what was going on around him. But natural inclination then took over. Moving inside, he scored one goal and helped in making two more. A few days later he withdrew his transfer request but, nevertheless, played several Second Division games at outside left before being chosen in his customary role. Then 31 years old, he relished what was his first opportunity to play at the higher level. His one-hundredth game for Barnsley was on 10th December 1955 against Liverpool at Anfield. He celebrated in style with a splendid goal – receiving the ball from Arthur Kaye and racing fully 40 yards through the home defence before shooting past the advancing 'keeper and providing the Reds with a share of the points. And in the following April, for the second time in three seasons, he was leading scorer.

In the 1956/57 season he was quickly on the goal-trail again. At Bristol City on 8th September he ran 20 yards through the opposing defence to beat the goalkeeper with a spanking drive from the edge of the penalty-area, but that was to be his last appearance with the Reds. A matter of days later, after 130 games and 58 goals, he was transferred to Rotherham United.

His debut for the Millers was against Swansea Town on the same day as Roy Stephenson, a much higher-priced player whom the club had obtained from the First Division, yet Bob scored twice in a 6 – 1 victory and Stephenson was not among the scorers. But the single goal he needed in order to record one hundred in the League was three months in the getting, principally because within a few weeks he contracted pneumonia and was out of the game for two months. Towards the end of that time the manager and the club doctor exchanged heated words over his fitness to play – the team were in a bad patch and his proven scoring touch was required – but when he eventually returned it was soon apparent the illness had taken its toll and he did not again play to his previous standard. Nevertheless, his century was reached by the first of his two goals which beat Leyton Orient in March 1957 and he had totalled 109 by the time of his departure from the Football League on leaving Rotherham United in the summer of 1958.

He then had two seasons at King's Lynn, after which he joined Scarborough. Two seasons there were followed by one with Selby Town and he then reverted to amateur status and played for a Working Men's Club in Rotherham until 44 years old.

On leaving Rotherham United he took employment with a company which constructed sports grounds and over the following five years he learned all aspects of the trade. In 1963 he was taken on a three months' trial as groundsman at Millmoor and was delighted to be again involved in senior football. During the summer he dug up the playing area with borrowed equipment – it had to be borrowed, the club didn't have any of its own – and created a new pitch which, by the start of the season, looked in better condition than anyone could recall. After a year he enquired about the pay increase promised when the trial proved satisfactory, but considered the subsequent offer of an additional ten shillings (50p) per week insulting and promptly left the club. For the next 13 years he worked as a boiler operator at Rotherham power station, then for a further seven years he was employed in the same capacity at Doncaster until 1984, when he took early retirement.

Bob Brown's goals against Darlington in January 1954 included a nine-minute hat-trick; the fourth coming when he seized onto a pass from Lol Chappell and raced through in brilliant style to crack the ball home. A four-goal feat is commendable at any time, but conversion of the 57th-minute penalty would, in addition to putting Bob in the record books, have created a unique hat-trick for the Barnsley club. For, of the five players who would then have scored five goals in a single game, three of them would have done it against Darlington!

John Thomas: An Exceptional Talent

A slip of the tongue by trainer Bob Shotton while introducing John Thomas to the staff at Oakwell resulted in the player's new colleagues knowing him as 'Joe'. But in the name in which he had been christened he was already well known in football, cricket, bowls and tennis arenas in the environs of Doncaster where he had spent his formative years. He was to have five seasons as a Barnsley full back and membership of the side who were runners-up in Division Three (North) in 1954 and champions in the following year, missing only two games in those two excellent seasons. It was while at Oakwell that he realized he had a natural aptitude for the game of golf, developing into a scratch player and one of the country's leading amateurs, and a regular winner of competitions at county and regional level.

A Lancastrian, he moved with his parents to Askern, near Doncaster, when work in the mines took his father to Askern Colliery in the aftermath of the 1926 General Strike. As a wing half John later played for Doncaster Boys and on leaving school he joined the Askern Youth Club side.

To say his first period of employment was brief is an understatement: it lasted until lunch time on the first day. At school his favourite subject was Art and, keen to pursue that interest, he obtained work with a Doncaster signwriter. His first task was not what he expected, for he spent the whole morning on a pedal-operated press, printing thousands of business cards. At the lunch-break he was with a colleague who had been working alongside him and who had joined the firm four weeks earlier. Anxious to know when he would start getting the kind of work he wanted, he enquired how often the other had done any signwriting. And on being told that the previous month had been spent entirely on the pedal-operated press he replied, 'Well I'm not doing that, so tell them I shan't be coming back!' On the following day he began work as an apprentice electrician at Askern Colliery. He remained there for the following 10 years, at one stage combining work with football until the Barnsley team he was eventually to join won promotion into the Second Division.

In 1948 he joined Wolves' nursery side, Wath Wanderers, and became a part-time professional with the parent club a year later. At that time, on Fridays, the Molyneux dressing room notice board displayed details of *seven* teams to be fielded on the following day. John began in the third team and progressed to the reserves, but his continuing to work at the colliery was not to the club's liking. It was not their policy to have part-time players and only John's determination not to give up his employment enabled Barnsley to obtain him in June 1952.

His debut was in September in a 3 – 2 defeat by Everton, and by winning a regular place in the following February he had the doubtful privilege of being in a side which ended the season in bottom place in the Second Division. Happily, team performances improved considerably in Division Three. At that stage of his career John became the subject of consistently favourable press comment. And it wasn't confined to the Barnsley area, for in reporting the Reds' FA Cup game at Norwich in November 1953 the *Eastern Daily Press* doubted that the home supporters would see a better full back than him in the remainder of the season.

The highlight of his soccer career came with the Reds' championship and promotion in 1955. He missed only two games and his performances were of such consistently high quality that manager Tim Ward, not a man to praise without good cause, was quoted as saying that within a year John would be good enough for the England 'B' side.

But that was not to be, for an injury against Notts County in the second game of the next season necessitated the removal of a cartilage and he was out of the side until the end of the following March. He retained a first team place at the beginning of the next season, that of 1956/57, but never regained the pre-injury form and the club's signing of his former Wolverhampton colleague John Short effectively ended his Oakwell career.

In March 1958 he was transferred to Mansfield Town. A season later he joined Chesterfield where, following another cartilage operation, specialist advice that he would always be susceptible to ligament trouble and should not risk further injury brought about his retirement from the game at the early age of 27.

John's happiest time in football was with Barnsley and he considers it an honour to have played for the club. The players were all good pals and enjoyed each other's company so much that there were times when the trainers actually had to *send* them home. And while he was an Oakwell player he met some of soccer's most renowned individuals – men who were masters of the game and held in a kind of awe by this impressionable young footballer. Once when the team were in London, staying at the Great Northern Hotel at King's Cross at the same time as the Blackpool side, Stanley Matthews came and chatted to them; after a game at Stockport, Tim Ward brought his former England colleague Frank Swift – who was to perish at Munich Airport three years later with some of the country's greatest players – into the dressing room and John recalls that Swift's hand was so big that it seemed to completely engulf his own as they shook hands; and once while he was waiting at a bus stop at Askern, Raich Carter, one of the greatest inside forwards of all time, spotted him and stopped his car to offer a lift. One of his most vivid memories from those years is of walking towards Oakwell for an evening training session and seeing people crying in the street – and learning, as they had just done, of the Manchester

United disaster at Munich. And the overriding impression of his time at Barnsley is the kindness of the local people.

On becoming a full-time player in 1956 he hoped to continue in the game until his early thirties and, having looked after his money, intended then to go into business as a sports outfitter. The curtailing of his career meant he hadn't accumulated the capital necessary for such venture, so, instead, he went into the insurance business. He joined the staff of the Pearl Assurance Company at Chesterfield, was eventually promoted assistant manager and remained with them until 1973. Then he went into business as an insurance broker, dealing in the full range of life cover and private and company pensions. Over the intervening years J C Thomas & Co has fulfilled all his expectations. It provides him with a pleasant living; enables him to have holidays whenever he wants to take them and, perhaps even more important, enables him to play golf to his heart's content.

The golf involvement began as part of the Oakwell training routine. The players had a weekly round at Staincross and those who didn't take part were required to carry the clubs of those who did. Having no intention of being a permanent caddie, he acquired some clubs and received tuition from team-mate Harry Hough. Harry has surely not had another pupil who took so easily to the game. John's driving had length and direction from the start; when he hit the ball it seemed almost always to end up where he wanted it to be, and before long his handicap was in single figures.

Two years after leaving Barnsley he declined an offer of the job of assistant professional at Coxmoor Golf Club, Chesterfield, and to this day he regrets that missed opportunity. But he was still in football and there was then no real indication that top-class golfers were soon to begin to accumulate considerable sums of money.

He has had membership of the Chesterfield club since 1959. Three years later, by which time he was a scratch player, he was chosen to represent Derbyshire and played for the county side on 80 occasions over the following 15 years. There was a year when he was only one stroke from entry into the British Open; the innumerable competitions he has won include the Derbyshire Open, the Derbyshire Amateur Championship three times and the Midlands Senior Championship – and he doesn't even have to practice. The game has been such a major part of his life over the last 30 years that he would willingly give up everything achieved in a successful business career if he could only put the clock back and take his chance as a professional golfer.

Golf and football are but two of a list of games at which he has excelled. For 10 years from the age of 16 he was an opening bowler and number 5 batsman with Askern CC in the Yorkshire Council; he played lawn tennis in the Doncaster and Barnsley Leagues, and his team in the Chesterfield Table Tennis League won consecutive championships in the two years he was with them. But one of his most noteworthy achievements was when, as a member of Askern Bowling Club, he was club champion when 13 years old!

John Thomas's strengths as a footballer were skills which came naturally plus speed and anticipation: if a winger beat him on the half-way line he could usually catch him before he got to the penalty-area. On joining Barnsley as a teenager he was of such slender build that skipper Norman Smith – himself no heavyweight – said John was the only one he'd ever seen who could hula hoop with a Polo Mint! Yet the exceptional talent which nature had bestowed enabled him to not only play any games he chose, but to play them exceedingly well.

George Spruce: A Manager's Fine Judgement

George Spruce was centre half in Barnsley's 1955 championship side, having joined the club three years earlier from Wrexham where he had the reputation of being one of the best centre halves in the Third Division. Time proved the esteem to have been well earned and at least one good judge of a player regards him as the most constructive centre half the Reds have had.

As a young teenager he was small for his age and football at school was as an outside left, in which position he represented Chester Boys, the sturdier build of a centre half not developing until several years later during service in the Royal Navy. On leaving school he obtained employment as a milk roundsman and, still a winger, he joined local side Heath Rangers. Playing football was then all he really wanted to do and, not being an ambitious individual, he was content to stay with Rangers and refused trials with half a dozen League clubs whose standing in the game ranged from the now long-defunct New Brighton to Arsenal and Liverpool. Yet a trial he was eventually persuaded to have, with Bolton Wanderers, was curtailed by the outbreak of the Second World War.

Work as a milkman and football with Heath Rangers continued until early 1941 when he was conscripted into the navy. Initial training was at the incomplete and commandeered Butlin's Holiday Camp at Pwllheli and, on qualifying as a gunner, he was posted to DEMS – defensively equipped merchant ships which had been fitted with Orelikon rapid fire guns as a defence against enemy air attacks. For the following four years he served in the North and South Atlantic, Indian Ocean and Mediterranean, sometimes in a convoy and sometimes not. The nearest he got to action was when his ship rescued survivors from a U-boat attack with wreckage from the sunken vessel still floating at the scene, but while sailing some of the most dangerous sea lanes in the world Ordinary Seaman-Gunner Spruce considered himself fortunate in never hearing a shot fired in anger.

In 1944 he played the first football of his naval service. Then based at Trincomalee, Ceylon, games were against sides from other ships and local sides who played in bare feet. His demobilization was, in fact, delayed for two weeks in order that he would be available for the base's football programme.

The autumn of 1945 saw him back on the milk-round and footballing with Heath Rangers, and that is almost certainly how it would have remained but for a particularly persistent Wrexham scout. After the enforced absence he was totally engrossed in the game, even to the extent of declining an invitation to his sister's Saturday afternoon wedding and, as in his younger days, was content to play it at local level. But the scout was also a neighbour and accosted him almost daily – at home, in the street and even at his place of work, continually urging him to have trials at Wrexham. Eventually he agreed. The scout was certainly perceptive, for after only three games in the 'A' team and two in the reserves he won a place in the first team.

That took place soon after the start of the 1948 season and he played 135 games over the next four years. He had been a centre half since his time in Ceylon, but the skills which had developed as a teenage winger provided him with a more constructive style than was the norm for defenders in the Third Division. It was doubtless an ability to work the ball out of tight situations rather than booting it up the field and the frequency with which his astute passes set attacks in motion which prompted the manager to use him as a wing half. However, it was a role he didn't want. He went so far as to ask to be left out of the team if he couldn't have the number 5 shirt, but that never happened.

It was disenchantment with things at Wrexham which made him responsive to Barnsley's approach in May 1952, even though manager Angus Seed made it clear that he would be joining the club as a reserve. Yet, in the light of the circumstances which brought him to Oakwell, one can well imagine his feelings when, three weeks into the new season, he made his Second Division debut at . . . right half.

He made a further five appearances that season – all at centre half – and following Matt McNeil's transfer in the following summer he took over in the first team at the start of the 1953/54 season. By that time the Reds were in the Northern Section of the Third Division; he played in each of the 46 games and the season ended with them in the runners-up position. In the following campaign they did even better, and being a member of Barnsley's championship side was the high-point of George's long playing career.

But a low-point came after only six weeks in the Second Division when, in October 1955 at West Ham, he had the misfortune to break his right leg. It was a measure of the friendliness for which the London club was renowned that some of its supporters beat manager Tim Ward to the hospital with condolences and fruit. The medical staff were equally prompt, for George was treated and, with leg in plaster, travelled back to Barnsley with Ward later in the evening.

He returned to the side in the following March and was captain during Norman Smith's long injury-absence in 1956/57. In that campaign he played 39 games but the manager was obviously looking to the future and in the final stages George made way for young Duncan Sharp. His final season at Oakwell was spent in the reserves and in April 1958 he was given a free transfer.

Then 35, he had no real expectation of remaining in the professional game and during the summer returned to live in his home town. Soon afterwards he was invited to take part in a testimonial for a Chester player. His display at left back was sufficient for the club to sign him and he had a more or less regular first team place for the following three seasons.

In 1961 he finally had to accept that his League career had come to an end. He was therefore delighted to be offered the job of groundsman-second team trainer. It was particularly pleasing because he knew a lot about each aspect of the role; his father had been a groundsman for 50 years and George, in his youth, had spent many an hour helping him, and two of his brothers had followed their father into that line of work. No longer being a player, he knew to expect a reduction in wages but was dismayed to learn the job paid only £6 per week. He took his concern to the chairman who asked what wage he had expected. On hearing George had hoped for at least £10 he said, 'We can't possibly pay you that, it's more than the first team trainer is getting!' He therefore left the club and had two seasons in non-League football with Runcorn and Prestatyn, thereby remaining a professional player until he was 40 years old.

On leaving Chester and full-time football he worked for the Gas Board as a meter-reader/collector. During six years in the job he did what he had hoped to do in senior soccer, albeit at a much lower level, with part-time work as football coach at a private school and groundsman at a works sports complex.

In 1969 he took over his father-in-law's hackney carriage business which the latter had had since the end of the First World War. But it had certain disadvantages; the occasional week-end reveller would sometimes infuriate him more than anything that ever happened on the football pitch, and an instance of bilking would sometimes make the difference between a profit and a loss on a day's work. Nevertheless, he enjoyed the involvement with the vast majority of his customers and retained the business for 17 years until taking early retirement in 1985.

When the young George Spruce reached manhood his weight remained constant, year in, year out. He was particularly thankful for the unvarying avoirdupois when pre-season training began; trainer Bob Shotton would put the others through strenuous and hated routines to shed excess pounds accumulated during the summer, yet George was allowed to train in whichever way he preferred. Even now, at 66, he has the same tall, lean build of the man who so effectively policed the centre of Barnsley's defence in the mid-1950s.

His joining the club in 1952 was somewhat surprising, for £10,000 was a big fee for a reserve centre half who, at 29, was appreciably older than the man he was to understudy. However, his signing proved to be another example of Angus Seed's fine judgement. The player became the most popular at Oakwell – for both his pleasant manner and the way he played, which had the style and polish of the then England centre half, Neil Franklin. He was far removed from the traditional 'stopper' and continually dribbled the ball out of the penalty-area before passing to a colleague. Tim Ward wanted him to clear his lines quicker and told him he was far too casual, but had to accept George's reply that that was how he was and he couldn't see himself altering. Yet there were others on the scene who liked to see some culture in the heart of a defence and wouldn't have had him change, and one of them, Gordon Pallister, regards him as the most constructive centre half the club has had in the last 50 years.

Arthur Kaye: An Aggressive Intent

Arthur Kaye was born at the Miners Inn at Higham where his father was the licensee and at 17 he became a Barnsley footballer, developing into a fiery, dynamic right winger and reaching the verge of the England team. Now, after a career which took him via Blackpool to Middlesbrough in the North-East and Colchester in the South-East, he is living a mere quarter mile from the first address he had in the town.

An outstanding schoolboy footballer, he won honours at county and national levels and his skills were of such natural origin that, without tuition of any kind, he could control a ball with his feet when only four years old. Football at Darton High School took him to membership of the Barnsley and Yorkshire Boys teams and a place in the England side against Scotland in 1948. In the same year he was in the Barnsley team which reached the semi-finals of the English Trophy – by which time he had attracted the attention of Sheffield Wednesday. He spent a week training there and his refusal to join them was a great disappointment to former Oakwell stalwart Johnny Logan who was then on the Hillsborough coaching staff and had encouraged him to go there, but the youngster was determined to sign for his home town club.

On leaving school he became an amateur at Oakwell and began a joinery apprenticeship with local builders William Goodyear & Son Ltd. In May 1950 he became a part-time professional and in the following January he made his Second Division debut in a 1 – 1 draw at Luton Town. During the season he had two further outings and became increasingly concerned that his career in football was being hampered and delayed by the apprenticeship and eventual National Service. His employers had a good relationship with the club in that they carried out much of the repair and development work at the ground, and were understanding in respect of his request to cancel the indentures. That done, he wanted National Service out of the way and early in 1952 he was conscripted into the Royal Army Medical Corps. Stationed initially at Aldershot and later at Fulford Barracks, York, he played for the Regimental, Northern Command, and British Army teams. During that time he won a regular place in the Reds' side and became a full-time player on completion of military service in 1954, by which time he was undoubtedly the Oakwell crowd's favourite footballer.

The following season saw Barnsley champions of Division Three (North), having attained top place on Easter Monday when a superb goal from Arthur helped towards a 2 – 0 success at Bradford City. The Second Division calendar began with a visit by Leeds United when he scored a splendid winning goal from a free-kick awarded for a foul on himself on the edge of the penalty-area. Within a matter of weeks he won his first senior representative honour by being chosen for the England under-23 team against Denmark – and acquitted himself well by having a hand in three of England's five goals.

Season 1956/57 was a splendid one for him. In August, in the last minute of the game at Swansea he collected the ball near the halfway-line and beat man after man to score the winning goal. Two weeks later he gave a superb individual display to score twice and make a goal for Malcolm Graham in a 3 – 3 draw with Blackburn Rovers. And the excellent performances went on throughout the season, continually drawing favourable press reports and suggestions of international honours and transfers into the First Division.

Against Ipswich Town in the early weeks of the following campaign he produced one of the finest individual displays Oakwell has ever seen. Time after time he cut through the visitors' defence and scored a fine solo goal and two fiercely-struck penalties in the Reds' 5 – 1 win. Soon afterwards he played for the Football League against the Irish League and was in the England World Cup squad at the first and intermediate stages but, to his bitter disappointment, was excluded from the final party. It was unfortunate that his three seasons in the Second Division had been in a side which in the main had been struggling, for there were many observers – some based far from Barnsley – who considered him to be the best right winger in the country, yet full international honours were to evade him.

In the summer of 1958 the maximum weekly wage of professional footballers was raised to £20, but at Oakwell the increase was implemented only partially, to £18. During Arthur's seasons with the club he had been totally committed to its cause; the board had refused substantial offers for him from Spurs, Newcastle United and Chelsea but, in any event, he would not have wished to be transferred. He was therefore totally disillusioned by the refusal to pay him the maximum wage. Several other players originally rejected the new terms but during the summer the number holding out gradually reduced until he was the only one who hadn't re-signed.

At first he felt sure the club would give him what he felt to be his due – after all, he was the star player – but eventually he had to accept the lesser amount offered to him. It left him feeling let down, by both the directors and his colleagues who could have supported him but failed to do so. His mind began to dwell on the really good players who had been allowed to leave in the past and the possible reasons for their departure. He linked his conclusions to his own experience and, not surprisingly, there was a change in the long-standing devotion he'd had for the club. Although he couldn't intentionally give less than his best, thereafter his play seemed to lack something of its previous 'bite'. It was a time of generally poor performances by the team and they ended the season in the division's bottom place, but Arthur was spared that final ignominy.

After a 3 – 1 defeat at Ipswich on 14th March 1959 he was dropped for the only time in seven years, and that was his last game for the Reds.

Within a couple of weeks of the season ending he was transferred to Blackpool for the quite modest fee of £13,000 – and there is no doubt his omission from the Barnsley team over the preceding two months lost the club several thousand pounds. His start with the Seasiders couldn't have been on a more appropriate day; Saturday, 22nd August was the beginning of Barnsley's annual Feast Week, and at that time the traditional holiday resort for local folk was the town where Arthur Kaye was about to make his debut as a First Division footballer. On that sundrenched afternoon the 30,000 spectators included about 10,000 from Barnsley – and they couldn't have been more delighted with their favourite player's performance. The disappointments of the previous year behind him, he was his old aggressive, abrasive, brilliant self and helped pull back an early 2 – 0 deficit with a hand in two goals in an exciting 3 – 2 victory over old rivals Bolton Wanderers.

He had been signed by Blackpool as replacement for the legendary but ageing Stanley Matthews. However, most of Arthur's games were at inside right as Matthews' partner and he came to regard the former England winger as a truly great player and the finest he ever saw.

His time at Blackpool ended unexpectedly in November 1960 when Middlesbrough made an offer for him which his club accepted, and the new terms were at a financial level he had not previously thought possible to attain. He remained at Middlesbrough for five years before joining Colchester United. Again, he hadn't been made available for transfer but Colchester, in the form of manager and former England centre half Neil Franklin, secured him by paying what was a substantial sum for a 32-year-old. His new team won promotion to Division Three in his first season, but a damaged Achilles tendon limited his stay to two years and brought his professional career to an end in 1967.

He then returned to Barnsley and worked again for Goodyears, and after five years with them he joined the Building Department of Wombwell District Council. Several jobs later he took employment with the NCB's Building Department, remaining there until taking voluntary redundancy in 1985. He is now a self-employed joiner, and he and a bricklayer colleague together involve themselves in every aspect of their trades, from routine repairs to building houses.

On returning to Barnsley in 1967 he worked part-time for two years for the County Borough of Barnsley Education Department as a football coach at schools and youth clubs. He was also player, manager and general factotum of the California Hotel team in the Barnsley Sunday League. He remained with them for two seasons, in each of which they were promoted to a higher division of the league.

Walking is his present form of recreation. On at least one evening during each week and on Saturdays and Sundays he tramps a 10-mile circuitous route from Higham via High Hoyland and Hoylandswaine, and one of the weekend walks is usually in the company of his younger son, John. John is a Physics graduate of Hull University, and elder son Steven – an Engineering graduate – works as a freelance artist in Colchester.

Arthur Kaye's attainment of under-23 international status is the highest post-war English acknowledgement the Barnsley club has had, and only one other player has received recognition at Football League level during that time. At 5′ 5″ he seemed almost as broad as he was tall, and against some full backs he would start the game by pushing the ball down the wing and running at full speed into them – willingly conceding a free kick, but he believed in getting his retaliation in first! He was a real crowd puller. Supporters loved his aggressive style and the way he tore into the opposition and the manner in which he could completely take over a game, and when he was grounded he was invariably back on his feet in a flash – he wanted the ball so much. Had his peak seasons of 1955–1958 been with a more fashionable club or perhaps even a Barnsley side of earlier years, he would have received honours in abundance but, be that as it may, he was an idol of the Oakwell supporters and his skill and determination would earn him a place in Barnsley's best-ever team.

Lol Chappell: A Record Well Earned

Larratt (Lol) Chappell was leading scorer in Barnsley's 1955 Division Three (North) championship season and his 21 goals included three hat-tricks. Indeed, in six completed Oakwell seasons he did the hat-trick on six occasions – more times than anyone else in club history – and his total of 94 League goals is the highest of any Barnsley player.

A High Green boy, on leaving school at 14 he worked in Wm Green's foundry at Ecclesfield and junior football was with the foundry side, Thorncliffe Welfare and Birdwell Rovers. It was while with the latter side in 1947 that Barnsley signed him as an amateur and he became a professional in May 1949, a matter of weeks before he was conscripted into the army for National Service.

Stationed at Catterick Camp in the 16th/5th Lancers, weekend leave enabled him to play fairly regularly for the 'A' team, but on the first occasion that such leave was not granted he absented himself in order to play against Sheffield Wednesday reserves. Monday morning punishment included a posting to Egypt, where he remained for a year before returning to the UK.

His debut in the first team was as stand-in at inside right for Tommy Lumley at Birmingham City in November 1952. The Reds lost 3 – 1, but it fell to Lol to score their goal and in the following March he succeeded Tommy Taylor on the latter's transfer to Manchester United. Thereafter he was always at centre forward.

It was a season which saw Barnsley relegated from the Second Division. In the following campaign, 1953/54, they were runners-up in the Northern Section, on 6th March Lol recording his first League hat-trick in a 4 – 2 success at Carlisle United. A week later, in a 5 – 0 beating of Accrington Stanley, he helped in the scoring of two goals and then lit up the final few minutes with two of his own – the first followed a 40-yard dash before planting the ball firmly past the 'keeper, and the second was a header which the *Sheffield Telegraph* described as being reminiscent of Tommy Taylor at his best.

A year later Barnsley were champions, and Lol's contribution was 21 goals. In the run-in he scored twice in a 3 – 0 defeat of Bradford City before a crowd in excess of 18,000 and a fortnight later he had two more in a 3 – 1 defeat of Carlisle United.

The opening season in Division Two was, in the main, a long struggle, in part due to Lol's injury-absence throughout the autumn. In the end they finished six points clear of relegation, an enormous help being his two goals – including the winner – against Swansea Town in April after the team had trailed 2 – 0 at the interval.

In November 1956 he sustained cartilage damage in a game at Oakwell against Huddersfield Town, and after he'd been carried from the pitch the visitors ran riot and scored five times without reply. The injury required surgery at Claremont Nursing Home, Sheffield, for which the club paid a surgeon's fee of £50 and an identical sum for the patient's 14-day stay there. Such charges may now be thought extremely cheap but, to put them in context, each equated to almost three weeks' wages for a Barnsley footballer. And the £520 benefit payment which Lol received after eight years as a professional would now barely pay *one week's* wage of a Barnsley player.

The 1957/58 season ended with him again top scorer, and in the opening week he must have delighted manager and former Derby County captain Tim Ward with a hat-trick in a 4 – 1 win at the Baseball Ground. The following season brought an end to his time at Oakwell; again he led the scorers but, just as his first appearances in the team had been closely followed by relegation, so were his last.

In the summer of 1959 a fee of £4,000 took him to Doncaster Rovers. However, a knee injury limited him to 34 appearances and at the season's end he wasn't retained.

Less than two months after surgery to the damaged knee, in August 1960, he joined Bath City in the Southern League. A year later he was set to return to his South Yorkshire roots and had arranged to play for Wisbech Town when, out of the blue, came an approach from Bideford. He had no intention of joining them but he, his wife Greta and their three children went to look at the place and promptly fell in love with it. So much so that, apart from a fairly brief spell when business took him to Portsmouth, Lol stayed in the area for the remainder of his life, and Greta and the now grown-up children are still there.

Four seasons with Bideford included membership of the 1964 Western League championship side. Following from that success he was appointed player-manager of Barnstaple Town, and he remained there until reaching 40. Then, although choosing the team, he felt unable to justify a place for himself and decided to move to a club where he could continue to play.

He then reverted to amateur status and joined Appledore FC in the North Devon Premier League. Although declining an official position, he was really the man in charge and instilled a professional attitude within the club. Much of what he introduced still continues – not least his insistence that the team ran onto the pitch together, in line, as though they meant business, rather than in the haphazard, 'whenever you're ready' fashion which appertained on his arrival. He refused payment of any kind, wanting only to give something back to a game which had provided him with endless enjoyment.

Appledore won at least one trophy in every season but one while he was with them, and on the only occasion when they missed out they were finalists in both the Westward Ho! and Devon Charity Cups. He continued to play until he was 47, and he did so much for the club that he is remembered with affection by those connected with it.

On leaving professional football, although still in the game with Appledore, he felt a need for a new challenge. Consequently he took up squash, receiving tuition from a professional coach and becoming a really good player. He represented Devon County Veterans, and on moving to Hampshire he joined Portsmouth Squash Club – one of the best on the South Coast – and won a place in their team despite being well into his fifties.

When football took Lol into the West Country he worked as an agent for the Wesleyan and General Assurance Society. He quickly found that being a popular figure on the local soccer scene was greatly to his advantage; people invited him into their homes to talk about football and before they knew what was happening he'd sold them a policy!

He was so successful that within three years he was a district manager and the Society's tutor in the South-West. In 1985 he was promoted to a bigger area covering Hampshire and the Isle of Wight, but a year later he left the Society and returned to Devon to become proprietor of the Barley Grove Service Station in Torrington. Sadly, the venture was short-lived. Within six months he began to tire easily and feel generally unwell, but he continued with both work and squash. Indeed, during that period he won the veterans' championship at the local Riverside Squash Club but the time came when he had to seek medical help. He was then found to have a brain tumour. After several months in hospital he returned to the family home at Little Torrington where he died a week later, on 19th February 1988, aged 57.

Lol Chappell was a man who thrived on an active involvement in sport, from junior days around Ecclesfield – which included cricket with Mortomley St Saviour's – through his best years with Barnsley and less demanding times in the West Country, and into the instant activity of squash to which he adapted so successfully in his mature years. He was even to the fore in games of poker which took place on the coach while travelling to away games. Although on one visit to Bristol he won £25 but lost that amount and more besides on the return journey, and Harry Hough had to lend him the few coppers needed for his bus fare home to Gawber!

He joined the Barnsley staff as a right winger, being converted to a centre forward while still a junior. Despite the coaches' best efforts he remained essentially a right foot player; the other eventually being used with some confidence in training but he never seemed to trust it on match days. Chairman Joe Richards publicly expressed a view that he was the greatest trier the club had ever had; certainly he was a non-stop worker who chased every chance that carried the merest hint of a goal. His being leading scorer is therefore an honour well earned, as indeed were six hat-tricks. Actually, there was another – in a pre-season friendly at Falkirk in August 1953, but the scoring day which should have given him most pleasure but, instead, ended in utter frustration was the occasion of Bristol City's visit on 27th August 1958. Then he scored four times – and rarely can a player have had such a personally successful afternoon yet been in a losing side!

Harry Hough: The Most By Far

Harry Hough's interest in football developed almost by chance. At High Green Secondary Modern School he took no part in the game, and in 1939 while serving with 262 Squadron Air Training Corps his offer to play in goal for their team was not taken up until the regular custodian was eventually drafted into the Royal Air Force.

Then his displays in ATC football came to the notice of those in charge of football at his place of employment, the Chapeltown-based Newton Chambers & Co, and he accepted their invitation to join the Thorncliffe Welfare side in a Sheffield amateur league. He remained with them for three seasons, in each of which they won the Wharncliffe Charity Cup and conceded fewer goals than any other team in the league.

On leaving school he had obtained employment at Newton Chambers' Barley Hall Colliery and four years later, at 18, he was working at the coal face. In September 1947 he became a part-time player at Oakwell and continued his work in the mine until becoming a full-time professional early in 1951.

With but three 'A' team games and a handful of reserve outings behind him he made his Second Division debut within seven weeks of joining the club. The first three-and-a-half seasons were spent as deputy to Pat Kelly and in September 1950 he was in the Barnsley reserve side which played a Central League game at St James' Park, Newcastle, in front of *20,000* spectators. And he excelled at saving penalty-kicks at some of the game's most exhalted grounds. In a goal-less draw at Villa Park in December 1948 he saved a penalty from former English international centre forward Dickie Dorsett; at Old Trafford in August 1949 he saved each of the home side's attempts to score from a twice-taken penalty, and at Goodison Park on Good Friday 1951 he saved each of two penalties awarded to Everton. In-between-times, at Oakwell in 1949, Bury reserves were allowed *three* attempts at taking a penalty: two missed the goal and Harry saved the one which was on target.

He won a regular place in the first team in the spring of 1951 and in the following year had the most disappointing experience of his career. His displays had been of such consistently good quality that he was chosen for the England 'B' side against Holland, but an arm broken against Sheffield Wednesday in the week preceding the international game prevented him accepting the honour. Surprisingly, another chance to do so did not come his way. He was the only player to be continuously in the Reds' team throughout seasons 1953/1955 when they were runners-up and then champions of Division Three (North). The unbroken run of games continued until Boxing Day 1956, by which time he had created a club record of 176 consecutive appearances.

In February 1959 he was dropped from the team after a 5 – 0 defeat at Sheffield United. Manager Tim Ward blamed him for all the goals and maintained he had become over confident. It was a view which Harry couldn't accept, and several months elapsed before he formed his own conclusions about the reason for his omission. When he lost his place the team were in a mid-table position but thereafter went steadily downwards and at Easter were in next-bottom place with relegation inevitable.

In such situations managers usually rely on experience to stop the rot. Prior to losing his place Harry had missed only two games in the previous five seasons, but he did not again play for the team. Yet shortly before he was cast aside chairman Joe Richards had made special reference to him at the club's annual meeting in the terms, '... He is a fine type of player with a wonderful record. We are fortunate to have him on the books.'

At the season's end Harry was placed on the transfer list ... and then things began to fall into place. A year earlier he and Bob Midwood, a local businessman and renowned amateur golfer, had formed a partnership as sports outfitters and, by competitive pricing and a lot of hard work, were getting the venture onto a sound footing. While he was available for transfer, Tim Ward arranged for him to visit the manager of Walsall with a view to moving there. He returned to Barnsley with things more or less finalized and told Ward what had taken place. He was then instructed to see the chairman at his office at Worsbrough. On being ushered into his presence the latter opened with, 'You've cut our profits to the bone since you started up.' Harry was nonplussed. The chairman had spoken to him on only two previous occasions in all his years at the club and this remark seemed to have no relevance to what he believed to be the purpose of his visit. Trying to steer the conversation in the right direction, he said, 'Mr Ward has arranged for me to be transferred to Walsall.' The chairman's response was, 'The manager had no right to do that without my approval. You're *not* going to Walsall, and since you and Mr Midwood have started in business you've cut our profits to the bone.'

Then the penny began to drop. Mr Richards must have a financial interest in Cleggs, another sports outfitters in the town, situated a mere hundred yards from Hough & Midwood in Sheffield Road. He was then dismissed, but believed he had discovered the reason for his omission from the team and being required to leave the club so soon after his worth had been publicly proclaimed.

In July he was transferred to Bradford Park Avenue. By then a qualified FA coach, he took charge of training during a managerial vacancy in 1962 and in the following year was appointed player-manager of Denaby United in the Midland League. He was chosen from a short-list of two – the other being fellow sports outfitter and Rotherham United player Danny Williams. And Harry feels the committee must have found his terms for the supply of kit more attractive than Danny's!

He remained at Denaby for three seasons and had a good working relationship with chairman Sam Peck. But when Peck retired, Harry found there were some on the committee who wanted to influence selection of the team. He therefore decided to let them get on with it. He resigned and spent the following season as player-manager of Wharncliffe Woodmoor in the Barnsley League. He used the club's excellent facilities for Sunday morning soccer schools; up to a hundred youngsters attended and he got considerable pleasure from seeing how they developed as the course progressed. At the same time he used his skills at schools in the local West Riding area, and Steve Daley, later a million-pound player with Manchester City, will say that Harry Hough was the first coach he ever had. His final three years in the game were spent as player-manager of Woolley Colliery in the Yorkshire League. It was a successful time in that the team had consecutive promotions to the league's First Division, and on that high note Harry retired in 1972 after 25 years as a professional footballer.

He was the Players' Union representative throughout most of his time at Oakwell and was elected to the union executive in 1957. Eleven years later chairman Jimmy Guthrie retired and it fell to Harry, as the senior member of the executive, to succeed him. However, the demands of business and a need for the chairman to be London-based made it impractical for him to take up an office he would have loved to have had and, reluctantly, he stepped aside to allow Jimmy Hill to become chairman.

Hough and Midwood continued in partnership until 1962 when Harry became a sole trader with premises in Barnsley Road, Cudworth. He remained there for seven years, during which time he supplied kit to almost every club in the Barnsley League. In 1969 he became sub-postmaster at Grimethorpe and later had offices at Sandal, Hipperholme and Cudworth. While at Sandal he and his wife, Joan, bought a holiday home at Filey. They liked the area so much that after two years they purchased a permanent residence there, and after moving back to South Yorkshire and Cudworth sub-post office for a brief period they returned to the east coast town in 1986.

Harry is now in semi-retirement with a part-time job in Action Sport, an organization formed by the Manpower Services Commission to provide sporting facilities for the unemployed, the disabled, and senior citizens. He is a team leader responsible for organizing training and coaching sessions in bowls, badminton, football, table tennis and swimming in Scarborough, Filey and Whitby.

His main interest is now golf. It is a game he has loved since boyhood but he didn't take it up seriously until becoming a Barnsley footballer. His home at Chapeltown was near Tankersley golf course and he and his pals would fashion clubs from sycamore sticks cut from the adjacent woods. And by carefully choosing their times and using balls which the woods also provided they taught themselves the rudiments of the game. His handicap is 8 and has been as low as 2, yet he's only had one lesson in his life. In 1960 Hough & Midwood arranged for Henry Cotton, a three-times winner of the British Open, to give a talk and demonstration to local golf enthusiasts, during which Cotton took it upon himself to spend some time adjusting Harry's rather quick back swing. And after that single lesson it took him nearly 12 months to get the swing right again!

He has played on every major course in England. He reached the finals of the annual PFA competition in each of the 20 years in which he entered and his best performance was in 1955 when he was runner-up to Don Revie. At Silkstone Golf Club he was Barnsley and District champion in 1956 and 1957, and if he has a regret about his life in professional sport it is that it was spent in football instead of golf.

The youthful Harry Hough was not one for strenuous physical activity: while with the ATC he volunteered to keep goal simply because the role didn't require him to run about. And although never a smoker, he had the young miner's propensity for drinking large quantities of beer. But his attitude towards both alcohol and exertion altered dramatically when he joined the Oakwell staff and realized the advantages to be had from a career in football. Then he cut out the drink and took pride in his fitness, developing great physical strength and always taking the lead in training – colleagues intent on showing how fit they were had to be able to keep up with him, and few were ever able to do so. Such wholehearted approach enabled him to be a professional player until he was 47 years old, and his 345 appearances for Barnsley is by far the highest of any goalkeeper the club has had.

John McCann: Beware Irate Goalies!

The first payments which John McCann received in professional football were determined by the number of spectators attending games in which he played. He was then with Bridgeton Waverley, a Glasgow semi-professional club: the players received £1 per thousand spectators, and the average payment was £1.10s.

Earlier he had played for St Gerard's Grammar School and the Glasgow Catholic Schools team, and on leaving school he worked as a trainee manager at the Berryknows branch of the Glasgow Co-operative Society. Then his football was as a wing half with a local junior side and a Bridgeton Waverley scout happened to be present on the only occasion he played at outside left. The outcome was that he joined them as a left winger. A year later he became eligible for National Service and, doubtless due to his civilian job, he was conscripted into the Army Catering Corps. At Bulford Camp in Dorset his duties were in the Sergeants' Mess, and regular involvement in service football included membership of the Catering Corps team which played in the 1954 Army Cup final.

On completion of National Service he returned to his former job with the Co-operative Society and regained a place in the Bridgeton Waverley team which he held until his transfer to Barnsley in December 1955. After being in the reserves until the following April he made his Second Division debut against Nottingham Forest and he also played in the season's final game.

Disappointingly for him, he was excluded from the side at the start of the next season but was back on 5th September against Lincoln City when his perfect cross provided the first goal and he scored the second in what became a 5 – 2 success. Thereafter, injury apart, he was never omitted from the team.

In the following month Liverpool visited Oakwell – and lost 4 – 1. John scored twice, and for the second he beat a defender on the touch-line and streaked towards the goal. The visitors' goalkeeper, Tommy Younger, was a Scottish international and a giant of a man: he advanced towards John who slipped the ball through his legs to score one of the cheekiest goals Oakwell has ever seen. Younger was made to look foolish and snarled an obscenity which made reference to his tormentor's parentage. The young winger knew better than to hang about, and the enraged 'keeper chased him fully 20 yards towards the centre circle before composing himself and returning to his proper place on the pitch!

John's displays were of such consistent quality that in the following February – within six months of winning a first team place – he won Scottish 'B' international honours against England. The Scots reported at their hotel on the morning of the game and played in the evening without having had an opportunity to practice together – and were soundly beaten. John didn't have a particularly good game, and although his personal standard was to rise even higher than at the time of that selection he didn't get another opportunity to play at international level.

In December 1958 the Reds were at home to Sheffield Wednesday. John always played well against their right back, Ron Staniforth, and during the game he went past him and was promptly knocked to the ground – and then his opponent fell on top of him. It seemed Staniforth was deliberately holding him down, and when he managed to struggle to his feet he was so incensed that he swung a punch at the full back. He was promptly grabbed by the visiting centre half, Peter Swan, who urged him to cool down or he would be sent off, and others joined in that angry scene. The consequent stoppage of play caused the game to be extended by four minutes and during the extra period Wednesday snatched the winning goal. It was one of a series of frustrating happenings in what developed into a disastrous season. At the end of November the team were in the top half of the table, but Easter saw them almost at the bottom from where they failed to extricate themselves.

Whereas the succession of poor results had a confidence-sapping effect on most of his colleagues, John had one of his best seasons. He was, therefore, unwilling to settle for Third Division football and in May 1959 was transferred to Bristol City in a three-player deal – in his respect the fee was £15,000.

In the previous season his new club had finished in a mid-table place in Division Two, but John soon decided they were a poorer side than the one he had just left. That may or may not have been the case but they couldn't have been much better, for in the following May he had the doubtful distinction of being the outside left of teams which finished in bottom place in the Second Division in consecutive seasons.

In the summer there was the customary post-relegation management change and the new man introduced a variation into pre-season training which John had not previously encountered and could not come to terms with. It entailed the first team passing the ball the length of the pitch and into the goal – without there being an opposing team to try to stop them doing it! His protest that practice should be as realistic as possible fell on deaf ears. He therefore refused to be part of what he felt to be a futile exercise and when he received the ball, in the absence of a defender to beat, he deliberately tapped it over the touchline and out of play. Needless to say, he was excluded from further training sessions. When the season began he was out of the side until October and then recalled for one game at the request of Huddersfield Town who were keen to sign him. Even then he was played out of position, and their manager's request to see him at outside left was dismissed with, 'You've seen him there often enough at Barnsley!'

Perhaps he had. In any event, John signed immediately after the game and made his debut on he following Saturday against Southampton. It was from his pin-point centre that Huddersfield opened the scoring and early in the second half he scored himself to put his new team on course for a 3 – 1 victory. In September 1962 he was transferred to Derby County and, after a spell on loan at Darlington, he joined Chesterfield for two final seasons in the Football League. Then followed three seasons in the Midland League – two with Skegness Town and one with Leamington Lockheed – and he retired from the professional game in 1969.

On joining Chesterfield in 1964 he returned to live in Barnsley, and on finishing in full-time soccer he joined the staff of Shaw Carpets Ltd at Darton as a trainee inspector. After two years he was in charge of a 12-man shift and later he became an inspector responsible for quality control. In the early 1980s the company reorganized its system of manufacture and reduced the workforce and, consequently the number of inspectors. The changes affected almost everyone, and John is now one of a pool of men who are required to turn their hands to any aspect of the manufacturing process.

The seasons at Oakwell had made him so well known on the local soccer scene that his election to Shaw Carpets' sports committee and into the football team was almost automatic. It was then necessary for him to be reinstated as an amateur but, in the event, it was hardly worth the bother. He found difficulty in adapting his own professional approach to the less committed attitude of team-mates and decided against continuing in the side when he realized the way he wanted the others to play was spoiling the enjoyment they wanted from the game.

His other sporting involvement is golf, but he regards it in a similar light to that in which his workmates view their football and he doesn't play well – only for fun. He was taught the game by Oakwell colleague Harry Hough and has been a member of the Silkstone club since returning to live locally in 1964.

He once commented in the dressing room at Oakwell that a Scottish international footballer was entitled to better facilities than the club was providing – and he was promptly thrown into the bath! It was a remark made in jest, yet that view was echoed by at least two First Division managers. Cardiff City tried unsuccessfully to obtain him immediately following the Reds' FA Cup success there in 1957, and the only reason he didn't join Aston Villa was that Bristol City were quicker with their bid. And confirming the esteem in which he was held by some in high places, in 1964 he received a 'name your own terms' offer from the Pan Helenic Sporting Club in Sydney, Australia, who said he had been recommended to them by the manager of Everton.

He was, and still is, a forthright individual and an inability to suffer fools gladly disadvantaged him at certain times in his career – yet Tim Ward knew him better than most and was glad to have him on his staff at both Barnsley and Derby County. As with a lot of outside lefts, his right foot was mainly for standing on but he differed from the majority in his absolute accuracy in crossing the ball: its exactness was the hall-mark of his game and is perhaps unequalled in Oakwell's history. Similarly, while 'B' international games have been in the soccer calendar since 1949 and are but one short step from full recognition, John McCann is the only Barnsley footballer ever to have played at that level.

Norman Smith: A Captain of Champions

Most of Norman Smith's adult life until his mid-thirties was spent fighting one cause or another. As a 19-year-old RAF sergeant air gunner in Lancaster bombers he fought off attacks by enemy aircraft during operations over Europe during the Second World War: he spent five years fighting for a place in Arsenal's first team before joining Barnsley; several times he fought his way back into sides after serious injury, and as captain at Oakwell he fought a losing battle against relegation in 1953 but two years later had the thrill and satisfaction of leading the team into the Second Division.

As a boy he played football for his school in the Lancashire cotton town of Darwen and for Darwen Boys, and then became a trainee mechanic in the textile industry. In 1943 at the age of 18 he volunteered for the Royal Air Force. He hoped to be a navigator but at the time there were no vacancies in that branch so he qualified as an air gunner and was posted to Bomber Command's 101 Squadron at Ludford Magna in Lincolnshire. Over the following two years he was promoted to Warrant Officer and his operational flights included 1,000-bomber raids on Cologne and Dusseldorf and an attack on munitions factories at Stettin in occupied Poland which entailed a hazardous non-stop flight of 1,500 miles. During an attack on Stuttgart two of his aeroplane's four engines and the undercarriage were destroyed, and after staggering back to England the 'plane crash-landed in Suffolk with, miraculously, no injuries among the seven-man crew.

In 1944 101 Squadron supported the D-Day landings in Normandy by flying overhead and jamming the enemy's ground radio communications. Later they prepared the way for the airborne landings at Arnhem by bombing the area in advance of the attack, and Norman was unaware that his brother Tom, a glider pilot, was to be involved in that ill-fated operation. He also took part in daylight attacks on flying bomb launching sites in northern France and by November 1944 had completed the maximum permitted number of 30 operational missions. His role of 'Tail-end Charlie' was the most exposed and dangerous in flying combat, yet despite many frightening and stressful experiences he came through without physical injury of any kind.

After completing the operational tour he spent the following two-and-a-half years on Flying Control duties in Northern Ireland. In the Province he played his first football since leaving school. During the week he represented Flying Control Command in inter-service games – all of which were on the mainland – and at weekends he played as a professional with Brantwood in the Irish League.

On the cessation of hostilities in 1945 he ended the Irish connection and joined Bolton Wanderers as an amateur, playing for them each Saturday and continuing his mid-week football with Flying Control Command until demobilization in March 1947. He then signed for his home town club, Darwen, in the Lancashire Combination and in the season's few remaining games he was spotted by an Arsenal scout and invited to have a trial with them in an annual charity game against their local non-League side, Hendon. It was an event in which Arsenal normally fielded a full-strength team, and the trialist lined-up alongside such illustrious footballers as Denis and Leslie Compton, Bryn Jones – once the game's most expensive transferee – Jimmy Logie and international full backs Laurie Scott and Wally Barnes. In fact, the only one who wasn't a household name was Norman Smith!

Arsenal was the most prestigious club in the land and Norman was manager Tom Whittaker's first signing. He started at right half in the reserves and after 12 months was switched to the other flank. On asking for an explanation he was told it wasn't expected that Joe Mercer, the first team left half, would go on for much longer. Captain and former England skipper Mercer was then 34 and the significance of the explanation was not lost on the young reserve. However, Mercer went on and on until he was 40 years old!

A business interest on Merseyside precluded the captain's involvement in anything other than League and Cup games. Consequently, and despite there being three other international wing halves on the staff, Norman was the one to deputise in friendlies and summer tours abroad. Yet Mercer's presence at the club prevented him playing in the Football League during five seasons at Highbury. Nevertheless, he enjoyed every moment with that famous club and it was only the realization that time was passing without any real indication of a first team place that he agreed to join Barnsley in October 1952.

At the time of his arrival the team were entrenched at the bottom of the Second Division. Early in the New Year he was appointed captain, but the tide never turned and the season's end brought relegation into Division Three. Having spent the previous five years in Arsenal's first team squad this was his first experience of continual poor results and the fears and anxieties associated with relegation. And he found certain aspects of the Oakwell scene, to say the least, surprising. This was his first awareness of directors having access to a dressing room at half-time and at the end of a game. Similarly, he had not previously known players who weren't striving to hold a place in the first team: most were on a fixed wage irrespective of which team they were in, and at reserve games there was an absence of jeering supporters and a chance of sometimes being on the winning side. Nor had his years in the capital prepared him for the close contact which at that time footballers with a town club had with the local people. On one occasion Barnsley had lost at Wrexham despite playing really well – the home side only had three shots at goal but won 3 – 0. On returning to the town that night Norman and goalkeeper Harry Hough were travelling together on a Yorkshire Traction bus to their respective homes and, while enjoying the recollection of an incident earlier in the day, a hand was placed from behind onto Harry's shoulder. Thinking it belonged to someone they knew, they turned to look into the face of a complete stranger who said, angrily, 'It's all right you two *laughing* when you've lost today!'

However, in the first two full seasons of Norman's captaincy defeats of that magnitude were infrequent occurrences. He had taken over as skipper for the simple reason that no-one else would have the job, but in the Third Division performances improved considerably. The first season ended with them in second-top place and in the following campaign they won the championship with four points to spare.

While still savouring the enjoyment of that successful season, disaster struck in the opening game in Division Two. Then, after 10 minutes against Leeds United, he damaged a thigh and didn't play again until the season's final match. In fact, in almost 20 years as a professional footballer he had four cartilages removed, shoulder and collar bones broken, groin trouble and serious ankle damage – and it reached the stage that he was no longer considered an injury risk because he'd already had everything that was likely to happen to him!

After resuming at right half at the start of the 1956/57 season he was dropped in September and was out of the side for almost 12 months. His return was at inside right and he quickly made his presence felt. On 28th September 1957 his diving header from Arthur Kaye's short cross won the game against West Ham and was later acclaimed as Oakwell's most spectacular goal of the season. And always previously having been a defender, his two goals a few weeks later in a defeat of Rotherham United was the first time he'd scored twice in any game.

Norman remained in the side until he was 34, and in July 1959 he joined Shrewsbury Town as player-coach to the reserves. For the previous two years he'd been a member of an International Managers' XI which toured the country playing charity games during the summer. A team-mate was Shrewsbury manager Arthur Rowley, and the player-coach appointment came from a friendship struck during that involvement.

Two years later he accepted an invitation to take up the new post of player-manager of the football team at Sankey of Wellington Ltd – motor parts manufacturers in Shropshire. They had just been admitted into the semi-professional Cheshire League and his first task was to recruit players for that higher standard of competition. The side he fielded contained several First Division names, and the half back line consisted of himself and former England defenders Neil Franklin and Henry Cockburn. The appointment also provided work for him at the factory and the combined wage was the highest income he'd ever had. The club's dressing and bathing facility was – at his instigation – designed on identical lines to that at Highbury, and his own living accommodation was a luxury flat overlooking bowling greens at the works' splendid sports complex.

He remained with Sankeys for two years before eventually becoming tired of certain committee members trying to influence his selection of the team. And when injury put him out of the side for a couple of months and it was suggested his pay be reduced accordingly he decided it was then time to leave.

He returned to Barnsley and over the following six years worked as a salesman at Grimes' Garage at Worsbrough Bridge, for M C Mills & Co in Castlereagh Street and in the plumbing department of Northern Ideal Homes. During that time he was a football coach and PE instructor at schools at White Cross, Darton and Darfield; he was a scout for his former Barnsley boss, Tim Ward, who was then at Derby County and he was player-coach with Worsbrough Bridge in the County Senior League. In 1969 he joined the staff of the United Friendly Insurance Co Ltd. As a member of the Home Service Department he worked in the Wath and West Melton areas before moving to Ward Green and Worsbrough, and he remained with the company for 20 years before taking early retirement.

He has had a 40-year involvement with golf and had a long friendly acquaintance with a former British Open winner, Dai Rees. Rees was the professional at South Herts Golf Club at Finchley where Norman learned the game and he trained with the players at Highbury. For many years Norman's favourite clubs were a Dai Rees set which were almost brand-new when he purchased them from Arsenal colleague Denis Compton. And by a mild deception which was aided and abetted by the elder of the Compton brothers he obtained them for £10 when it was Denis's intention to toss a coin with him to determine whether the price was to be £10 or £20! He has been a member of Silkstone Golf Club since first coming to Barnsley. His handicap is now 11 but has been as low as 5, and over the years he's won every trophy at the club.

Despite his expertise at golf, his favourite leisure-time activity is Magic. It is a subject which intrigued him as a boy from the moment he saw a friend of his father's make a ha'penny vanish from the palm of his hand and reappear at the end of his nose! Initially he learned something of the art from books, but the interest really took hold when he was in lodgings in London and a next-door-neighbour was a professional magician. He has had membership of the Barnsley Magic Circle for many years and is a member of the International Brotherhood of Magicians. His first public performance was as a schoolboy and he entertains regularly at school Christmas parties, house-parties and Masonic dinners. Yet despite the applause he receives for performing the seemingly impossible he knows how difficult it is to satisfy everyone in an audience – as exemplified by a conversation which was related to him a few days after one of his school party presentations:

'Mum, that magician at our party this afternoon wasn't a real magician.'

'Why wasn't he?'

'Well, he was very good but he can't be a *real* magician because he's the man who calls at my grandma's every Friday tea-time to collect her insurance money!'

Norman Smith signed for Barnsley on Friday, 24th October 1952 and spent the night at the Royal Hotel. The place seemed almost empty, and about 9 o'clock he walked to the bottom of Market Hill in the town centre. It was a wet, miserable evening with hardly a soul in sight, and as he retraced his steps to the hotel he thought of Friday evenings in London and told himself he had made the biggest mistake of his life. He would have given anything to have called the transfer off, but he knew there was no turning back. Yet there were brighter days ahead and, far from the move North being a blunder, it provided the best thing that ever happened to him in meeting Adéle, the lady who was to become his wife. And on 4th May 1955 he became one of only three men in the one hundred year history of Barnsley Football Club to captain a side which won a divisional championship within the Football League.

John Short: A Style to Enthuse About

It may well be that John Short is the only footballer to have played at Oakwell for two different clubs on consecutive Saturdays – he having that experience in October 1956. On the 20th of the month he played there for Stoke City reserves and a week later he made his debut for Barnsley in a 4 – 1 defeat of Liverpool. He had begun his career with Wolverhampton Wanderers with whom he won a League championship medal, and the move to Barnsley returned him to his South Yorkshire roots.

He had schoolboy representative honours while at Darfield Foulstone School, from where he got a job as a haulage hand at Dearne Valley Colliery and played for the colliery football team. Then an inside forward, in that capacity he joined Upton Colliery FC and was later recruited for Wolves' nursery side, Wath Wanderers, by their manager Mark Crook. Indeed, Mark's initial high regard for his young protégé was later to develop into a close friendship.

In the spring of 1948 he went to the parent club for trials, immediately after which he became a full-time professional. Still an attacker, it was two years later while captaining the reserves from the centre forward position that manager Stan Cullis converted him into a full back – a role which he was to have for the remainder of his career.

Wolves were then one of the leading clubs in the land and John achieved a regular place in the First Division side in 1952. He had already won a championship medal with the Central League side and further award came his way in 1954 when Wolves were champions of the First Division.

In the summer of that year he was made available for transfer, and although Barnsley's Tim Ward enquired about him he backed off on learning the size of the fee required. In the event John joined Stoke City, remaining there for a little over two years.

On 3rd March 1956 John married Margaret Bridges at St Andrew's Church, Bolton-upon-Dearne, the ceremony taking place at 10.30am. It seems that getting to Stoke in order to play in the afternoon game against Middlesbrough was not the bridegroom's main objective of the day, for he telephoned the manager from The Hollies at Wath where the reception was being held and said he might have difficulty in getting there on time. One can only guess at the reply he received. Nevertheless, when his car arrived at the city boundary he found a police escort awaiting him and he was rushed through the football traffic and was thus able to take his place in the team. But perhaps he wasn't the only one to be ill-prepared for the game; Stoke were beaten 5 – 2 and in the following week he was omitted from the side.

He was already hankering to return to South Yorkshire and was therefore unwilling to set up a matrimonial home in the Potteries. Margaret remained at her parents' home in Bolton-upon-Dearne while her new husband continued at his lodgings in Stoke and, during the summer, sought his club's permission to live in the Barnsley area and train at Oakwell. When that wasn't forthcoming he took matters into his own hands and effectively went on strike; he didn't report for pre-season training and was still absent when the League programme began in August. However, the club stood firm and simple economics ensured John was the one to back down. He presented himself at the ground in mid-September and asked to be placed on the transfer list. The player having been brought to heel, the club would see no point in continued refusal and, consequently, he was transferred to Oakwell.

The fee of £4,000 was considerably less than Barnsley would have expected to pay. John went straight into the side, forming part of a defensive trio of Short, Sharp and Swift which became as effective as the names suggest. He held a regular place for the following three seasons, in each of which he represented Sheffield and Hallamshire FA in the annual match against Glasgow. His last game was on 5th September 1959. On that day during the Reds' 4 – 1 beating of Southend United he sustained damage to knee ligaments which effectively brought his playing career to an end.

On leaving Oakwell he returned to the mining industry at Houghton Main Colliery, working initially as a miner and later as a foreman on the pit top. He had a brief spell looking after Barnsley juniors on match days, but quickly decided a 'watching' role was not for him. For 10 years he played regularly in the Colliery Welfare side and thereafter filled-in when required until reaching his mid-forties. By that time his three sons were teenagers and he obtained a lot of pleasure from sometimes being in the side when the eldest, Kenneth, was at centre half. Steven and Robert were also promising players; the latter declined invitations to join Barnsley and Rotherham United on schoolboy forms, and Steven had a couple of seasons on Aston Villa's books. Yet dad, at 45, was so fit that he could beat them all over 80 yards and was so supple that from a standing position he could lean forward and press his forehead onto his shins.

Post-Oakwell involvements included management of the Houghton Main WMC side, scouting for Wolves, playing charity games with the ex-Barnsley XI and membership of the Yorkshire TV team which included his pals Norman Smith and Charlie Williams, and Roger Greenwood and Richard Whiteley from the *Calendar* programme.

Football was John Short's life: sadly, it also precipitated his death. On Sunday, 10th October 1976, after a game between the ex-Barnsely team and Charlie Williams' XI at Wombwell Sporting Club, he blacked out in the changing room. An ambulance was summoned but when it arrived he had partially recovered and flatly refused to go to hospital. It was a most unwise decision. A little later and while still at the ground he again lost consciousness; the ambulance was recalled, but he was pronounced dead on arrival at hospital.

At that time the ex-Barnsley team played every fortnight, but following John's death no games took place for nearly three months. Doubtless some were pondering the wisdom of footballing at forty-plus, but activities resumed early in 1977. Yet for the remainder of the season, in memory of a former colleague and friend, the team would line-up for the kick-off without anyone standing in the right full back position.

John's untimely death generated considerable local sympathy for Margaret and her sons, and Barnsley FC hosted a testimonial game in which such illustrious names as Danny Blanchflower, Johnny Kelly and Gavin Smith were in an ex-players' side which opposed the first team. The family also benefitted from three concerts organized by Charlie Williams – then at the height of his career, hosting ITV's *Golden Shot* after a long run in *The Comedians* at the London Palladium. Duties as MC enabled Norman Smith to display his conjuring skills and the bill included two of the funniest men in show business – Charlie, and Stan Richards – and former England winger Colin Grainger who was then making a second career on the Northern club circuit.

Throughout John's years in football, from when he was with one of the leading clubs in the land to his final season with Barnsley which was his only experience of life in Division Three, people within the game were impressed by his abilities and style. In 1951, while he was still primarily a Wolves reserve, former international Charles Buchan, in his authoritative *Charles Buchan's Football Monthly*, described him as an England player of the future. Team-mate Duncan Sharp reckons he was the hardest, longest and most accurate kicker of a dead ball he ever saw, and Gordon Pallister, perhaps the most cultured full back Barnsley has had, still enthuses, even after 30 years, about the classical style of John Short.

Don Leeson: Irony Upon Irony!

Don Leeson was a goalkeeper at Oakwell for almost four years before having a regular place in the first team and, even then, 10 weeks elapsed before he finally ended up on the winning side. Once in the team he went on to play exactly 100 consecutive games and his voluntary premature retirement from football a few weeks later was very much against the club's wishes and at a time when arrangements were in hand to transfer him into the First Division.

Born at Askern, near Doncaster, in schoolboy football he was a forward and had trials for the town's boys' team as an outside left. Unfortunately for him, the other number 11 in contention was David Pegg who went on to play for Manchester United and England – consequently there was no place in the Doncaster Boys team for Don Leeson. On leaving school he worked as an apprentice fitter at Askern Main Colliery and played at inside forward in the colliery reserve team. He was also required to deputize for the goalkeeper, little knowing the role would be a stepping-stone into professional football.

The inevitable happened early in 1953. The reserve goalkeeper was injured at a time when the first team 'keeper, Billy Tarr, was having trials with a senior club and this resulted in Don being drafted into the first team. He was needed for only one game, at the end of which he was approached by a scout who thought he'd been watching Billy Tarr. Nevertheless, he invited Don to have a trial with Nottingham Forest on the following Saturday.

However, word travels quickly in small communities and during the weekend Don was visited by a pal, Askern CC colleague and Barnsley full back John Thomas. John called to say, 'If Forest will give you a trial I'm sure Barnsley will, too. Leave it to me, I'll speak to John Steele.' The outcome was that instead of going to Nottingham, Don presented himself at Oakwell and after demonstrating his abilities in a junior game he joined the club as an amateur.

Starting in the Northern Intermediate League side, within a few weeks he was playing in an FA Youth Cup quarter-final at Old Trafford in front of a crowd considerably bigger than the Reds' first team currently attracts to Oakwell. The youngsters put up a creditable display before losing 3 – 1 to a side which included the prodigious Duncan Edwards – and that young Pegg again.

The following season was spent in the 'A' team and at the end of it he became a professional player. The signing-on fee was £10 and even now he remembers his great excitement as strong, 18-year-old legs raced him almost a mile through the streets of Askern from the bus stop to his parents' home in order to show them the first two large white bank notes that he'd ever seen.

A year later he won a regular place in the reserves – and the remarkable consistency of Harry Hough kept him there for almost five consecutive seasons. His first team debut in a 1 – 1 draw at Rotherham in December 1956 was his only League appearance of that season. Another came in the following year and his breakthrough was on St Valentine's day 1959 against Brighton & Hove Albion when Hough was dropped in the aftermath of a 5 – 0 drubbing at Bramall Lane.

Don had long awaited his preferment but the accompanying circumstances were far from what he would have hoped for. Apart from two draws, each of the following 12 games was lost; Don wasn't in a winning team until Swansea Town were beaten 3 – 1 on 20th April and the season's end saw Barnsley in bottom position in the Second Division.

In the first season at the lower level he played in each of the 46 games, during the course of which there was a 'Acrobatic Leeson in great form for Reds' headline to a *Green 'Un* match report of a 0 – 0 draw at York City. Later in the year in the second round of the Football League Cup's inaugural season the Reds lost 3 – 0 to First Division Derby County – and 'Rufus' of the *Yorkshire Evening News* said Don was in great form and only his grit and determination kept the score within reasonable proportions. A few weeks later 'Brilliant Leeson Barnsley's Hero' headed a *Green 'Un* report of a goal-less draw with Brentford, but his unbroken occupancy of the goal was nearing its end. On 4th February 1961 he sustained a ruptured blood vessel at Bournemouth and was out of the side for a month until the FA Cup quarter-final at Leicester City. In the replay the visitors' winning goal resulted from a misunderstanding between himself and Duncan Sharp, following which he was dropped from the team.

But he was already disenchanted with the Oakwell scene. Due to be married in the summer, he had been given the keys to a club house at Staincross. However, just before Easter manager John Steele requested that they be returned as he had to provide accommodation for a player he intended to sign from Accrington Stanley. Don protested vehemently but to no avail. 'There'll be another,' said Steele, and there the matter rested.

But the injustice of the situation rankled. He'd given the club everything he'd got, yet he was being disadvantaged for the sake of a man who hadn't even joined them. The more he thought about it, the angrier he became and within a couple of days he'd submitted a request to be transferred. It was then the turn of the manager to be annoyed. He berated Don at length but the latter stood his ground and insisted the request be passed to the chairman. But it seemed the club intended to hang on to him, for he found he'd been transfer-listed at £5,000 – about double the usual asking price for a Third Division goalkeeper.

The team's progress in the FA Cup had won them the *Sunday Pictorial* Giant Killer Trophy which carried with it an expenses-paid visit to Eire for a match against a Glenmore Select XI. The opposition included England's Ron Clayton, Charlie Hurley – then probably the best centre half in the country – and Dave Mackay and Cliff Jones from Spurs' double-winning side of that year. The game proved to be Don's last for the club and the *Sheffield Telegraph* match report said he was a splendid goalkeeper, bringing the house down on one occasion with a fantastic leap to turn away a full-blooded drive from Cliff Jones.

By then he had been on the transfer list for almost three months and was anxiously awaiting news of an approach for his services. Since his recent marriage he and his wife, Ann, had lived at her parents' home at Askern. On returning there from Dublin he was greeted with, 'I've got you a new job while you've been away. It's at Grimsby.'

'Oh, Grimsby Town. They're a good club.'

'No, Grimsby Police. There's a house for us and they have one of the best police teams in the country. They're coming back to see you on Sunday.'

Until then Don had not considered leaving professional football. However, after meeting two representatives of the Grimsby Borough Police he began to like the idea of a secure, interesting job which provided ample opportunity to play football, albeit at a level far removed from that to which he was accustomed. After talking things over with Ann he decided it was the job for him and within a matter of days he had passed entrance and medical examinations and been accepted into the force.

He then went to Oakwell to inform the club of his decision, and secretary Raymond Vicary listened in apparent disbelief as Don told him of his intention. He was then asked to wait, and 20 minutes later chairman Joe Richards was on the scene. Without uttering a word he held out the keys to the house at Staincross. Don shook his head. 'It's too late now, Mr Richards. I'm leaving.' Yet the club retained his registration for six years, thus ensuring first claim on him if he was to leave the Police during that time.

Don's career in the Grimsby Borough and Humberside forces saw him first as a uniformed constable and then a detective for 15 years until his retirement in 1985. Although Grimsby was one of the country's smaller forces it had one of the best football teams because chief constable Butler – son of a former chief constable of Barnsley – was a football enthusiast who encouraged like-minded young men to join his force.

Don played in police football until he was 37 years old. During that time the force team reached the Police Athletic Association Cup final on three occasions – each of which was against Birmingham City Police. And in each final only one goal was scored: in the last it was scored by Don's side, enabling him to have a Cup-winners' medal among his soccer memorabilia. Six times he represented England in an annual match against Scotland, and in 1964 and 1969 he played for the English forces in the European Police Cup. The finals were held, respectively, in Marseille and Stockholm and on each occasion England finished in third place.

He was also a club cricketer. A wicket-keeper and left handed middle-order batsman, he was in the Askern first team in the Yorkshire Council when 13 years old. Apart from two seasons with Doncaster Town in the Yorkshire

League he remained with Askern until moving to Grimsby and throwing in his lot with the police team. His most successful period was in 1953 when he was 18 years old. Then, playing against Ackworth, he had five victims behind the stumps and scored 107 at a run-a-minute. And on the following Saturday he scored a not-out century against Leeds Zingari.

Looking back almost 30 years, Don Leeson has no regrets about leaving professional football. It enabled him to embark upon a varied and well paid career which provided almost as much football as he'd previously had. Yet one can understand Barnsley FC being displeased by his premature retirement. He was their first team goalkeeper with his best years still ahead of him and, irony upon irony, Nottingham Forest had just agreed to pay them quite a hefty fee for his transfer!

Frank Beaumont: A Name in Soccer History

Frank Beaumont's career in professional football never reached the heights which it once seemed certain to do, yet it had some notable achievements. His debut in Barnsley's first team was while still a groundstaff boy, having made the jump from Yorkshire League to Second Division without even a single game in the reserves. In November 1959 he created a club record for the quickest goal in FA Cup football by scoring in 20 seconds against Bradford City. And later, in non-League football and still under 30, he had the distinction of being player-manager of the team who were the first Wembley winners of the FA Challenge Trophy.

A Hoyland Common boy, he joined the Oakwell ground staff in 1955 on leaving Kirk Balk School and won English youth international honours in the spring of 1957 against Belgium, Holland and Luxemburg. Early opportunity in the first team came in the summer by way of an injury to George Spruce in a pre-season private practice at Sheffield Wednesday. Frank had gone along solely to assist the trainer, but when Spruce was hurt manager Tim Ward shuffled the team and sent him on in his usual inside forward position. He did well enough to be kept in the side for the return game, when another good performance put him into the first team in Oakwell's annual public practice on the last Saturday of the close-season.

Almost needless to say, and doubtless to the dismay of the reserve team's inside forwards who would have considered themselves in line for promotion, Frank's display was sufficient to keep him in the team against Bristol Rovers for the opening game of the season. Twenty-fourth of August 1957 was therefore the date when a groundstaff boy scored an equalizing goal for Barnsley by collecting a rebound from his shot which had hit the post and hammering the ball into the net via the underside of the cross-bar.

It would have been unrealistic to expect a 17-year-old Yorkshire League footballer to hold a regular place in the Second Division, and that proved to be so. Nevertheless, just as he'd scored in his first game as an amateur, on becoming a professional on Christmas Day he marked the occasion with a goal in a 3 – 2 win at Notts County. And personal festive joy continued when he opened the scoring three days later in a 3 – 0 defeat of Derby County.

During that season and the one which followed he was primarily a reserve player, but his potential was always evident. In April 1959 when he scored against a Fulham side destined for Division One, the *Sheffield Telegraph* described him as the most dangerous forward on the field, even though the opposition had Scotland's Graham Leggat and England's Johnny Haynes. The season ended with relegation and the departure of several leading players. However, offers for Frank from West Brom and Liverpool were refused, chairman Richards saying that he was one who had to be kept in order that the team could get back into the Second Division.

From August 1959 until his departure more than two years later Frank had a regular place in the team. However, a 2 – 0 win at Bury in September perhaps had a bearing on his eventual destination, for he scored the second goal with a fine volley from the edge of the penalty-area. He was also to the fore in a home tie against Bradford City in the FA Cup when both Jack Lunn and skipper Jimmy Baxter missed penalties. Later, with the Reds trailing 3 – 2, they were awarded another. A confident Frank Beaumont placed the ball on the spot, and with Tim Ward on the touch-line screaming, 'Jimmy, Jimmy, you take it', he hammered it high into the net to earn a replay at Valley Parade.

It was there that Frank put an entry into club records with his goal in 20 seconds. Unfortunately that was the team's total score and less than the home side got, consequently the Reds fell at the competition's first hurdle.

In February 1961 he resumed his maltreatment of Bradford City with two goals in a 5 – 2 success, but in the following game his youthfulness made way for the experience of Frank Bartlett in a fifth round tie against Luton Town. He returned for the next game, was again among the goals, and ended the season as second highest scorer.

There had already been a period in Frank's career when his slightest mistake had prompted barracking from a noisy element on the terraces and it began again in August 1961. He decided the time had come to move on, and asked to be transferred. The chairman expressed both sympathy and confidence, but Frank was adamant that a change of club would be to his advantage and he wanted to be away.

A fee of £15,000 took him back into the Second Division with Bury, and on his debut on 19th September he scored the winner in a 3 – 2 success over Sunderland. A fortnight later Bury played with 10 men throughout the second half when Frank's gem of a goal brought victory over second-placed and previously unbeaten Rotherham United. And in January 1962, in the FA Cup at Bramall Lane, after Sheffield United had led 2 – 0 he scored his side's first goal which helped take their First Division opponents to a second replay.

However, enjoyment of being with the Lancashire club was short lived, ending abruptly with the appointment of Bob Stokoe as manager. Frank just couldn't get on with him. Their lack of compatibility resulted in periods in the reserves and his absences from the team brought letters of complaint to the local press. Indeed, there was an occasion when supporters seemingly brought about reinstatement by giving him a standing ovation at the end of a reserve game.

The crunch came early in 1964. On 1st February Bury played at Plymouth: Frank was continually in the thick of things and thought he'd had a particularly good game. The second half was broadcast nationally by the BBC, and on visiting his parents next day Frank was pleased, but not surprised, when dad said that the commentator had been almost continually mentioning his name. That was doubtless so, but it wasn't to be mentioned by Bob Stokoe when planning for the next game, against Manchester City. Frank was to travel but not play, and on seeing the team-sheet he sought out the manager and hard words were exchanged. When the situation calmed, having no wish to travel if he wasn't playing, he asked to be in the reserves. Stokoe, unbending, replied, 'The reserve team's already picked.' 'Alright, I'll go in the 'A' team then.' The player having been suitably humbled, the manager expressed no objection.

However, come Saturday, when the team coaches were filling in readiness for journeys to Manchester, the seniors bound for Maine Road and the 'A' team for a rather less imposing ground at the Avro Vulcan factory, an objection was raised – by the chairman. He thought it totally inappropriate for Frank to be in the third team and said so, forcibly, to the manager. Then he boarded the third team coach and asked Frank to go with the others to Maine Road ... and Frank refused. There could only be one outcome: at the season's end he was not retained and, as a result, joined Stockport County.

His first Cup-tie with Stockport was quite momentous. He scored twice to give a two goal lead over divisional leaders Bristol Rovers but the advantage was lost, yet in front of 20,000 spectators his team went on to win what the *Stockport Express* described as the greatest Cup-tie ever seen at the ground. The next round took them to Liverpool where, against all the odds, the eventual Cup winners were held to a 1 – 1 draw. But Frank was unable to play, having been suspended after being sent off at Doncaster Rovers on Boxing Day when his display had been so pleasing to the travelling supporters that they clapped him all the way to the dressing room.

In 1966, after two seasons at Stockport, he was made available for transfer. There was opportunity to remain within the Football League but the offer which most attracted him was from Macclesfield Town. Consequently he threw in his lot with the Cheshire League club and, the first few seasons at Oakwell apart, the six years at Macclesfield were the happiest of his career.

The high standard of organization within the club contributed towards the successful period which Frank had there. In 1967 he had great satisfaction from being in the team which beat his previous club in the first round of the FA Cup. Next victims were fellow non-Leaguers Spennymoor, and then Macclesfield were drawn at Fulham. There they led twice, and it took a penalty from future Oakwell manager Allan Clarke and two goals late in the game to put them out of the competition. Indeed, John Arlott, reporting in *The Times*, said that it was not until the last quarter-hour that Macclesfield began to look inferior to their First Division opponents.

The Cup run was no flash in the pan. At the season's end Macclesfield were

Cheshire League champions and winners of the North-Western Floodlight League Cup, and the championship provided entry into the newly-formed Northern Premier League.

At that stage Frank was appointed player-manager. The success continued, and under his direction the team became the first champions of the Northern Premier League. Even greater reward came in the following year when they were again champions and experienced the delight of winning the FA Challenge Trophy. Then, on 2nd May 1970 at Wembley Stadium, Frank led Macclesfield to victory against Telford United in the first final of the competition.

He remained with the club for two more years, but left when a new chairman insisted on involving himself in matters which Frank considered to be the manager's responsibility. A man who had resisted a chairman's persuasions on a much lesser issue certainly wasn't going to tolerate that! Thereafter he had spells as a player with Bradford Park Avenue and Frickley Colliery; player-coach with Gainsborough Trinity and player-manager of Dodworth Colliery Welfare – thus remaining a professional footballer until 40 years old.

After leaving the full-time game in 1966 he worked initially as a salesman in office equipment and photographic materials. Towards the end of his time at Macclesfield he joined the staff of Lancashire Shopfitters Ltd of Accrington, from where he progressed to his present position with the Wholesale Division of W H Smith & Son. His employers provide a shopfitting service for the retail newspaper trade, and Frank is a shop development adviser responsible for an area stretching from Leicester to Newcastle-upon-Tyne. The role requires him to advise retailers on the best use to be made of their premises, and plan and sell a shopfitting package.

On retiring from football he joined Higham CC in the Huddersfield League. Cricket is a game he hadn't played since schooldays, but his agility in the field saved a lot of runs and he was usually good for a quick 20. He remained with them for three years until sustaining a fractured cheekbone in a game at Holmbridge. Then 46, he decided the time had come to play a less dangerous game. He took up golf and adapted to it so well that after only a couple of years his handicap was down to 14. Football involvement now continues with a Saturday afternoon role as scout for Coventry City.

Frank Beaumont was a 'muck or nettles' player whose wholehearted attitude put him continually in the thick of things – chasing, tackling, shooting or just running off the ball as part of the next move. With Barnsley, Bury and Stockport County he had a happy if undistinguished career, but with Macclesfield Town he put his name permanently into football history as the first captain to receive the FA Challenge Trophy in the game's first non-League Cup final.

Henry Walters: Memorable Sporting Debuts

Henry Walters was born only a few miles from Oakwell, yet he had been a professional footballer for 10 years before an opportunity arose for him to join his home town club. His career spanned almost two decades and began at Villa Park on the opening day of the 1942 season when he was the 17-year-old right half in the visiting Wolverhampton Wanderers side, playing alongside the England centre half and skipper, Stan Cullis.

He was also a well known club cricketer whose introduction to the game was even earlier than his entry into senior soccer. At the age of 12 he played for the first time in the Yorkshire Council; later he had trials at the county nets at Headingley, and he was a member of a Cortonwood championship team and played in Council cricket for 30 years.

A native of Wath-upon-Dearne, he played in the same Brampton School football team as the Reds' future player, George Robledo. He also represented Dearne Valley Boys and on leaving school he became an apprentice joiner at Cortonwood Colliery and played for the Wolves' nursery side, Wath Wanderers.

During the Second World War colliery workers were exempt from military service but in 1944, along with dozens of other joiners from the South Yorkshire Coalfield, he was directed to work in London on the repair of properties damaged by enemy action. He had played fairly regularly for Wolves and, then living in the Metropolis, transferred his allegiance to Clapton Orient. That was at a time when the capital was being subjected to raids by V1s – pilotless jet-propelled flying bombs launched from Northern France. When their fuel was expended they plunged to the ground, causing their warheads to explode, and work was continually interrupted by the need to take cover during those indiscriminate attacks. There were occasions when football matches had to be halted while a high explosive missile passed overhead, and his work in London and games with Orient continued until the end of the war.

In 1946 he resumed his employment at Cortonwood and joined Walsall as a part-time player. There were no floodlights at football grounds in those days and the first post-war season had to be extended because of postponements during the exceptionally hard winter: Henry made his debut in the Football

League on 24th May 1947 – with Walsall having three games still to play!

He made 253 appearances for Walsall and his employers were accommodating regarding the club's demands of him. For pre-season training he was granted four weeks' unpaid leave each summer – until 1951. Then, one week into training, a management change at the colliery resulted in him receiving a letter terminating his employment. At that point Walsall got what they would have preferred all along: he became a full-time player and was granted the privilege of being allowed to continue to live at Brampton and train at the colliery sports ground.

Two years later, even with the convenience of a motor car purchased with a £249 benefit, he had had enough of weekly 200-mile round trips to the Midlands. Walsall were prepared to release him and in July 1953 he visited the managers of Rotherham United, Sheffield Wednesday and Barnsley with the intention of joining whichever club would have him. Wednesday and Barnsley were interested, but each stipulated that Walsall would have to reduce the transfer fee – which had been fixed at a very modest £750.

On a Friday afternoon later in the month he resumed his previous employment at Cortonwood Colliery and on the following day he was summoned unexpectedly to Oakwell to be told a fee had been agreed with Walsall. However, on his earlier meeting with Tim Ward he hadn't been completely honest about his age and the manager thought he was younger than he actually was. Nevertheless, Henry joined the Oakwell playing staff and remained with the club for seven seasons until he was 36 years old.

His debut was delayed by an injury sustained in a cricket match during the summer. Opening the innings for Cortonwood at Denaby, after scoring 26 runs he broke a finger. A hospital was adjacent to the ground and after treatment there he resumed his innings and scored a further 26. The injury kept him out of the Reds' team until mid-September, but he then held a place for the following four years which included the 1955 Third Division (North) championship and the two following seasons in the Second Division. Between 1957 and 1959 he was used as player-coach in the reserves and then he returned to the first team to spend most of season 1959/60 at right full back.

In October 1955 Lincoln City visited Oakwell and Henry was at centre half opposing Andy Graver, a man who less than 12 months earlier had changed clubs for the very high fee of £30,000. Yet Barnsley's £250 centre half completely outplayed the expensive centre forward and twice cleared off the line goal-bound shots from him. At Swansea in August 1956 he was presented with the match ball after his two goals – one a fierce drive from 35 yards – helped beat the home side 3 – 2. And again in Wales later in the season he captained the team which caused one of the biggest surprises of the third round of the FA Cup by inflicting a 1 – 0 defeat on First Division Cardiff City.

Early in 1960 Tim Ward left for Grimsby Town and Henry could have joined him as trainer-coach, but he felt the schooling of four children had to take precedence over pursuing his career on the East Coast. After spending the 1960/61 season as player-coach with the reserves and 'A' team he accepted an invitation to become player-manager of Wombwell in the Yorkshire League.

He had a particularly successful time there, for in 1963 the team were champions of the Second Division and won the Division One championship twice in the following three years. It then seemed he had achieved all that was then possible at Wombwell, and after five enjoyable seasons he left the club and severed his connection with the game.

He has had a love of cricket since boyhood. Then his summertime Saturday afternoons were spent at the Yorkshire Council ground at Brampton where he involved himself in anything that required doing, from putting up the score to taking collections. And he took part in a game much earlier than he could have expected, for in 1937 Swinton arrived with only 10 players and he, at 12 years of age, made up the team for them.

He was in the Brampton team by the time he was 16 and remained with the club, through its name-change to Cortonwood, for 30 years. The captain of the Swinton team for which he had made the earlier emergency appearance was the Yorkshire player, Richard Denton. Denton later joined Cortonwood and for several seasons he and Henry were the team's opening batsmen.

In 1951 he had trials at the county nets at Headingley and received an offer to play professionally in the Huddersfield League. It was something he would have loved to have done, but as eight months of each year were fully taken up by work and football commitments he felt it unfair to his family to further extend the time devoted to cricket.

He was a member of the team which won the Yorkshire Council championship in 1961 and during that season he made his highest-ever score of 133 not out. And in the same summer an unbeaten 116 was scored after he'd been dropped off the first ball of the game. During his later seasons he moved down the batting order, and he had the pleasure of his two eldest sons being in the team with him. Since then his second son, John, has been a county cricketer with Derbyshire and is now with Rotherham Town.

In 1984 he took early retirement from his work at Cortonwood Colliery and now assists John at the latter's motor body repair business at Rimmington Garage, Wombwell. In anticipation of his retirement he bought an electric organ which he learned to play under the tuition of the Wombwell Parish Church organist. He has a long-held interest in classical music and the newly acquired expertise provides him with a great deal of pleasure from playing the works of his favourite composers – Beethoven, Tchaikovsky and Grieg.

Despite joining the Reds late in his career Henry Walters played 172 games for them and was selected for every outfield defensive position. In 1960 he received a £600 benefit – a generous and unexpected payment so far as a part-time player was concerned. Many of the full-timers didn't get such reward, but chairman Joe Richards said it was an acknowledgement of the player's hard work for the club. Henry was physically very strong and did indeed have a tremendous work rate, but he didn't regard what he did as being hard work – it was just a joy for him to be playing football.

Duncan Sharp: The Best of Both Worlds

Most of Duncan Sharp's 238 games for Barnsley were in the Second Division and he was perhaps the most fiercely combative centre half the Reds have had during the post-war period. Tall, dark and handsome, he was the ultimate stopper and a great favourite of the supporters: from the club's point of view it was unfortunate that a desire to expand his business interests caused him to retire from football when at the peak of his abilities.

During his early years he was often anxious and on edge before games started, but manager John Steele cured that by appointing him captain and thereby giving him more to think about than just himself. Off the pitch he was a quiet, mild mannered man but, like Fred Trueman and Freddie Mills, in his sporting role he was a snarler. With growled instructions and biting reprimands he drove his team throughout every 90 minutes but afterwards in the dressing room one wouldn't have known he was there, and although his style contained an abundance of passion and aggression he was a credit to the game in every way.

The constant determination to win was instilled in him by the late Web Swift – a master at Barnsley Grammar School and, eventually, father-in-law to his team-mate and close friend Norman Smith. Duncan was centre half in the grammar school side and, like Liverpool in the present professional game, they were the team which all the others were keen to beat and the blood-and-thunder encounters with Raley, Longcar, and Barnsley Central were meat and drink to him. On one occasion Web Swift – a strict disciplinarian and commanding personality – told Duncan he felt the team weren't scoring enough goals and he was moving him to centre forward for the sole purpose of getting the ball into the net. An instruction from Swift had to be obeyed and it was as much the apprehension of what might happen to him if he failed as the wish to succeed which spurred him to a hat-trick against arch-rivals Penistone Grammar School.

On leaving school he signed amateur forms at Oakwell and became a part-time professional in 1950, soon after his 17th birthday. He remained a part-timer for eight years, working initially in the laboratory at Wharncliffe Woodmoor Coke Ovens and later as a fitter at Haigh Colliery. The first two seasons were spent in the junior sides and during that time an altercation with player-coach Tim Ward had what he felt to be a long-term detrimental effect on his career. The conflict stemmed from frayed tempers during a 9 – 0 debacle at

Stocksbridge but on the day Duncan was disenchanted with Ward before the game even started, from what he saw as the latter's negligence in failing to ensure his boots were included in the skip. Consequently he played in a borrowed pair which were two sizes too big, and when Ward shouted at him during the heat of battle, he shouted back! The fact that the coach was a former English international and his senior by 15 years cut no ice with the young centre half. But the coach was soon to become manager, and over the following seven years there were times when Duncan was to rue that row in the mud at Stocksbridge.

His first team debut was against Mansfield Town in November 1953, but the manner in which Ward told him of his elevation ensured no pleasure was gained from what should have been one of the happiest moments of his career. 'I'm going to have to play you, there's no-one else, but you can't kick with your left foot, you can't head a ball and you're slow at turning,' as a briefing for a new challenge is not to be found in any text book of management practice. Duncan was broken hearted. It was something he had looked forward to for years, yet he almost wept. Nevertheless he gave his best and the *Barnsley Chronicle* reported none of his alleged shortcomings, saying that he made only one mistake in the whole game, prevented Mansfield's leading scorer from adding to his tally and did not let the side down. Later in the season he again deputized for George Spruce and the fact that each game was won suggests there was nothing badly amiss with the stand-in centre half.

A low-point in his career came a year later when he began to be troubled by a painful right hip. The trainers and physiotherapist couldn't alleviate the problem so he arranged to be examined at a hospital in Wakefield. Opinion there was that there was tuberculosis in the joint and, in desperation, he sought a second opinion from a consultant in Barnsley. Some mental relief came from being told the hip was perfectly sound, yet the intense pain continued. It was so severe that when pre-season training began he was unable to take part. The manager, aware of the consultant's view, washed his hands of him and the trainers wouldn't talk to him – they thought he was malingering. He was so fed up that instead of being at Oakwell when the season opened, he was on holiday at Blackpool with his wife, Pat. While there he heard of a stallholder on the South Pier who sold remedies for aches and pains and, although sceptical, he was prepared to try anything that might ease his suffering. He and Pat went onto the pier and, when he was sure there was no-one in sight whom he knew, he described the symptoms and was sold a red compound which had to be applied twice daily. On the following day, somewhat to his surprise, the pain seemed to have lessened. By Wednesday there was a definite improvement and on Thursday he was so much better that he cut short the holiday and returned to Barnsley and was training at Oakwell on the following day. He had to pick up his career in the 'A' team, but by mid-season he was back in the reserves. To this day there has been no recurrence of the painful hip and the previous scepticism for those who purvey patent medicines has long since disappeared. Certainly the man on the pier at Blackpool accomplished what several trained professionals had failed to do.

He was in the first team for most of the 1955/56 season while Spruce was incapacitated with a broken leg and he eventually succeeded him in 1957. He retained the centre half position throughout the following two seasons, but in 1959 he was again out of favour. Perhaps significantly, Tim Ward departed for Grimsby Town on a Friday in the following February and Duncan was back in the side on the Saturday. At the start of the next season he was appointed captain, retaining the role until leaving the club two years later.

Duncan has been in business since he was 25 years old. His first venture was as a newsagent at Lundwood and in the spring of 1962 he felt a need for additional capital in order to diversify his interests. He therefore approached manager John Steele with the suggestion that although he was still some time away from a benefit entitlement, the amount accrued to his credit was £1,400 and, if he could have it at that time, he would settle for £1,000. The proposal was fruitless, for Steele responded with, 'You'll settle for nowt, Duncan, we've no money.' 'Fair enough' he replied, 'I've finished then.' No-one at the club believed he really intended to retire, but when it became apparent that one of their greatest assets was to be prematurely lost the manager sent for him. 'You can have your thousand pounds, Duncan, it'll come from the transfer fee and you can have your pick of half a dozen clubs.' But the player was already at the only club he wanted to be with and had no intention of joining another. He therefore forfeited the cash on offer and at the end of the season he retired from football at the age of 29.

In close-seasons he had worked at Redfearns' Glassworks at Old Mill and on leaving Oakwell he negotiated a contract to transport the company's products. Yet for several years afterwards he hated every minute of it. He was a home-loving man; the life of a professional footballer had enabled him to spend a great deal of time there, but his new career saw him away from home for three or four days on end with little time for his family. He found himself driving past hotels in Bristol, Birmingham and central London which brought back memories of happy times spent in them as a Barnsley footballer, although he'd not previously seen what they looked like at 3am. But he persevered and, as on the pitch, threw himself wholeheartedly into what he was doing. The result was that, under his direction, Duncan Sharp & Son (Transport) Ltd eventually had 60 HGVs, a head office at Carlton Industrial Estate and depots at Manchester, Cardiff and Tilbury Docks and was one of the largest family owned transport contractors in the country. That is, until the spring of 1989 when the business was sold for a substantial sum to a Hertfordshire company, Eleco Holdings. The former proprietor's time is now devoted to other interests which, in the main, centre on his estate at Carlecotes.

Just as Duncan's business developed from small beginnings to quite considerable proportions, so has his place of residence. The first home which he and Pat had was a two-up, two-down terrace house at Haigh which they purchased for £500. Now they live on the edge of the Pennines at Carlecotes Hall – a splendid property with courtyard and stables which dates back to 1650. It was built as a residence for a Colonel in Cromwell's army and stands in 40 acres of lawns, woodland and pasture.

Duncan severed his connections with soccer many years ago but his present sport is equally as physical and considerably more dangerous: he now has a chestnut hunter and at weekends he rides with the Rockwood Hunt. Learning to ride at that level was, at times, a painful experience, for the ground can seem awfully hard on falling from a jumping, 17-hands horse. Yet centre halves don't come any harder than Duncan Sharp and four international centre forwards would doubtless testify to that. For in December 1955 he played consecutive games against Stan Mortensen, Billy Liddell, John Charles and Bedford Jezzard, and they didn't manage a single goal between them.

Chairman Joe Richards was not renowned for being financially considerate towards the players, but his helpfulness towards Duncan made the latter regard him with the same kind of affection that he had for his own grandfather. In 1958 he was so involved in work connected with the recently obtained newsagency that he completely overlooked the date by which he was required to sign the next season's contract. Three weeks elapsed before he signed and the manager was adamant that he wouldn't be paid for the lost period. Indeed, Tim Ward went so far as to say it would be contrary to the League's rules for the club to pay wages for the period he was not committed to it .. yet *someone* paid, for an amount equating to the lost weeks was in his next wage packet. And it was the chairman's consideration which enabled him to start in business in the first place, by responding favourably to a request for an accrued share of benefit long before the entitlement became due. Consequently Duncan has long been quite open in his belief that everything achieved has stemmed from Joe Richards' help at a time when without it his hopes would never have got off the ground.

No centre forward relished a duel with Duncan Sharp and as he rarely inspected the pitch before a game his team-mates frequently received enquiries from opponents about whether he was playing: a centre forward's face would drop if they said he was. The supporters loved his straightforward style, and after a tackle they would sometimes turn to each other and laughingly say, 'What's the verdict – murder or manslaughter?' At the age of 17 he could have gone to a university of his choosing and from there into a rewarding career in almost any direction he wished, for the 10 subjects in his School Certificate included Greek, Latin and physics. Indeed, on starting his first job at the coke ovens the manager was at pains to point out that he was far too highly qualified to be working there, but all the youngster wanted was something to tide him over until he could become a Barnsley footballer. And although it may be his scholastic attainments were not put to best use at that time, it now seems he has had the best of both worlds. A combination of business acumen and sheer hard graft has provided a life-style comparable with anything that might have developed from the academic career once open to him, and he has had the enjoyment and satisfaction of being a leading footballer of the only club he ever wanted to be with.

Herbert Tindill: Finishing with a Flourish!

Bert Tindill was a footballer who would not have been out of place in the First Division, but opportunity to display his skills at the game's top level never came his way. His professional career spanned 18 seasons, from teenage years with Doncaster Rovers to May 1962 at Oakwell when his goals on a warm, early summer evening were primarily responsible for the Reds retaining Third Division status.

Born at South Hiendley on New Year's Eve 1926, the small and wiry 'Tich' Tindill was by two years the youngest in the school football team and, as the only son of the steward of South Hiendley Village Club, was the only lad for miles around to have a football and a bicycle. The family's comparative affluence was again apparent when he left school. Then he obtained an engineering apprenticeship which paid 10s 6d weekly, yet 14-year-olds could earn three times that amount from pit-top work at the local colliery.

He joined Doncaster Rovers in 1943, making his first team debut in an 8 – 1 success at Hull City. He retained a place for most of the season, but conscription into the army in late 1945 took him to the West Country for most of the following two years. During that time he played for Yeovil Town, missing his own club's triumphant season of 1946/47 when they won the Division Three (North) championship with a record number of points and goals, thereby beating the previous divisional record created by Barnsley in 1939.

He was back at Doncaster in time to have membership of their Northern Section championship side of 1950. He remained with the club for a further eight years and totalled 402 peacetime appearances – one of which was in October 1956 when he scored twice in a 5 – 2 defeat of the Reds. Nearly two years earlier it had been his superb display at Middlesbrough which resulted in Rovers making their first-ever appearance in the fifth round of the FA Cup. Then his 74th minute goal came from beating six opponents before lobbing the ball into the net, and the 41,000 spectators had already seen him involved in the other goals in his team's 4 – 1 victory.

Bert had begun his career as a right winger, but by then had operated to good effect in all the forward positions. In that respect he had had considerable help from manager Peter Doherty – a man accepted as one of the finest inside forwards of all time. Doherty had joined the club as player-manager in 1949 and led the team to promotion in his first season, and Bert openly acknowledged how he had improved by playing alongside such a master craftsman. The appreciation was, apparently, mutual. In February 1958, soon after moving to Bristol City, Doherty returned to Doncaster to sign Bert immediately after he'd scored in a 2 – 1 success over the manager's new side.

At that stage of the season Bristol City weren't doing at all well and relegation seemed a real possibility. Bert soon altered that. In 14 games he scored 10 goals – including a hat-trick against a Fulham side who were going for promotion. Another memorable occasion was on 12th April when he again scored twice in another five-goal defeat of Barnsley and at the season's end Bristol were well clear of the relegation places. Yet Doncaster Rovers, the team he'd left 12 weeks earlier, were firmly entrenched at the bottom of the division. In the following year he continued his torment of the Reds, scoring twice and having a hand in all but one of the other goals when his team beat them 7 – 4 at Oakwell in August 1958.

Bert joined Barnsley in October of the following year. He stayed for three seasons and was almost always at centre forward. During that time an Oakwell 'first' took place when Reading were the visitors in the FA Cup and extra-time became necessary. It had never previously occurred at Barnsley, and Bert broke the deadlock for the Reds to go into the fourth round at Huddersfield Town. There his lob beat the goalkeeper and rebounded for Ken Oliver to score in a 1 – 1 draw in front of more than 44,000 spectators.

His final season was 1961/62. Not only did his goals in the last game ensure Third Division survival, but it was his winner against Hull City on 23rd April which had provided that last-gasp opportunity to avoid the drop.

Bert and Peggy Hannan – a girl of a devout Roman Catholic family – met in April 1949. Peggy's mother had distinct reservations about this young man who was paying regular attention to her daughter and who didn't seem to have a proper job. She had such little awareness of matters appertaining to sport that on being told Bert was with Doncaster Rovers she replied, 'Doncaster Rovers – what's that?' She couldn't believe that a living could be made from playing football but, nevertheless, she came to adore her future son-in-law. Bert became a convert to Catholicism, making his first communion on the day he and Peggy were married – less than a year after their first meeting.

Football and family apart, Bert's main interest was horse-racing. It began when he was a young player at Doncaster, in regular contact with jockeys attending meetings on the adjacent racecourse who used the treatment facilities at Belle Vue and responded with tips and complementary tickets. He retained a love of the sport for the rest of his life, taking his growing family on regular outings to racecourses in the North of England.

On returning to South Yorkshire in 1959 he succeeded his father as licensee of the Sun Inn at South Hiendley and when his playing career ended he moved to the Lundwood Hotel on the outskirts of Barnsley. Seven years later he left the licensed trade in order to spend more time with Peggy and their six children.

He went into business as a motor body repairer at South Elmsall, later buying a partnership in Magnet Motors, a car body repair business in Wakefield Road, Smithies. On leaving Lundwood the Tindills lived at Brierley and, later, at Hemsworth. Bert was a man who had never had a day's illness in his life, but on 10th July 1973 he was at home at Hemsworth when he collapsed and died. He was 46 years old.

In his last game for Barnsley, against Torquay United on 2nd May 1962, anything less than a victory would have consigned the club into Division Four. Bert played with the same spirit and enthusiasm he had shown in his first game as a stripling with Doncaster Rovers and, with the Reds trailing 2 – 1, he equalized just before half-time and clinched the issue with his second and the team's fourth goal mid-way through the second half. It was a fitting finish to a fine career, and at the end of the game and amid scenes of great jubilation, team-mates and supporters carried him shoulder-high from the pitch.

That last game had special significance for both Bert Tindill and his club, yet his approach to it was the same as to every other game in which he played, for he knew no other. He continually gave everything he'd got, and his managers always knew that from him they would get 90 minutes of wholehearted endeavour and, very possibly, a winning goal.

Colin Swift: The Last to Leave

Barnsley-born Colin Swift was a member of the town's boys' team for two years and in the second, 1949, they won the Yorkshire Shield and the English Schools Trophy. Normally he would have left Raley School at Easter 1949, but he remained there for two further months in order to continue with Barnsley Boys as they moved purposefully towards winning the two competitions.

After success in the national trophy the team attended a civic reception at the Town Hall, and Barnsley FC organized a celebration for them and their parents at the Queens Hotel which included a presentation of blazer badges to the team. The club also took the unprecedented step of attempting to sign all 11 players. Colin was one of three who were taken onto the ground staff and the remainder – with the exception of one whose allegiance lay with Sheffield Wednesday – joined the club as amateurs.

As the only groundstaff boy who was a full back, he was favoured by trainer Bob Shotton – himself a former full back. He assisted Shotton with the kit and occasionally travelled with the first team. At such times he was allowed to sit with the trainer, and at splendid grounds like Hillsborough and Maine Road he watched his idols in the heat of battle at the closest possible quarters – an exciting experience for a 15-year-old.

His own career began in the most junior of the club's five sides and he'd graduated to the third team in the Yorkshire League by the time he was required for National Service in 1952. Stationed at Tonfanau in North Wales with 55 Training Regiment, Royal Artillery, he played at right back behind future England captain Ronnie Clayton of Blackburn Rovers in the regimental side which won the championship of Division One of the semi-professional Welsh League (North).

Saturday soccer in North Wales kept him away from Oakwell for two years, and he had been back at the club for a further year before getting an opportunity in the first team. That came in August 1955 at Fulham. There the Reds faced a side which had five internationals and two men – Ron Greenwood and Bobby Robson – who were to become managers of the England team. The debutant right back was directly opposed by Charlie Mitten of Manchester United fame and received favourable comments in newspaper reports which were unanimous that the visitors played splendid football – despite losing 5 – 1!

In the following year Colin had a regular place in the side and was the only member of the 1949 Barnsley Boys team who was still at the club. At that stage he had an opportunity to move to First Division Cardiff City. Jimmy Moore, outside left in the Reds' FA Cup-winning team of 1912, was then scouting for the Welsh club and frequented the Coach and Horses in Sheffield Road. It was a place where Colin had an occasional mid-week drink and he got to know Jimmy quite well. One evening it was suggested that a transfer to Cardiff could be arranged, but he was established in the Barnsley team and the maximum wage then in operation meant there was little financial gain in such a move.

Over the next six years he was involved in all the team's triumphs and disappointments, which included the 1959 relegation and historic FA Cup games at Cardiff and Leicester – the latter encounter was in the sixth round of the competition and earned them the *Sunday Pictorial* Giant Killer Trophy.

After being first choice at right back for four consecutive seasons Colin was switched to the other flank in 1959, remaining there until a game against Northampton Town in October 1961, which was to be his last appearance in the team. Then he sustained knee ligament damage which was not correctly diagnosed, and a year's absence from the game took in three operations and removal of cartilages before the real trouble was identified. That was not until he'd had a few outings in the reserves – then only with the aid of pain-killing injections – at which stage medical opinion was that his career was at an end.

The condition of the knee prevented him turning quickly and he was unable to meet even the less demanding requirements of non-League soccer. Consequently he has not played at any level since departing Oakwell in May 1963.

On leaving the club he worked first as a salesman with DER Ltd – the TV rental company – at their Barnsley branch before moving within the same field to Joseph Peck Ltd in Doncaster Road. Remaining there until 1978, he then became a milk roundsman with the Co-operative Society Dairy in Stocks Lane. He works an area bounded by Summer Lane, Shaw Lane and Dodworth Road, and his style of delivery has impressed his customers to the extent that it has even cropped up in a pub quiz. Quizes are a popular form of entertainment in the town's pubs, and a question posed one evening in premises in Dodworth Road was, 'Who is the fastest milkman in the West?' The expected answer was, of course, *Ernie* – the speedy, amorous milkman of Benny Hill's 1976 comic song. But one of those present shouted out, 'It's Swifty, he never stops running!' Colin's working day begins at 5am and about four miles of his route, from float to doorstep, is done on foot when he runs continuously. On a good day he can finish soon after 10 o'clock, but the actual time depends on how quickly he runs!

Tommy Taylor, Colin's club-mate before being transferred to Manchester United, had also been a fellow pupil at Raley School and during schoolboy football Colin became friendly with David Pegg and Mark Jones who went to Old Trafford as juniors. Years later the four were together in the Royal Artillery and their friendship flourished during the 12 months in which they played in the regimental side. Therefore one of the saddest periods of his life stemmed from an occurrence in February 1958 when his friends were among those who perished in a tragedy at Munich Airport. Yet football provided him with endless enjoyment, and one of his most thrilling experiences took place even before his professional career began – on the evening of 7th May 1949 when the Oakwell attendance of 27,700 at an English Schools' final was almost double that at the Second Division fixture in the afternoon. In fact, his years as a Barnsley footballer, from the age of 15 to 29, were the best of his life, spent doing what he was good at in the company of some of the best players the club has had – many of whom remain his friends to this day.

Frank Bartlett: Every 90 Minutes Non-Stop

Frank Bartlett considers himself fortunate to have had a career in professional football. As a teenager in Durham he twice gave up the game, and halfway through a month's trial at Oakwell he packed his bags and went home. He was persuaded to return and straightaway became a professional player, but two years later he was still unhappy about being so far from his native North-East and tried unsuccessfully to obtain his release from the club. Yet from such hesitant beginnings stemmed an Oakwell career which had more than 300 games, a goal scoring record, the team captaincy and membership of the 1955 Third Division (North) championship side. As much as anything it was his popularity with the supporters which brought about the change of heart and he still lives in the town, although his 12 years with the club ended as long ago as 1963.

The second youngest of seven brothers, he played football for his Chester-le-Street school and after leaving there two years elapsed before he took up the game again. He was then invited to play for Kimblesworth – one of the best junior sides in Durham. It was October when he joined them but he scored 45 goals and the team won each of the four competitions in which they were involved. Kimblesworth were an under-18 side and at the end of the season he was too old to continue with them and, despite his success, he had no overriding urge to join another club. He might therefore have been lost to the game altogether but for elder brother George leaving the Blackhall Colliery Welfare side in order to have trials with Notts County and recommending Frank as a replacement. Blackhall were a semi-professional team in the same league as the reserve sides of senior clubs in the North-East, and although Frank was an amateur his displays at inside forward attracted the attention of a Barnsley scout.

Consequently he visited Oakwell for a month's trial during pre-season training in 1950. However, it was the first time he'd been away from home and after a fortnight he was so homesick that he left his lodgings at Darton and, without telling anyone at the club, returned home to Chester-le-Street. But promising young footballers are not given up easily, and within a couple of days the scout was back at the Bartlett family home. He arrived on a Friday at 10am and spent all day trying to persuade Frank that the first two weeks were always the worst and with those already behind him he could look forward to a career seemingly full of promise in what was really a welcoming and friendly town. The lad wasn't at all convinced but by 4pm had weakened sufficiently to return to Barnsley. On the following day he played in a public practice match, immediately after which he was offered, and accepted, professional terms. And to ensure there were no further unauthorized departures, manager Angus Seed accommodated him at his own home, the White Hart Hotel, for the first weekend and then arranged lodgings for him with club-mate Johnny Kelly at Ward Green.

In the early post-war years physically fit young men were required to perform National Service in HM Forces. It came at the age of 18, but for those in apprenticeships it was delayed until that aspect of their training had been completed. Frank's apprenticeship within the motor trade was severed when he became a professional footballer, and early in 1951 he was conscripted into the Royal Air Force. For the following two years he served at RAF Full Sutton, near York, and the station team won the Fighter Command Cup in each of the two seasons he was with them. As a retained professional he continued to receive a weekly wage from the Barnsley club, but throughout that time he rarely showed his face at Oakwell. There was as much football as he wanted during each week, and weekend leave was almost always spent in his home town. When National Service ended in February 1953 he sought his release in order to return there but Angus Seed, perhaps having in mind the weekly outlay over the previous two years, was adamant in his refusal.

His debut was in the following month in a 2 – 2 draw with Leeds United when he deputized at inside right for the injured Eddie McMorran and had the pleasurable experience of scoring in his opening game in the Second Division. After retaining a place for the remainder of the season it was disappointing for him that he made very infrequent appearances during the following campaign. However, he established himself in the team at outside left during the 1954/55 championship season when he twice did the hat-trick – at Gateshead in November and at Oakwell against Workington Town in the following February. His season's total of 15 goals was the highest ever by a club winger but, despite that, he hated having to play in the position. He continually brought his feelings to the attention of manager Tim Ward who, during the period that Frank was in the role, signed several specialist left wingers. On one occasion he scored twice in a 5 – 2 FA Cup win over York City and was excluded from the next game in favour of newcomer Bill Wardle. Yet Wardle, like all the others, was eventually dropped for Frank to be restored to the team, but it reached the stage where he would rather be omitted than play at outside left.

In the autumn of 1956 an injury to skipper Norman Smith enabled him to play at right half – the position he'd always wanted to have. His first game in it was against Nottingham Forest, whose inside left was Doug Lishman who had just joined them after a long and illustrious career with Arsenal. Tim Ward's pre-match instruction to his right half was, 'Stick to Lishman like glue.' Frank obeyed to the letter, so much so that as the two men walked off the pitch together at the end of the 1 – 1 draw the Forest player said, 'I'm going to the lavatory now – I suppose you're coming with me!' He had the right half position for two years and it was the happiest time of his whole career. In 1960/61 he moved to inside forward and was leading scorer with 17 goals – which included a hat-trick in a 6 – 1 beating of Notts County.

The 1962/63 season was his last with the club. In July he joined Halifax Town, but injury limited his stay there to one season. He then moved into the Midland League to have two seasons with Goole Town, and long spells in local football with Kexborough Rovers and the Star Paper Mill team enabled him to continue to play until he was 46 years old. It was never his intention to remain in the game when his playing days ended, and after leaving Halifax Town he took employment with the Barnsley Optical Company in Shambles Street. From there he moved to the Star Paper Mill in Old Mill Lane, remaining there for 13 years until it closed in 1981. He now works at the BOC warehouse on Carlton Industrial Estate where Marks & Spencer's foodstuffs are received from manufacturers and dispatched to stores throughout the North of England.

The brown wavy hair which Frank had as a Barnsley footballer has now disappeared but the same ready smile is still much in evidence. The lean look has also gone, no doubt because he takes the view that strenuous physical activity is for the young and the fifties is a time for enjoying the comforts of life. The few extra pounds he now carries have given him a definite resemblance to the former heavyweight boxing champion, Henry Cooper. Surprisingly, the similarity does not arouse comment in Barnsley, but when on holiday away from the town he is either asked if he is Henry Cooper or he overhears someone referring to him by that name. Yet any misapprehension disappears immediately he speaks, for the native North-Eastern accent, which almost 40 years in Yorkshire have failed to diminish, cannot possibly be confused with the Cockney tones of the famous boxer.

Frank's intense dislike of the outside left role was because, by its very nature, there were periods when he was not actively involved in the game – and he wanted to be everywhere on the pitch. The ability to keep running throughout 90 minutes stemmed from boyhood days in Chester-le-Street; his home was within a couple of minutes of open countryside and the River Wear, and every spare moment was spent in the Great Outdoors, running, climbing and swimming. Those activities provided him with endless stamina, but when Tim Ward first saw him at inside forward he was concerned that he would burn himself out before his career had gone its natural course. Time proved the manager's fears to be groundless, for it was the player's natural style to be continually up having a crack at goal and straightaway be back defending. He actually scored more goals as a wing half than as a forward – one of which was the winner at First Division Cardiff City in 1957 when the Reds created the biggest surprise in the fourth round of the FA Cup. And although he feels he was fortunate in being allowed to overcome the obstacles which he himself placed in the early years of his soccer development, it may be that Barnsley Football Club was equally fortunate in having such a versatile and one hundred per-cent player as Frank Bartlett.

Billy Houghton: The Long Range Specialist

Billy Houghton played in the Barnsley Boys team which won the 1954 Yorkshire Wylie Shield and was one of eight members of that side to join the Oakwell staff. In the same year and while a pupil at Littleworth School he won county representative honours and became an outstanding footballer at youth level. Indeed, in all the years that junior competitive football has been played, few of the town's youngsters have received as much international recognition as Billy. After 10 years with Barnsley he continued his career at four other clubs – with Ipswich Town he won a Second Division championship medal and played in the First Division – and he remained within the Football League until he was 35 years old.

On becoming an amateur at Oakwell he was apprenticed to a local building firm, C D Potter & Sons, where Mr Ralph Potter was, and still is, a director of the club. He started in the junior side at left half and, soon afterwards, scored 10 goals in four games at centre forward. But he was a wing half until late in his career and played for the English youth team on 10 occasions in 1957 and 1958, alongside Jimmy Greaves and John Lyall who later managed West Ham. Those games brought him to national notice and in the spring of 1958 manager Tim Ward was anxious to secure him on a part-time professional contract, although he was still eligible for one more game with the youth team. Becoming a professional would have disqualified Billy from that final honour so he declined to do that, but the manager was persistent and persuaded him to sign a post-dated contract, to become effective in June after the game against Austria. Ward certainly knew what he was doing. Immediately Billy had signed, Manchester City were on the scene and, had he not then been committed to Barnsley, their tempting offer would have taken him to the First Division set-up at Maine Road.

He became a full-time player on completion of his apprenticeship and after only four reserve team games he made his Second Division debut in October 1957 against Blackburn Rovers. And although the Reds lost 2 – 0, he was the one who came nearest to scoring when he rattled the visitors' cross-bar with a fierce drive from 30 yards. He played 20 games in that season and won a regular place in the following August and, injury apart, was never omitted from the side.

In the summer of 1964 the terms he was offered were less than he had expected and, on telling the manager what he hoped to receive, he also pointed out that he qualified for a benefit payment. The result was that a fee of £10,000 transferred him to Watford. His new manager was Bill McGarry and Billy had been aware that he had been on his wanted-list for some time because former team-mate Ken Oliver, who had joined Watford in the previous season, had told him that McGarry had stated an intention to secure him. The manager was a man who liked 'hard' players and no doubt remembered his first contact with Billy – as player-manager of the Bournemouth side which drew at Oakwell in February 1962 when he was at the receiving end of a really shattering tackle from Barnsley's young, tough, left half.

He found McGarry to be a man who would do anything for those who gave one hundred per-cent and after the boss moved to Ipswich Town he joined him there in the summer of 1966. The three seasons at Ipswich were the happiest and most successful of his career and during that time he was converted to full back. His team won the Second Division championship in 1968 when he missed only one game in the whole campaign, and it was a happy coincidence that as they were being promoted the club with which he began his career was experiencing the delights of promotion into the Third Division. He relished every moment of the season in Division One and there was a lot of satisfaction in being in the side which achieved success at such places as Highbury, Nottingham Forest and West Ham.

In the summer of 1969 he was keen to return to South Yorkshire and a transfer he was able to arrange to Leicester City was intended to be of a temporary nature until a more convenient move became possible. That occurred six months later when he joined Rotherham United. He might have returned to Oakwell instead, but, recently out of the First Division, he felt almost insulted by a requirement to prove himself on a month's trial.

He played 139 games for the Millers and when his career drew to a close in 1974, manager Jim McGuigan – a man respected as a coach throughout football – offered him the position of reserve team coach. It was a job he would have loved to have had and it was not surprising that it was offered to him, for one of his previous Rotherham managers, Jim McAnearney, had said that any youngster wanting to progress in the game could do no better than model himself on Billy Houghton. But when told that the wage for which he'd asked was appreciably more than the first team coach was getting he realized he would be better off by returning to the joinery trade.

Initially he worked for the Kershaw company at Barnsley, then he was with Barnsley MBC for four years before buying a newsagent's business at Wombwell. He had that for four years and is now employed by British Coal's building department.

As a player, Billy's special skill was in passing the ball. He preferred to pass rather than beat a man and, even as a junior, it was said of him that he could land a football on a sixpence. He played 235 games for Barnsley and in the last one, at Queen's Park Rangers in the season's final game in 1964, it was essential to obtain a point in order to avoid relegation but the team trailed 2 – 0 at the interval. The tide began to turn in the second half when his 30-yard shot was blocked on the line, from which a scrambled goal enabled them to fight back and equalize and so retain Third Division status.

Although the scoring of goals was not a major part of his game, those he did score were usually from well outside the penalty-area. In October 1960 he celebrated his 50th appearance with a glorious 25-yard volley into goal in a 2 – 1 win against Tranmere Rovers. On the last day of that year he sent a piledriver into Bristol Rovers' net to help towards a 2 – 0 success, and on a freezing night in January 1964 he scored from nearly 30 yards in a draw with Hull City. Two months later a great first-time shot from the edge of the area put the Reds on course for a 2 – 1 win against Notts County. Another long range shot put him among the scorers in a 6 – 2 second leg League Cup defeat of Darlington; in the first his volley from 25 yards had entered the net but was disallowed – and then he missed from the penalty-spot. The power of his shooting, like the accuracy of his long pass, was readily acknowledged by team-mates, who sometimes added the wry comment that the nearer he got to goal, the less lethal he was likely to be! His skills were those of a top-class player and it was no surprise to people at Oakwell when he went on to the First Division. Likewise, his attitude was always right and the manager who was seeking a coach had correctly assessed Billy Houghton as a model professional footballer.

Tony Leighton: A Wholehearted, Genuine Man

Tony Leighton was top scorer in each of three seasons at Oakwell and his 24 goals in 1963/64 is a post-war Third Division record for the club. He went on to be a leading scorer at Huddersfield Town, but before joining Barnsley he'd been given away by both Leeds United and Doncaster Rovers. Yet progress with Barnsley was such that on his transfer in December 1964 the club received £20,000 for someone who, two-and-a-half years earlier, they had got for nothing.

Born in Leeds, the youngest of nine children, he won representative honours at both football and cricket with Leeds and Yorkshire Boys. On leaving school in 1954 he could have had a position on the Leeds United groundstaff but, instead, went along with a parental wish that he learn a trade. He became an apprentice plumber, but two years later was able to persuade his parents that football was what he really wanted and he took up the previously offered appointment to the Elland Road groundstaff.

Earlier he'd been a right winger, but with Leeds United juniors he became a centre forward and progressed to the reserves. In his final season he scored 34 goals in the Central League, but in two-and-a-half years his only appearance in the first team was in a pre-season friendly in 1958.

Twelve months later a free transfer took him to Doncaster Rovers. Within a matter of weeks, in a rare appearance with the reserves, he equalled a 40-year club record by scoring all the goals in a 6 – 0 defeat of Stockport County reserves. Over the following three years he played at full back, wing half and in all the forward positions, and he led the scorers in each season. In his final season he was out of the side for 12 weeks following a cartilage operation – yet his 28 games produced 24 goals.

It seems quite incredible that such a consistent scorer received his second free transfer by the time he was 22 but, in May 1962, that was Tony's experience. Barnsley's John Steele pondered Rovers' reasoning and, instead of signing the player immediately, invited him to spend a few weeks at Oakwell in order to have a look at him.

What impressed Steele most was Tony's enthusiasm, but as a centre forward he wasn't really what the manager was looking for. Nevertheless, he was signed on full-time terms and the coaches got to work on him. He was a fitness fanatic, exceptionally strong with a rather unorthodox style and he could outjump anyone on the field. Expert opinion was that he was an out-and-out striker who should get into the penalty-area as often as possible – yet his inclination was to range all over the opposition's half of the pitch. 'You end up crossing to yourself, Tony,' Steele once said in some desperation, 'and you're never there!' Tony got the message and then went from strength to strength.

His first Oakwell season – that of 1962/63 – ended with him having scored 22 goals. In the next he did even better. His goals included two on 6th September 1963 in a victory over leaders Luton Town and two against Queen's Park Rangers in October when he lobbed the Reds' future 'keeper, Peter Springett, for the first and jinked past two defenders to score the second with a fierce left-foot drive. At Crewe in November he provided the first away success of the season and on the following Saturday his scorching 30-yard shot confirmed the Reds' 2 – 0 victory over new leaders Crystal Palace.

The transfer to Huddersfield Town took place on New Year's Eve 1964. He was his new team's fifth centre forward of the season, the others having managed only five goals between them in the previous 24 games. Tony quickly showed how it should be done, on 2nd January scoring on his Second Division debut in front of 45,000 spectators at Newcastle United.

Despite the season being more than half over when he got there he ended it as second-top scorer. Again second-top in 1965/66, in the following season – his last at the club – he led the scorers with 20 goals.

He was transferred to Bradford City in March 1968, in the following year being part of their team which won promotion into the Third Division. In the summer of 1970 he was appointed player-manager of Bradford Park Avenue – the club then being outside the Football League. By then he was a centre half, in which position he played against the Reds at Oakwell in the first round of the 1971 FA Cup.

He was the PFA representative at four consecutive clubs and was elected to the management committee in 1965. In fact, he always felt his heavy involvement with the PFA to be the reason why he was never retained anywhere for longer than three years. From 1969 until retiring from the game in 1973 he travelled regularly throughout England and Wales defending players at FA disciplinary hearings. The manner in which he carried out that responsibility earned him the respect of disciplinary committees and those he represented, and the expertise which he developed brought upon him the nickname, Leighton QC.

In the early summer of 1976 Tony experienced the onset of serious illness. Having participated in sport since boyhood, it was to be expected that any physical impairment would manifest itself when he was in competition with others. He had been in senior league cricket from the age of 16, playing professionally in the Huddersfield and Bradford Leagues and Yorkshire Council and spending the summer of 1964 in the Leicestershire second XI. A number 3 batsman, he was a big hitter of such renown that, during his time at Oakwell, spectators flocked to Shaw Lane in their hundreds to see him in action with Wombwell Main in the Barnsley Cricket Club's annual knock-out competition.

It was some 12 years later while playing for Liversedge in the Bradford League that he began to have difficulty in co-ordinating his movements. He had been an outstanding fielder – there were no liberties with quick singles when Tony Leighton was about – but he realized he wasn't picking up the ball cleanly. At first he thought he perhaps needed spectacles, but a visit to an optician revealed nothing amiss in that respect. However, the problem persisted and when his speech began to slur he knew something was seriously wrong. After a series of tests, muscular sclerosis was diagnosed. Although that in itself was bad enough, the speed of his physical deterioration puzzled the doctors and further tests revealed him to be suffering from the incurable motor neurone disease. He learned this, and the inevitable, progressively worsening nature of the illness, on his 37th birthday.

At that point the determination within his character was never more in evidence. He had always been a hard working man. To provide a good living for his wife, Pauline, and their two daughters he supplemented football income throughout most of his playing career. At Doncaster he did evening-time work at the Green Tree Hotel at Hatfield and on attending for training each morning he'd already spent two hours bagging coal for a local fuel merchant, and while with Huddersfield he had a part-time job at a sports outfitter's shop in the town centre.

On leaving professional football he was employed as North-Eastern representative for the textile manufacturers, Courtaulds. Five years later he was promoted to Special Accounts Manager at the company's Nottingham office, to which he travelled daily from his home at Heckmondwike. It was while in that post and, ironically, when he was about to be promoted to Sales Manager, that he became ill. Nevertheless, he was determined to carry on and exchanged his car for one with automatic transmission in order to conserve his flagging strength. Eventually he felt best able to cope by spending the working week in Nottingham and returning home on Friday evenings, but after a few weeks even that was too much for him. He became confined to a wheelchair and Pauline gave up her job in order to care for him.

Medical opinion was that Tony's long involvement in sport was not to his advantage, for there is apparently some evidence which suggests that the stronger the muscle, the quicker the disease destroys it. Yet he never accepted that he was going to die; he exercised as best he could and gave himself a variety of interests. The ex-Leeds United Players' Association provided continual support. Two of them, Roy Ambler and Derek Powell – they and Tony had been pals from junior days at Elland Road – took him to their fortnightly meetings and arranged for him to have a Possum machine – a piece of electronic equipment which enables the severely physically disabled to communicate with each other. By using it, Tony contributed an article on his career in football to the April 1978 edition of *Possability* – the Possum Users' Association Magazine – but he didn't see it published, for he died on 4th April, aged 38.

Tony Leighton was a friendly, outgoing man who loved people. He was always the first to greet a new player, and youngsters coming into a side could rely on him for help and encouragement. Ever-willing to make presentations at junior clubs, he organized annual visits to Blackpool illuminations for the Oakwell families and they also attended fireworks parties which he and Pauline held each 5th November at their home in Dodworth Road.

On match days at Oakwell he couldn't wait to get onto the pitch: he would dash down the tunnel and with knees up and elbows working like pistons he'd race to the Pontefract Road end in readiness for the kick-in. There was purpose and determination in his every movement and, just as he loved the crowd, the crowd loved him, too. Indeed, it was perhaps a combination of spectator approval and good management which created the turning point in his career. He was always appreciative of the fillip he got from John Steele. In February 1964, during the week preceding Manchester United's visit to Oakwell in the fifth round of the FA Cup, the Manchester *Evening News and Chronicle* published an interview with Tony. In it he said, 'John Steele picked me off the midden heap and got me going again. I shall always be grateful to him and Barnsley for that.' On the last day of that year, on saying his farewells prior to departing for Huddersfield Town, he held out his hand to Steele and said, 'Thanks, boss. I was nothing when I came here and you made me a centre forward.' It was something which didn't have to be said, but such openness was typical of the wholehearted, genuine man who was Tony Leighton.

Bobby Wood: A Fruitful About-Turn

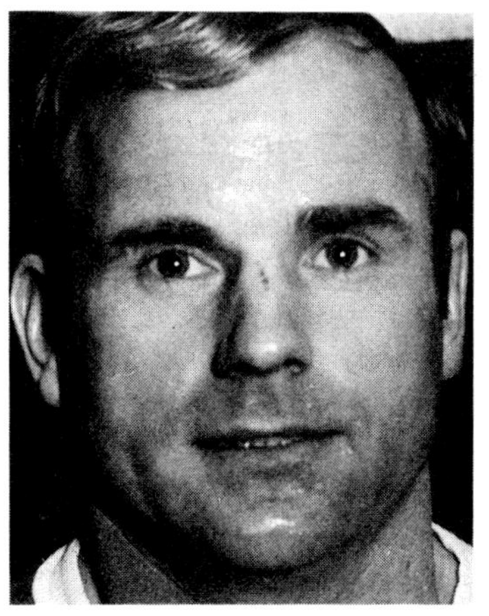

When Bobby Wood's career ended in 1965 he had created a new Barnsley record for number of games played. And it can truly be said that no player has ever been closer to the club than he, for his home in Belgrave Road is a mere 100 yards from the main entrance to the Oakwell ground. He came into the side in 1951 alongside some of the club's most renowned names – Pallister, Baxter, McCormack and McMorran among them – and over the following years he became a mainstay of the team and a fine example to its younger members.

He is a native of Elphinstone, a village 10 miles from Edinburgh, and joined the Reds as a 21-year-old from Hibernian. He was then a part-time professional and worked at Woolley Colliery, and although he won a place at the opening of his first Oakwell season – and provided the first victory with a spectacular flying header almost on the stroke of time at Doncaster on 1st December – he played only spasmodically before beginning National Service in the army in 1952.

While serving in the 7th Training Regiment, Royal Signals, he played regularly in army football and captained the regimental side which beat the RAOC in the 1953 Army Cup final. Throughout that time he played for Barnsley reserves and occasionally for the first team and he became a full-time player on completion of military service.

As an inside forward he was a member of the 1955 Division Three (North) championship side and his 12 goals included the winner at Tranmere in March and two against Rochdale on 3rd May which ensured the championship came to Oakwell. At the commencement of the following season he scored Barnsley's first Second Division goal in a 2 – 1 success over Leeds United, and at the higher level his standard of play kept him continually in the sporting headlines and there were suggestions that he was being considered for international honours.

Season 1957/58 was particularly satisfying for him. He represented Sheffield & Hallamshire FA against Glasgow and scored in the Reds' 3 – 2 win at Notts County and in their 5 – 0 success at Huddersfield Town – displays which brought comment from the respective managers, Tommy Lawton and Bill Shankly, that Barnsley were the best team in the Second Division. On 19th October Charlton Athletic visited Oakwell as leaders of the division and left wondering what had hit them after Bob had been among the scorers in an exciting encounter in which the Reds administered a 4 – 1 thrashing. And on 28th December he scored what was considered the best of Barnsley's three goals when Derby County were beaten in front of 22,000 spectators who formed Oakwell's biggest crowd of the season.

On the evening of the 5 – 0 victory at Huddersfield he and team-mate Frank Bartlett – the two have now been close friends for almost 40 years – set off to spend what was left of the weekend with his parents. At 2am, when 30 miles from Edinburgh, the car ran out of petrol and as there was no likelihood of obtaining any at that hour they pushed it into the side of the road and slept. Some time later they were awakened by a member of the local constabulary whose suspicions had been aroused by the car being parked miles from anywhere. On being questioned about their identities, Bob said they were Barnsley footballers on their way to Elphinstone to see his parents. The constable then looked more closely at him and said, 'You're Bobby Wood, aren't you? I remember you playing for Hibs. Wait here.' He then left, and 10 minutes later returned with a gallon of petrol, saying both he and the garage proprietor whom he had got out of bed were pleased to perform a small service for a player they had always liked when he was with Hibernian.

In 1959 the club paid him the maximum £750 benefit, but not before originally saying it could not be afforded and he had responded with a request for a transfer. He was presented with the cheque immediately before a game against Stoke City, and he celebrated by scoring the winning goal.

In the following spring he was placed on the transfer list. A nagging knee injury had limited his appearances during the previous season and it was suspected he had cartilage trouble, consequently the club decided it was time to part company. Mansfield Town enquired about signing him but withdrew on learning about the knee and, thoroughly despondent, he returned to Edinburgh. There he took matters into his own hands. He presented himself at the city's Princess Margaret Rose Hospital for surgery on his right knee, and the removal of a cartilage rectified all the previous problems. Two months later he returned to Oakwell where, after satisfying the manager about his fitness, he was re-engaged.

He remained with the club for a further five years. During that time he became captain; he scored the goal which beat Huddersfield Town en route to the quarter-finals of the 1961 FA Cup and his availability enabled the club to obtain a very substantial fee from the transfer of wing half Dave Barber to Preston North End.

In February 1964 a testimonial game was arranged for him. But just as his earlier benefit had had its problems, so did this. The game was organized by the Supporters' Club and well attended, but the Inland Revenue's demand for a share of the proceeds was unexpected and argued for 12 months before being resolved. The problem arose through the tickets being printed from the block used for the club's games which bore the secretary's signature. The Inland Revenue's case was that the official nature of the admission ticket indicated the game was part of Bobby's employment with Barnsley FC rather than an act of appreciation by the supporters and was, therefore, taxable. In the event the demand had to be paid, but a substantial amount remained for the intended beneficiary and he was appreciative of all the hard work which had gone into making the testimonial such a successful event.

When his playing days ended in 1965 he had created a club record of 371 League and Cup appearances. He was then 35 and, not wanting to get involved in the hurly-burly of football at lower levels, he left the game and took up employment as a rent collector with Barnsley County Borough Council. This was retained for 24 years, until 1989, when he took early retirement.

Some players go through an entire career and suffer little more than minor cuts and bruises, but that was not Bobby's experience. His first footballing misfortune was as a 13-year-old who travelled back to Edinburgh in the guard's van of a train because the carriage seats couldn't accommodate his leg which was stretched in front of him in splints. It ended his season's football and also his schooling, for by the time he was out and about again it was time for him to find a job. While at Oakwell he was absent for long spells with thigh and shoulder injuries yet he always came up smiling – little wonder he was one of the most popular players the club has had.

Bobby Wood played in all three inside forward positions and at wing half. The latter was his favourite role – his long range shooting could be quite spectacular and brought some memorable goals – and the team always seemed to play well when he and Frank Bartlett were in the wing half positions. His time with the Reds extended from the tail-end of the immediate post-war years, through the despair of the 1953 relegation and back again into Division Two. There were problems again in 1964 and the fact that the team escaped relegation was to a large extent due to him pulling them out of trouble. Throughout that difficult time he played consistently well and his courage and determination were a fine example to his colleagues who could count themselves fortunate in having such a grand skipper. And it was apparent to all that the about-turn which brought about his re-engagement in 1959 was one of the best decisions the club had ever made.

George Kerr: Brilliant, But . . .

George Kerr has an approach to life which is based on principles instilled into him as a child. His mother, Mary, a Scottish Presbyterian, impressed upon him that he should never hold back from telling the truth and whatever he believes he should not hesitate to say. It is therefore easy to understand why he has made enemies. Indeed, Reg Brealey, chairman of Sheffield United and a friend of long standing, once said to him, 'I know you shoot from the hip, George, but why do you have to empty the chamber?' Nevertheless, he is still continuing a career which began at Oakwell 30 years ago – his playing days ended through injury when he was 28 and the intervening years being spent as coach and manager. During that time he's had his share of promotions and relegations together with the almost inevitable consequence of the latter. In the places where he has worked his lack of discretion is almost legendary and it may be he has brought some dismissals upon himself. Yet he is one of soccer's survivors: a club has always come for him and he bounces back, as full of confidence and immoderation as before.

George Adams MacDonald Kerr is a Scot from the banks of Loch Lomond, one of six children and the second of three brothers. The eldest, Billy, represented Scotland in international police football and Bobby played almost 400 games for Sunderland and captained their 1971 FA Cup-winning team.

George's junior football was with a Dunbartonshire side, Renton Select, from where Barnsley obtained him in 1960 when he was 17 years old. Quickly winning a place in the second team, in the following year he scored a hat-trick at Oakwell against Manchester United reserves in a game which Barnsley lost, 11 – 5. At that time in the Central League heavy defeats were not uncommon. Whereas Barnsley usually fielded players who were, hopefully, destined for the first team, the majority of clubs seemed to have sides consisting mainly of old pros whose first team days were behind them. For George it was an education to compete against some of those once great players – and if you were really keen you held your head high even when you were losing heavily. And there was plenty of that. In the same season that Manchester United reserves reached double figures, six goals were conceded against Burnley and Derby County, and seven against Newcastle United. During that time a Central League record was surely created at Hillsborough when the young Reds were beaten 14 – 0, following which John Steele told them they were going the right way to get football done away with!

George's debut in the Third Division was in September 1961 when Reading won 3 – 2 at Oakwell, but he lost his place in the following week after a 6 – 2 defeat at Torquay. During the season he had four other outings and became first-choice inside right in the following August, holding a place continuously for the remainder of his time at the club.

His enthusiasm was boundless. He trained in the mornings with the first team, in afternoons with the groundstaff boys and was back in the evening to train with the part-timers. But he had no time for coaching and discussing tactics, believing natural skills and an ability to improvise were the keys to success. Indeed, when team talks were in progress he didn't hide his impatience, wanting only to get onto the pitch with a football.

He was to the fore during a somewhat unexpected surge to the fifth round of the 1964 FA Cup. Scoring twice in a second round defeat of Rochdale, he got the winner which beat Bury to provide a home tie against Manchester United. Almost needless to say, that game brought an end to the Reds' interest in the competition. But the gate receipts were like manna from heaven, more than 38,000 spectators paying for the privilege of seeing the Cup-holders win 4 – 0.

In 1965 he was switched to centre forward as replacement for the transferred Tony Leighton. In his new role he scored more goals than ever before, starting by recording Barnsley's first Fourth Division goal in a win at Crewe Alexandra on 21st August. On 26th February his total reached 20 when he scored against Colchester United from a free kick on the edge of the penalty-area, but that was his last for the Reds. In March, on the transfer-deadline day, he joined Bury – the fee of £10,000 being a lifeline to a club which, in financial terms, was living from day-to-day. The move took place at the last minute because for the previous several weeks Barnsley had been under the impression that Fulham were going to have him. Instead, they obtained Allan Clarke from Walsall. As George says now, 'Who can say they made a mistake?'

It was at Bury that he experienced the first of what, over the years, were to be a series of personality clashes. He had been signed as replacement for Colin Bell who had moved to Manchester City and was to play many times for England, but he soon got at cross-purposes with chairman Bill Allen. Consequently he stayed only six months before being transferred to Oxford United.

Eighteen months later he was on the move again. This time to Scunthorpe United where he held a first team place for four years until injury ended his playing days in 1972. He admits to having an element of unpredictability within his character; others cannot know what he is going to do next because he rarely knows himself. This was never more in evidence than at this point in his career. For in the summer of 1973 this firm believer in full expression who had no time for coaches and tactics joined Lincoln City . . . as trainer-coach. Back at Oakwell, John Steele couldn't believe his ears. The next meeting between the Barnsley boss and his former player was on Lincoln's visit on 18th September. 'What's all this, George,' Steele said in feigned surprise, 'you a coach?' The jest was taken in good part, and the reply was in typical style: 'I know, John, but a bloke's got to eat, hasn't he.' And he had the last laugh, for his team won 1 – 0.

Under manager Graham Taylor, George's first spell as a coach ended when Lincoln City won the 1976 Fourth Division championship with a record number of points. Taylor then moved on and George succeeded him as manager, but in mid-December, after barely six months in the post and with the team in third-bottom place in the division, he was dismissed.

He was soon back, joining Grimsby Town as coach in July 1978. In the following year the players made successful representations to the board for him to replace the departed John Newman as manager, they no doubt being influenced by the part he had played in their recent promotion to the Third Division. That support was well placed, for the first season under his direction ended with the team winning the divisional championship and him receiving a substantial cheque and silver salver as the Third Division's Manager of the Season. In 1981 the team came close to being promoted from Fourth to First Division in successive years – in March they twice held third place – but eventually finished seventh. Nevertheless, George had done a quite remarkable job with players who had cost next to nothing.

Yet he felt there were some directors who would have been happier if the club had remained in the Fourth Division. Needless to say, he had brushes with them. But vice-chairman Mick McGarry had been a continual support and when he had to leave the board George knew the writing was on the wall for him too. He expressed his displeasure about McGarry's departure to chairman Middleton, saying he didn't approve of what had occurred and inviting the other to sack him there and then. That didn't happen, but the confrontations continued and at one point he was banned from writing in the match programme because of his outspokenness. On the first day of 1982, with the team in bottom place in the Second Division, he learned of an intention to dismiss him after the next game, an FA Cup-tie at Millwall. However, Grimsby won 6 – 1; hardly an appropriate backcloth against which to dismiss any manager. But the axe fell in the following week when Grimsby lost at home by a single goal to Orient.

Fifteen months later, on 21st March 1983, he became manager of Rotherham United. The appointment was made by the chairman, a self-styled millionaire named Anton Johnson who had acquired the majority shareholding in December 1979. The situation which George inherited was desperate on two fronts: debts totalled a quarter-of-a-million pounds and the team were in 18th position in the Second Division.

Despite there being only two victories in the remainder of the season, a win at Leeds United in the final game would have ensured survival. However, an interval lead was lost and the single point obtained was insufficient to avoid relegation. He had already assessed the extent of the task he'd taken on: what he hadn't realized was that he was about to begin the most traumatic period of his whole career.

It was apparent that income at the lower level would not meet the wages of the staff he had inherited and a priority was to make savings in that area. More than half the team were transferred during the summer but the situation was such that fees received were already accounted for, and replacements were in the form of free-transfer players who had previously been with him at Grimsby Town. In the following season there were times when it appeared there was to be another relegation – at the end of March the team were in next-bottom place – but five victories in the last six games avoided the ignominy of continuing descent. The generally poor performances were, however, off-set to some extent by stirring displays in the Milk Cup when First Division opposition in the shape of Luton Town and Southampton were dispatched from the competition. But anticlimax came with a fifth round home defeat by Walsall and, overall, his first full season was disappointing. Nevertheless, the next brought great improvement and the team held third place for most of November and December 1984.

Earlier, his arrival at Millmoor was at a time when supporters were concerned about the chairman's reported involvements with other clubs while showing, apparently, scant regard for his own and the team were not doing well, to be quickly followed by termination of a fairly brief stay in the Second Division. The favourite and expensive players transferred were replaced by men uncomplimented by large price-tags and even in the lower division the team were largely unimpressive. Those happenings caused considerable anger among some of the supporters and this was perhaps compounded by the area's worsening social climate brought about by the on-going coal miners' strike. The bitterness was expressed by shouting insults at the new players which ranged from jeering calls of, 'Come on, Grimsby reserves', to the filthiest personal abuse. In an attempt to take the strain off the team George made a conscious effort to attract the venom towards himself. And how well he succeeded! In replying to criticism on a local radio phone-in programme, he told one irate caller that team selection was nothing to do with anyone but himself – and supporters had better get used to him being manager, for he was going to stay for 15 years. In a pre-Christmas statement to the press, he said he had told his players to fully enjoy the festive season, for they should be able to eat, drink and make merry in *every* respect and still play football – and if they couldn't, they should look for other means of making a living! And taunts from the terraces were sometimes responded to in kind.

Not surprisingly, no other man connected with the club had ever generated such hostility. The feeling against him was such that he continued to live on Humberside – commuting to Rotherham daily – and his life was threatened on more than one occasion. Yet he did a lot of good things. The initial movement of players which caused such displeasure was, nevertheless, essential towards the main aim of continuing in business; he reintroduced a youth policy which had been allowed to lapse and did preparatory work in respect of two major outgoing transfers which were finalized after he left.

In September 1983, only a matter of days before chairman Johnson disposed of the controlling interest during an investigation into his affairs by the Football League, George signed a contract which secured his future with the club for the following four years. But in the spring of 1985, despite the still difficult financial situation and cost involved, the antipathy towards him convinced the board that he had to leave. For his own part, he felt he had done the job he had been engaged to do. Departure took place at the end of the season and in December, for the second time, he became manager of Lincoln City.

Again he was joining a club in a dire position and he was unable to improve the 21st place in Division Three which he inherited. In the following season he was involved in a second successive relegation. This consigned the club to non-League football and its manager to another period of unemployment.

But again, not for long. Seven months later, in December 1987, he was appointed manager of Boston United in the GM Vauxhall Conference – the premier non-League competition. At the end of his first full season Boston were in third place – their best-ever performance – but eight months later, in January 1990, when they were near the bottom of the table, he was dismissed. Yet if his previous experiences are anything to go by, this current absence from the professional football scene is of a purely temporary nature.

George was a player of tremendous vision in that he could always see two moves ahead, but he never felt that his physical response to what he knew was going to happen was as quick as it could have been. Nor would he listen to advice: he had a lazy nature, ignoring the coaches and others who urged for more application. He didn't really start to work at his game until he was 27 – which is perhaps one reason why this very gifted player had only half a season at a level higher than the Third Division.

He was as extrovert then as he is now. Oakwell's long-serving Norman Rimmington recalls being in charge of the juniors in a Northern Intermediate League match against Doncaster Rovers when George, on taking a penalty-kick, ran to the spot, turned, and *back-heeled* the ball into the net! And many a time he would walk nearly 200 yards from training ground to dressing room, keeping a ball continually in the air with foot, thigh and head while chatting nonchalantly to a team-mate. Rimmington reckons George Kerr had every conceivable skill and could have been the most brilliant player the club has had – all he lacked was consistency.

Alan Hill: The Leader of the Pack

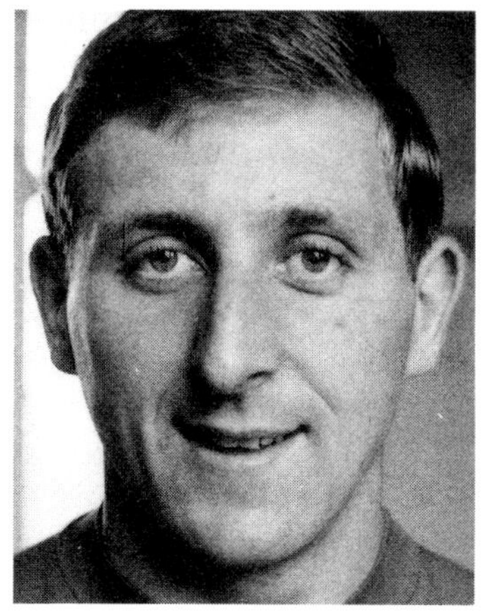

Beginning at Oakwell in 1959, Alan Hill's playing career took him from Fourth to First Division and he now has a staff position with one of the leading clubs in the land. Yet he freely admits that good fortune has played a leading part in his success. As a schoolboy centre forward he became a goalkeeper by chance and went on to play in the position for Barnsley, Rotherham United and Nottingham Forest; he was lucky that Barnsley had faith in him when he was incapacitated for long periods while still a teenager, and when he had to cease playing through injury he slipped into a coaching job which might not have been available to him had his career run its expected course.

While a pupil at Ardsley Junior School he played for the Barnsley under-14 side at full back and outside right. In the following year he attended a schools' trial as a centre forward – the position he held with his school. However, the organizers were short of a goalkeeper and Alan was asked to stand in. His performance was sufficient for him to be chosen in the position for both Barnsley and Yorkshire Boys during his final school year while continuing at centre forward for Ardsley. In that season, 1958/59, Barnsley Boys won the Yorkshire Shield and reached the semi-finals of the English Trophy. It was at that stage, against Brierley Hill Schools at Oakwell, he sustained the first of what were to be four shoulder dislocations.

During that season he had opportunities to join Manchester United and Wolves, but he was a home loving lad and didn't intend to leave it. Therefore, Tim Ward's offer of a job on the Oakwell groundstaff was just what he was hoping for.

His first team debut came less than two years later, within a fortnight of becoming a professional, in a 2 – 1 defeat at Tranmere Rovers in April 1961. He also played in the following game – the season's last – at Newport when a collision with a future Barnsley manager, John McSeveney, dislocated a shoulder for the third time.

In the following season he played 24 times and won a regular place in August 1962. By then he was coming to national notice. After a 2 – 0 defeat at Coventry City in the following February their manager, Jimmy Hill, said Alan was one of the most promising prospects in England. Those comments followed quickly upon a *Daily Mirror* report of a 2 – 1 defeat at Queen's Park Rangers which referred to a standing ovation he'd received from a normally partisan crowd. It went on to say that he alone had prevented the match becoming a rout.

But there was a cloud on the horizon. At Colchester in the opening game of the following season, 1963/64, the Reds lost 4 – 1. Manager John Steele held Alan responsible for all four goals and was, seemingly, still annoyed when the team coach reached the outskirts of Barnsley. It was customary for those living out of town to be dropped at a convenient point near to their homes, but on this occasion Alan was told to get out at Worsbrough and make his own way home to Kendray. He knew that the manager usually thought highly of him but, as he walked nearly two miles in pouring rain in the early hours of a Sunday morning, he also realized that Steele had no favourites. As if to emphasize a point, he was left out of the side for the following nine games.

He and his fiancée, Janice Watson, were married later in the season, on 25th March 1964. On that evening his parents held a party at their home, the Central Working Men's Club, which was attended by the Barnsley players and staff. As it was drawing to a close and Alan and his bride were dancing together, John Steele sidled up to him and said, 'Don't enjoy yourself too much tonight, Alan, you're playing tomorrow.'

'What do you mean? We haven't a game tomorrow.'

'*You* have, you're playing in the reserves at Liverpool – at centre forward!'

Steele meant what he said. Consequently, on what he'd expected to be the first day of his honeymoon, Alan journeyed with the reserves to Anfield. But it might have been better had he been used in his normal role, for although he scored the Reds' goal, they lost 5 – 1. It was his first competitive game following a shoulder injury at Christmas – and his second outing of the season as reserve team centre forward, the other being after an earlier injury to the other shoulder.

It may be that Barnsley's relegation in 1965 was at least partly due to Alan's absence from the side. Another dislocated shoulder and hospitalization for a second tendon tightening operation limited him to seven appearances in the whole season. Twelve months later, in June 1966, a fee of £12,500 took him to Rotherham United.

Three months into his second season there, in November 1967, with the team in next-bottom place in Division Two, a whirlwind called Tommy Docherty swept into Millmoor. Immediately adopting a practice which was later to be his hallmark, the Doc brought in new players and began transferring established ones. They were all on tenterhooks, wondering who would be the next. A month after his arrival the manager summoned Alan to his office and opened with, 'Do you like it here, son?' Fearing the worst, Alan replied that he did. He was relieved to hear, 'Well, we like you, too. I'm giving you a new contract and doubling your wage to £35.' It seems Docherty really did like him, for after he departed Millmoor he tried to obtain him for his next two clubs, Queen's Park Rangers and Aston Villa, but Rotherham rejected each approach.

Ironically, it was a game against Barnsley which marked the beginning of the end of his time at Millmoor. On 31st August 1968, when the Reds were there for a Division Three match, he broke a finger while the teams were warming-up on the pitch. He played throughout the game but when the extent of the damage became known the Doc promptly replaced him with Jim Furnell from Arsenal. Alan was out of action for six weeks and when he was again fully fit he had to agree that Furnell was playing too well to be dropped. Consequently he was in the reserves until the following March when, on the transfer-deadline day, he joined Nottingham Forest.

In finalizing the transfer their manager, Matt Gillies, asked Alan if a basic wage of £65 would be acceptable. Having been receiving little more than half that amount for the previous 15 months he was completely taken aback and said, 'Sixty five pounds, you must be joking!' Unperturbed, Gillies replied, 'Okay, eighty five pounds, then.'

After one reserve game he made his First Division debut in a 3 – 0 win against West Bromwich Albion. Therefore, in 10 days he had experienced soccer's extremes – appearing in front of a handful of spectators at a North Midlands League match at Millmoor and playing in the First Division in a game which, as the main feature of ITV's *The Match*, was viewed by an audience of several million.

At that time Forest's place in the top flight was looking precarious, but Alan's displays in the remaining games helped them remain there and endeared him to the supporters. He had been signed as a stand-in for the regular 'keeper, Peter Grummitt, who was about to be hospitalized, but he acquitted himself so ably that the other was eventually transferred without returning to the side.

Therefore, having established himself in the First Division, it was a tragedy when injury struck on 28th February 1970. On that day against Everton his right arm was broken in four places.

A year later, despite him having had the best possible treatment, expert opinion was that there was insufficient movement in the arm for him to continue to play. Yet manager Gillies was as generous as when he had originally signed him, giving a further year's contract which was tied to first team bonuses. Others were equally helpful. A testimonial committee was formed, chaired by Maurice Rowarth – a supporter who is now chairman of the board of directors. The committee arranged a match against Notts County which attracted 16,000 spectators, thus indicating the esteem the player had earned in a comparatively short time. The receipts enabled him to enter business as a hotelier in the city and the dual career enables him to be independent of football for a livelihood.

The high regard which made that possible was also evident within the club, for he was then appointed youth team coach. He remained in the role for 18 months until November 1972 when Dave Mackay succeeded Gillies as manager. The new man gave all the coaches a fortnight's notice and brought in his own staff. Yet a month later he met Alan and told him that everyone said he was good at his job and he'd like him to come back. He remained in post until October 1973. Then Mackay was appointed to manage Derby County and Alan went with him as youth team coach.

Fifteen months later, in January 1975, he was at home when he received a telephone call from Brian Clough, the newly-appointed manager of Nottingham Forest.

'Brian Clough here. Come to see me, I want you to work for me.'

'No thanks. I've never met you but I've seen you on TV and I don't like you.'

'I'll come to see you, then.'

'No you won't, I'm on contract with Derby County.'

Alan then replaced the 'phone. But Clough was persistent. Two days later he rang again.

'I want to come round to see you.'

'No.'

'Then you come here to see me. I'll make it worth your while. Come round now.'

So Alan went to the Forest ground for his first meeting with Brian Clough.

'I want you to take charge of my youth policy. When can you start?'

'I can't. I'm on contract at Derby County.'

'I'll double what you're getting there.'

Perhaps detecting a weakening in the other's resolve, Clough picked up the telephone and rang the Derby County manager.

'Now, David, I want no trouble from you but I've just signed your youth team coach.'

Alan tried to interrupt but was waved down and a raised voice at the other end of the line suggested to him that there was every likelihood of trouble. However, Clough replied firmly and put the 'phone down. 'That's fixed then, son. Working for me will be the best thing you've done in your whole life.'

That has proved to be true. The two get on like a house on fire and in the first six months Alan learned more about football and footballers than in all his previous years in the game. As in any relationship, difficulties have arisen from time to time but these have usually been resolved after little more than a ruffling of feathers.

The first real problem arose over Clough's choice of assistant manager. Alan had said he didn't want the job, so Peter Taylor – a former Middlesbrough team-mate of Clough – was appointed. Alan just couldn't get on with him. Matters came to a head when he passed some post-match comments about Taylor on Radio Trent after a Cup-tie in January 1977. He believed he'd been complimentary but Taylor didn't like what had been said and took him to task. By then he'd had his fill of the assistant manager. He resigned, devoted more time to his hotel, did some scouting for Wolves and occasional match commentaries for Radio Trent. A year passed before he and Taylor again met. Then, at the latter's invitation after an admission that he'd earlier formed totally wrong impressions, Alan resumed his previous role.

When Taylor himself left, in May 1982, Clough asked Alan to take over the duties of assistant manager without having that official title. He was happy to do it and combined the job with his existing responsibilities. But a year later, having been abroad with the youth team, he returned to find that the first team coach, Ron Fenton, had been appointed assistant manager. For the first time in all his years at the club he felt let down. On tackling Clough about it the explanation he got was far from convincing. The meeting ended in acrimony and despite Clough asking him not to leave he resigned, sure in his own mind that his years with Forest had finally come to an end.

On the following day he became assistant to John Barnwell at Notts County. But Clough kept asking him to come back. On one occasion he went to a Forest reserve game at Leeds, simply because every member of the side had been signed by him as a junior. Clough spotted him inside the ground and sent a message, asking to meet him in the team coach. 'You've seen them out there,' he said, 'you signed them all. How can you not be with them?' But Alan was adamant that he would not return.

That's how things remained until February 1988. Then Clough asked to see him and showed a letter he'd received from the Welsh FA. It was an invitation to manage the national side. 'I'm going to have this. I'll be part-time and I want you to be my full-time assistant. Will you take it?' Alan knew it was an opportunity of a lifetime. He agreed. Clough promptly telephoned Doug Sharpe, chairman of the Welsh FA, to tell him of their decision. Alan cleared things with John Barnwell and, within days, financial terms had been agreed. But the two were halted in their tracks when the Forest directors refused permission for Clough to accept the position. Not surprisingly, they expressed the view that managing their club was, in itself, a full-time job. Yet Alan had already resigned from Notts County. 'Where does this leave me?' he asked. 'Here with me' was Clough's reply.

The Notts County chairman maintained the whole affair had been nothing but a ploy by Clough to get Alan back to Forest and he threatened to take action in respect of the alleged illegal approach. In the event the dispute was resolved by Forest making a payment of £17,500.

Alan is now Youth Development Officer and in charge of scouting with responsibilities for signing players for every level of the club's involvement – from under 10s to the first team. He reckons he's too soft hearted to be a manager but he is certainly a good assessor. Almost all the club's 54-strong playing staff were signed by him. His first was Tony Woodcock who went on to play 42 times for England and over the years a dozen other future internationals have passed through his hands. Indeed, one of them, Chris Woods, a current England goalkeeper, was signed by him as a 14-year-old.

Fortune is said to favour the brave, so it is not surprising that it helped Alan Hill. The injuries he received while at Oakwell would have put many men out of football for good, but strength of character enabled him to overcome them and reach the game's highest domestic level. He also had great physical strength. Goalkeepers in training are usually to be found at the back of the pack. But this one, all six feet and 13 stones of him, was always the one to set the standard. The others said he was like a maniac and they hated to be grouped with him. His torment of them continued after normal sessions ended. Then, for sixpence a go, they would try to score from the edge of the penalty area. No-one ever did but they never learned, and in a fortnight he could earn himself almost an extra week's wage.

John Steele considers Alan could have had an equally successful career as an outfield player; he'd spotted him as a 14-year-old and had decided to take him onto the groundstaff even before seeing him play in goal. But as a goalkeeper, he was brilliant. Timing on crosses and in leaving his line was perfection and Norman Rimmington, the coach at the time and a former 'keeper himself, rates him the best the Reds have had in the post-war years. In fact, he goes further and says if Alan Hill was playing today he would be the England goalkeeper without a challenger in sight.

Dick Hewitt: A Constant Favourite

A life-long footballing ambition was realized shortly after 5pm on 28th April 1973 when Dick Hewitt received a Cup-winners' medal at Wembley Stadium. It was the most exciting moment of his playing career, although he'd thought his chances of treading the famous turf had gone for ever after being with four League clubs and not getting anywhere near the twin towers. But he eventually made it with Scarborough, who upset the form books by beating Wigan Athletic to win the FA Challenge Trophy.

A Moorthorpe boy, he played football for South Elmsall and District Boys and Moorthorpe St Joseph's Boys Club, and won representative honours with the All-England Boys Club side against Scotland, Wales and Ireland. On leaving school he had a trial with Arsenal from which nothing materialized, and he then joined the ground staff at Huddersfield Town.

He became a full-time professional on his 18th birthday in 1961, by which time he had a regular place in the Central League side. Then an inside forward, on one occasion he experienced the delight of scoring in the first minute against Liverpool reserves at Anfield – and then suffered with the rest of the team while Liverpool scored seven without reply.

After being a professional for three years without sampling first team football he joined Bradford City on a free transfer in 1964. He went straight into the League side and scored in each of his first two games – and was then dropped. During the season he made a further 18 appearances, but again suffered the bitter disappointment of a free transfer. Yet he was unshaken in a belief that he could make the grade, and in the summer he presented himself at Oakwell and offered his services to manager John Steele.

After a few practice games the manager shared his opinion and included him in the team, in the unaccustomed outside left position, at the start of the 1965/66 season. In the light of experiences at Huddersfield and Bradford it was satisfying for him to retain a place in the side and he played in all the 51 League and Cup games.

In the following campaign he was moved to wing half, where his displays were even more effective. By then, regular newspaper reports that he was being watched by bigger clubs prompted the manager to tell the press, 'I would not sell Hewitt at any price, I'm trying to build a side, not sell one!' Dick's own view was that he was enjoying being at Oakwell so much that he wouldn't have left anyway.

Although never much of a goalscorer, those he did get were either quite spectacular or scored at a decisive stage of a game. In a 4 – 2 victory over Bradford City he put a 20-yard lob over the goalkeeper's head; a 4 – 0 success against Tranmere Rovers saw him hammer a 20-yarder into the net in front of Oakwell's biggest crowd of the season, and in a 4 – 0 win over Southport he opened the scoring with a gem of a goal from all of 40 yards.

Against Port Vale in the 1967 FA Cup he got the equalizer in the 85th minute, and in the replay the penalty which he hit high into the net went a long way towards the 3 – 1 success. In reporting the game the national dailies were unanimous that Dick had a magnificent night and was the mainspring of continuous attacks which never allowed the home side to get into their stride.

After two seasons in which he had been one of the team's most consistent performers it was a blow to both player and club when he was injured in the summer of 1967. In pre-season practice he sustained ankle damage from a tackle by Pat Howard. The irony of the situation was that Howard replaced him in the team and then went on to a long career in the First Division, while he spent the next two years in the doldrums. Nevertheless, it is indicative of Dick's good nature that Pat Howard's soccer scrap-book contains a telegram of good wishes from his former club-mate, sent to him at Wembley Stadium seven years later prior to his appearance there for Newcastle United in an FA Cup final.

Dick was out of action for three months before returning to the side to score twice against Lincoln City, but the ankle gave almost constant pain. It was one of those injuries that wouldn't clear up, consequently he lost confidence and his place in the team. Managing only seven further games that season, it was a measure of the esteem in which he was held that he was retained. But his form did not justify increased selection during 1968/69, and in the spring a modest fee took him to York City.

It seems the new challenge was what was needed to provide an uplift in both confidence and form. He held a regular place during two seasons at York and was a member of their promotion-winning team of 1971. He also had a leading role in the FA Cup competitions. In 1970 he played in each of the three games which finally dispatched Second Division Cardiff City and in the following year, against Southampton from Division One, and after York had trailed 3 – 1 in what Malcolm Huntington of the *Yorkshire Evening Press* described as the greatest Cup-tie it had been his privilege to report, it was Dick who scored the equalizing goal.

In 1972 he joined Scarborough in the Northern Premier League. He could have moved elsewhere in the Football League but, in view of his long-term ambition, it was manager Colin Appleton's stated intention to build a team to win the Challenge Trophy which decided him to throw in his lot with Scarborough. It was the best decision he ever made, for the move brought the most successful period of his whole career. On an equally important note, income from part-time football and full-time employment provided the highest income he'd ever had which was supplemented by the Hewitts providing bed and breakfast accommodation at their new home in the seaside town.

Following closely upon the elation of Wembley success, on the following Monday Scarborough won the North Riding Cup and the season also saw them runners-up in the Northern Premier League and winners of the Vaux Cup. It was Dick's winning goal at York which put them into the North Riding final and continued his long established practise of scoring winners against previous clubs, having done so for Bradford City against Huddersfield Town and for Barnsley against Bradford City. And in the final his goal in the last minute provided Scarborough with their second trophy in three days.

A further Wembley appearance came in the 1975 final of the FA Challenge Trophy. This time Dick was on the losing side when Scarborough were unexpectedly beaten by Matlock Town, and a year later he was denied the rare achievement of a third Wembley final when he failed a fitness test on the morning of the game. It was the long-damaged ankle which let him down and, at 34 years of age, effectively ended his professional career.

Workwise, on moving to Scarborough he was employed by Post Office Telephones as a cleaner. A long period of study followed, at the end of which he qualified as a technician, and as a faultsman he had Saturday duties which ruled out further involvement in organized soccer.

Football is the only game Dick has ever wanted to play and he's been mad-keen since boyhood. In fact, he has a treasured photograph, taken on Blackpool's Golden Mile, of himself when nine years old, and his dad, with the former England star, Stanley Mortensen. His pastime is now five-a-side football, and he plays for the Dynamos in an over 35s league at Scarborough Sports Stadium. One of his proudest moments occurred in 1986 when he and his three sons, Richard, Mark and Craig, formed almost an entire team in the annual Eastfield five-a-side festival – and only a disadvantage in corner-kicks prevented them reaching the semi-finals.

Although the most successful period of Dick Hewitt's career was at Scarborough, his happiest seasons were with Barnsley, so much so that the family home – a hundred yards from picturesque Peasholme Park – is affectionately named 'Oakwell'. He was versatile and creative with excellent dribbling skills and lots of stamina – he seemed able to run for ever and was one of those busy players who look at their best when in the thick of things. His feelings about the time spent at Oakwell are easily understood, for his never-say-die spirit and willingness to give 90 minutes' endeavour in every game made him a constant favourite of the club's supporters.

Eric Brookes: The Youngest-Ever Starter

A Staincross boy, Eric Brookes was the youngest ever to hold a regular place in Barnsley's first team. In fact, in January 1961 he was pulled out of trials for the English youth team because he was required for a third round FA Cup game – and he was then 16 years old. And although he trained and played with the first team he was otherwise treated like the other groundstaff boys; he helped mark out the pitch, swept terraces and cleaned his team-mates' boots. He went on to hold a place at full back for nine consecutive seasons, playing his one-hundredth game soon after his 19th birthday and totalling 200 by the time he was 21.

While a pupil at Kexborough School he played for Barnsley Boys but, perhaps surprisingly in view of his quick progression to professional status, he never received recognition at county level. Joining the Oakwell groundstaff at 15, he had only the briefest stay in the junior side before moving into the reserves. That, too, was of short duration. After eight games in the Central League he made his Third Division debut at Bradford City in September 1960. The Reds won 4 – 1 and Benny Hill, writing in the *Sheffield Telegraph*, expressed amazement at the cool and calculating manner in which Eric had faced his first outing in the hurly-burly of League soccer.

It was therefore perhaps understandable when manager John Steele felt that the Cup match against Reading had to take precedence over an England youth trial. Indeed, few 16-year-olds can have begun a sequence of FA Cup games which continued to the sixth round and ended with but a single goal deficit after a replay against a First Division side. And withdrawal from the trial, in the event, wasn't detrimental. A few weeks later Eric played against Scotland and over the following year he was chosen on six further occasions. These took him out of the country for the first time and, remarkably, none of his seven games for England was *in* England.

By the end of the 1968/69 season he had played 325 League games – only 20 fewer than the record number of appearances then held by Harry Hough. In the following June he was transferred to Northampton Town, and it wasn't a move he was keen to make. He even considered backing out during the journey to Northampton with John Steele when the latter's conversation seemed to indicate that he didn't want to lose him, but knowing the directors had accepted the offer he decided there was no point in trying to stay.

The transfer fee was £8,000. Northampton thought they'd got a real bargain, manager Dave Bowen later saying that in 1967 Barnsley had refused to accept £30,000 which he'd then offered for him. After two years at the club he was transferred to Peterborough United where he sustained the first real injury of his career. In late 1972 ligaments in his left knee were damaged; he missed the rest of the season and at the end of it he was given a free transfer.

Then 29, he received invitations to play in Australia and South Africa and to become player-manager of Dundalk in the League of Ireland – but no others. He was keen to stay in mainstream football and the absence of interest from League clubs is perhaps best explained by John Steele. He says Eric had been on the scene for so long that managers could have been excused for thinking he was nearly 40!

In August 1973 he joined March Town in the Eastern Counties League, remaining there for five years, the last 18 months of which were as player-manager. Seventeen years on – and still not much above 40 – he continues to play competitive football in East Anglia. Having worked as a fitter for Perkins Engines at Peterborough since leaving Northampton, in 1978 he joined the works' side and took charge of training. There was a two-year spell when they were undefeated in the Peterborough Premier League and in 1987, whilst retaining employment with Perkins, he moved to the London Brick Company's team in the same league.

During 13 seasons in League football he scored three goals and shared them out equally – one for each of his three clubs. The Barnsley goal helped towards a 3 – 0 win against Wrexham in February 1964, but he still feels aggrieved that his total was not allowed to double. For against Newport County in the last game of the 1967/68 promotion season he fired in a fierce shot from the edge of the penalty-area which entered the net to equalize the score and enable the team to go on to crown a triumphant season with a 4 – 2 win. However, he was most displeased to find his shot had been adjudged to have struck a defender and recorded as an own goal.

Eric was a cultured defender who used the ball to advantage whenever possible rather than indulging in a big kick upfield. Neither was he one to go diving into a tackle – he waited for the winger to make the first move. Occasionally he struggled against a really fast one but in his entire career he has never intentionally kicked an opponent. Not being a flamboyant player, his value to the team was not always recognized on the terraces, but the same Benny Hill who had written of his debut in complimentary terms was a constant admirer. Three years later he opined that Eric was playing like a veteran while still a teenager and was the best left back the Reds had had since Gordon Pallister. Maybe that was true, but it begs an obvious question . . . which Eric answers with, 'I just didn't have enough ambition.' It would have been to his advantage if, once established, he'd moved to a bigger club where he would have been stretched; at Oakwell, there just wasn't any competition for him. Yet to his own generation of groundstaff boys he was an inspiration. Two of them,

Hill and Winstanley, have had much career success from beginnings at Oakwell and they, along with the other juniors, would watch Eric play in the first team – and while they could only hope what their own futures would be, they saw that their 16-year-old pal had style and class, and in their eyes he'd made it already.

Johnny Evans: A Considerable Contribution

Although it is almost 20 years since Johnny Evans departed Oakwell he can rightly claim a major part in putting the club into a position from which it has been able to attain its present high standing within the Football League. In the autumn of 1966, with the team firmly fixed at the bottom of Division Four, there was a real possibility that Barnsley FC would go out of business. It was saved only by two new directors making money available for new players and manager John Steele choosing wisely by signing Johnny Evans and Barry Thomas who revitalized the whole team by the skill and purpose of their play. Yet Johnny considered himself fortunate to be in a position to do that, for six years earlier, while with Bournemouth, he had been so badly injured that the club insisted his professional career was over.

A Liverpool boy of an Everton-supporting family, he was a mad-keen footballer who used an early morning paper round as a means of training – racing up and down flights of stairs in high-rise flats to deliver newspapers from a heavy satchel hanging from his neck. In local junior football he was exceptional in that he became a professional with Liverpool without having graduated through the Liverpool Boys side. In that respect he had the opportunity, but fate in the form of inclement weather was against him. He played in a trial at Penny Lane – of Beatles fame – in pouring rain; the ball was like lead, a sodden jersey swamped his slight frame and he barely got a kick.

On leaving school he joined a Birkenhead youth team with whom he spent a fortnight in the summer of 1953 footballing in Germany, Holland and Denmark. Determined to break into the professional game and having a pal who played for Liverpool Colts, he went along with him to a training session at the club's Mellwood practice ground. He did that for several weeks and was eventually chosen for the Colts' team. Liverpool's youngsters were certainly brought up the hard way for, as 15-year-olds, they played against seasoned professionals in Lancashire Combination clubs' reserve sides. At 17 he became a part-time professional, signing on the same day as his pals Ian Callaghan, Jimmy Melia and Tommy Smith, along with whom he held a regular place in Liverpool reserves.

Early in 1956 he began National Service, spending the following two years as a laboratory clerk in the Royal Army Medical Corps. Still available for Liverpool reserves, he played army representative football with the Northern Command side.

On returning to civilian life he became a full-time professional at Anfield. Army service had improved his physique and back at Liverpool he trained under the supervision of coach Bob Paisley. The latter devised exercises for him involving the use of a cement-filled length of scaffolding, from which Johnny developed into the strong, chunky player who was to become such a great favourite at Oakwell.

In the summer of 1959 he was transferred to Bournemouth where the manager was a former Anfield manager, Don Welsh. He had been heartbroken by Liverpool's willingness to let him go; a few months later further misery descended upon him when Bill Shankly took charge there and promoted many of his former second team colleagues. They quickly became household names and Johnny has often wondered how his whole future might have changed had he not been required to leave when he did.

In October 1960, in a game against Torquay United, he sustained cartilage and ligament damage in his right knee. After an operation in the following January he felt he was on the road to recovery until, six weeks later, Welsh called him to one side in the gym. Without any preamble the manager said, 'You're finished, Johnny, you won't play professional football again.' He felt his whole world had fallen around him. He pleaded to be given a chance to prove himself and Welsh, seemingly sympathetic, included him in the second team for a game against Bristol Rovers. Things couldn't have worked out better. He scored a hat-trick, but on seeing Welsh immediately afterwards was dismayed to be told, 'I don't care, you're still finished!' Over the following fortnight his right knee was examined by two specialists, each of whom was of the opinion that it would not withstand the rigours of professional football. Consequently the club released him at the end of the season. And in the light of the medical evidence, the possibility of spending a further 10 years in the Football League was the furthest thing from his mind.

He'd been back in Liverpool for nearly six months, working on the docks, when he met a former team-mate from Liverpool reserves, Alan Banks, who was then with Prescot Cables. As a result of their conversation Johnny had trials there, following which he joined them as a part-time professional.

In his only season with the club he scored 42 goals and helped win the Lancashire Senior Cup by scoring the goal which beat Chorley in the final. Still working at Liverpool docks, he was earning good money but he hated the job and had a consuming desire to prove himself in senior football. One day in August 1961, almost on the spur of the moment, he gave up his job and told Prescot Cables that he'd become engaged to a Bournemouth girl and was going there to live. The club may or may not have believed him but, in any event, they insisted he signed an agreement to rejoin them if he returned to the North-West.

He immediately signed for Salisbury in the Western League. Spending one season there, he got another Cup-winners' medal – for the Hampshire Senior

Cup – and totalled 38 goals. One of his last games was against Bournemouth reserves. After scoring twice in a 3 – 0 win he asked the Bournemouth trainer – a man he knew from his time with the club – if he could arrange for him to return there. By this time Welsh had left and his successor, Bill McGarry, was prepared to let him show his paces. Yet after two months in the reserves he was told, 'I'd be glad to have you, John, but we would have to repay £25,000 insurance. We can't do that so I can't keep you.' Nevertheless, the manager was helpful. He got in touch with a pal, Reg Flewin at Stockport County, and arranged for Johnny to spend a month there. But even then things didn't go smoothly. In the third week, 20 minutes into his first game in the first team, he dislocated a shoulder and was out of action for six weeks. However, Flewin had seen enough to convince him he'd got a player worth having and Johnny was signed on full-time terms. He never looked back. Remaining at Stockport for a season-and-a-half, he held a first team place and averaged almost a goal in every other game.

In February 1964 he was transferred to Carlisle United. Playing in the last 15 games of the season, his 16 goals had a big part in winning promotion into Division Three. In the following season the team did even better; Johnny was leading scorer and the Third Division championship provided Carlisle with two consecutive promotions.

March 1966 saw him on the move to Exeter City. But he didn't stay long, for in November of that year John Steele paid £4,500 to bring him to Oakwell.

Johnny is one of those few, fortunate people who look younger than their age. Steele had been told he was 26 when, in fact, he was nearly 29. Nevertheless, it must have been the best four thousand pounds the manager ever spent. The team then held 92nd place in the Football League and gates were less than 4,000. However, the signing of Johnny and Barry Thomas generated such interest that when the new strikers ran together onto the Oakwell pitch for the first time, on 12th November 1966 against Port Vale, more than 8,000 spectators were present. Barnsley won 1 – 0 and the feeling of despair which had hung over the club for weeks began to lift. For his own part, Johnny could not understand how a side which had players as good as John Bettany and Dick Hewitt had got into such a desperate plight in the first place. Be that as it may, a season which began so ominously ended with the Reds in a mid-table position. In the FA Cup he scored a last-gasp equalizer against First Division Cardiff City. The game was into injury time and his goal came from the very last kick – the players having to ask the referee for confirmation that he'd signalled the goal before the final whistle. It was the first time Johnny had played in the third round of the competition and he told the *Barnsley Chronicle* that scoring in such circumstances had been the proudest moment of his life.

The following season, 1967/68, was the first of three in which he was top scorer. Even more important, it ended with Barnsley winning promotion into the Third Division.

The championship had been won by Luton Town, but on visiting Oakwell six weeks into the new season they were beaten 3 – 1. Johnny scored the first goal, quite spectacularly, by meeting a cross on the turn and volleying first time into the net. Three months later in the FA Cup he scored to earn a replay against Leicester City – who had the future England goalkeeper, Peter Shilton, and Allan Clarke who was later to manage Barnsley. A week later he had great satisfaction from getting the winner against Bournemouth, and in the following game he scored a splendid goal in a 4 – 1 victory at Crewe. Then, in the fifth minute, he intercepted a back pass and rounded the goalkeeper on the edge of the penalty-area to curl a glorious lob into a top corner, quite out of reach of two goal-line defenders.

In September 1969 Walsall were beaten by two goals from Johnny – the first, a powerful drive from the edge of the area and the second when, 25 yards out, he fastened onto a partial clearance to hammer in a rocket of a shot which was climbing the back of the net before the astounded 'keeper could move.

Showing considerable versatility, when the second round of the FA Cup was played two months later he was at outside left, having already in that season played in all the other forward positions. Against Fulham in February he scored a 13-minute hat-trick after the Reds had trailed 2 – 0, only for the visitors to equalize three minutes from the end. A month later he scored the winner against Rochdale in a game which had a snowstorm and a 10-minute break when smoke from a nearby chimney fire completely engulfed the pitch. But in the return game with Rochdale, less than three weeks later, he sustained an injury which was to end his career. Having scored the goal which was to win the match, soon after the interval he was the victim of a cynical tackle from a man who had been a team-mate at Stockport County which severely damaged ligaments in his left knee.

A few weeks later, with leg in plaster, he hobbled onto the Oakwell pitch to receive the club's first Player of the Year award. He was back in action in September 1970, soon after the next season began, but he was only a shadow of his former self. He'd lost a lot of pace, he couldn't turn and so much of him seemed unable to react to the messages his brain was transmitting. He managed only 29 games but, nevertheless, was top scorer with nine goals.

Knowing it was time to call it a day, he retired at the end of the season to become the club's commercial manager. It was an opening which took him into a sales environment in which he is spending the remainder of his working life. Staying at Oakwell until November 1972, he then worked as a sales surveyor for Rentokil Property Care before moving into publishers' sales. Starting with Wm Collins & Sons, he is now an area manager with Fowler & Co of Romford, Essex, covering northern England and southern Scotland.

Johnny Evans had a remarkable work-rate and was a master at seizing half chances. His tactical awareness was in advance of his time and his unselfish running off the ball continually made space for others. He never wanted to train after Thursday: he knew when he was at his peak and would invent excuses why he shouldn't train on Fridays and the coaches went along with what he said, thereby getting the best out of him. The recovery from the depths of Division Four was, of course, a team effort but John Evans' name being the first to be engraved on the Player of the Year trophy is a fitting tribute to his own considerable contribution towards that achievement.

John Bettany: The Highest Tribute

John Bettany was one of soccer's vast majority – men who pursue their careers with the utmost dedication but never get within touching distance of the honours and rewards obtained by some more fortunate but not necessarily more capable fellow professionals. For him the high-point of 18 years in professional football was membership of Barnsley's 1968 promotion side. In the following season manager John Steele reckoned there was no more inspiring player in the Third Division, for he had a driving will to win and was a super craftsman, yet there was a period in his early twenties when he had given up hope of having a career in the game.

He was a Laughton Common boy who attended Dinnington School and represented Rother Valley Boys at football. On leaving school he obtained employment as a pony driver at Dinnington Colliery, remaining there for two years until moving to Thurcroft Colliery as a miner. Football was with a local under-18 side having the improbable name of Thurcroft Cowboys, from where he joined Wolves' nursery side, Wath Wanderers. Anxious to become a professional, after a year without an offer from Wolves he hoped for better things from an amateur registration with Sheffield Wednesday. But two years later pro terms were still not forthcoming, so he invited himself for trials with Lincoln City. That brought only a repeat of previous experiences: they were willing to have him as an amateur but not inclined to put him on the paid staff.

He therefore joined Thurcroft Miners' Welfare, remaining with them for almost two seasons until January 1960. By then he was thoroughly dejected by his inability to break into professional football. There was a move within the Thurcroft MW committee to take the quite illegal step of paying him to play for them, but even that came to nothing so he left the club and had no intention of continuing in the game.

And that's how it may have remained but for a chance visit, a month later, to a fish and chip shop in Thurcroft. There he met a Huddersfield Town scout, Wilf Blockley – a quite remarkable man who has coached school sides in the Antipodes since 1964 and still plays in staff *versus* student matches despite being over 80! Blockley knew John as a Thurcroft MW player and, on learning he was no longer with them, offered to get him a trial with Huddersfield Town. Deciding to have one last go, John agreed and, on the following Saturday, he and Blockley travelled by taxi to a Huddersfield third team game at Heckmondwike. The scout had such confidence in John's abilities that he told the taxi driver that he would be in the first team within six months of becoming a professional – but John began to think luck was still running against him when they arrived at Heckmondwike to find the game had been postponed because of the frozen state of the pitch. Nevertheless, later in the year a three months' trial was arranged beginning on August Bank Holiday Monday. Within six weeks he was a professional footballer and Blockley's prophecy was fulfilled when John made his Second Division debut on New Year's Eve. Achieving the long-cherished ambition was particularly pleasing when, in that first game, he scored in his side's 4 – 1 win against Lincoln City.

The initiation should really have come two months earlier. At the end of October he had been chosen for a game at Bristol Rovers but within 15 minutes of the team sheet being pinned-up in the dressing room he limped off the training pitch with a pulled muscle. But, for a man who had once despaired of getting into senior football, that opening spell in the team was particularly enjoyable. A few weeks after his debut he scored two first-half goals in a 4 – 2 defeat of Sunderland, and he and future Oakwell colleague Bob Parker were in the side which knocked holders Wolverhampton Wanderers out of the FA Cup.

He remained at Huddersfield for four-and-a-half years until March 1965, during which time he was in the team on 68 occasions. Understandably, it was the prospect of regular first team football which prompted him to accept the suggestion to join Barnsley. The move took place only hours before the transfer deadline, but he was unable to check the Reds' slide towards Division Four. Yet right from the start he was a favourite of the supporters. They loved his busy, all-action style and the way he strove to overcome a lack of height and weight. Historically, he was in good company at Oakwell in having to conquer such physical disadvantage.

Not only did he impress the supporters but the press also found him to their liking, regularly awarding him Star Player ratings at local and national levels. Keith Lodge, in reporting a County Cup semi-final in the *Barnsley Chronicle*, said his rocket of a shot from 25 yards produced the finest goal he'd seen all season. 'Wonder goal for Bettany' was a *Daily Mail* headline relating to a 1 – 1 draw with Swindon Town when he 'brought the house down with an incredible equalizer, catching the ball inches from the goal-line and lashing it across for it to crash against the inside of the far post and drop over the line'. And in a drawn FA Cup-tie with First Division Leicester City, Frank Clough of the *Daily Herald* said John dominated midfield as though he owned it and his through passing had the cutting edge of an open razor. Indeed, on that widely reported occasion the national dailies were unanimous that he had been the star of the game. His 150th appearance was in April 1969 against Mansfield Town when the *Morning Telegraph* said he produced the kind of sparkle that lights up any game and his passes continually unhinged the visitors' defence and contributed greatly towards the Reds' 2 – 0 success.

There was also an occasion when, quite unintentionally, he was involved in an incident at Oakwell which caused hilarity on the pitch and considerable interest among the readership of a national newspaper. During a game against Crewe Alexandra in April 1967 he went up with the goalkeeper for a high ball and was amazed to see the cross-bar fall to the ground. *The Sun* published a photograph of the scene, showing John staring in puzzled fashion at the wrecked goal, and invited readers to suggest what he might be saying. His actual words have been forgotten in the passing of time, but the newspaper awarded a £5 prize to a Prescot, Lancashire, reader who offered, 'So that's what they call a snapshot!'

His departure from Oakwell in June 1970 was unexpected and disappointing. Having held a regular place during the previous season and been re-engaged for 1970/71, he was surprised to receive a home visit from Rotherham United's manager, Jim McAnearney. The next emotion was dismay, for he learned that his visitor had John Steele's permission to offer a move to Millmoor.

The most enjoyable years of his football life thereby came to an abrupt end. Deciding the approach could only mean he was no longer wanted at Barnsley, he agreed to be transferred but soon realized he'd made a terrible mistake. Then 32, he had been well treated by the fans at Oakwell throughout more than five seasons there and, consequently, found it hard to fit into a new environment where supporters have rarely been generous to even their proven players. An ageing newcomer – from Barnsley, of all places – could expect little encouragement from them. To make matters worse, he soon began to feel that the manager wasn't all that keen on him. He held a place in the side until mid-October but was then dropped and totalled only 17 games in the whole season, at the end of which he was given a free transfer.

There was no opportunity to remain within the League so he spent the next season with Goole Town and the following two with Frickley Athletic. By then he was nearly 38, and the legs had gone. He knew he couldn't hold a place in anyone's first team and having no wish to be part of the hurly-burly of local football he terminated his connection with the game. He loved it while ever he was playing, but has had little interest since and apart from accepting an invitation to play at Oakwell in a benefit game for John Steele, his last visit to a League ground was in 1975.

On leaving full-time football he and his wife, Kath, bought a lock-up newsagency at Maltby. Two years later when their only child Lisa was expected it was impractical for John to continue footballing and retain the business. They therefore disposed of it, and from that time he has managed a newsagency in Wickersley.

John Bettany was a sharp, assertive midfielder with a driving will to win and his passes, swiftly delivered, seemed unfailingly to be placed where they would cause most disruption. Indeed, when more than 17,000 spectators saw the Reds beat Doncaster Rovers on 6th April 1968, Benny Hill of the *Morning Telegraph* reported that there surely couldn't have been a better midfield performance than John's in the whole of the Third Division. Team-mates paid him the greatest compliment by nicknaming him 'Billy' because he buzzed around in the same positive, aggressive manner as Leeds United skipper Billy Bremner –

and if there had been a prize at Oakwell for consistency and creative artistry with a football, he would certainly have won it.

Yet several years after departing Oakwell he received a tribute to prize above all others. John Steele, in his benefit year of 1977, was asked by the *Green 'Un* to name a Select XI from his 40 years with the club. He admitted it was an extremely difficult task. The final choice included such legendary names as Blanchflower, Baxter, Tommy Taylor and John Kelly. And, in that specialist line-up of Oakwell's finest players, the left half was . . . John Bettany.

Pat Howard: Surprising Friend and Foe!

Pat Howard's debut in Barnsley's League side was at Southport on Guy Fawkes' Night 1965 when he suffered the acute disappointment of the game being abandoned after only 10 minutes. But the brevity of that first appearance was in complete contrast to his career as a whole: a member of Barnsley's promotion side of 1968, he remained in League football for nearly 17 years, spending eight seasons in the First Division and playing in two Wembley finals in the mid-1970s.

He was centre half in the 1961 and 1962 Barnsley Boys sides, becoming an Oakwell apprentice a year later on leaving Keresforth Road School at Dodworth. Then his preference was really for Sheffield United where a schoolpal, Alan Woodward, was already an apprentice. There was even some family persuasion to go to Bramall Lane as the two lads' fathers were close friends, but in the end Pat joined his home town club. The deciding factor was the influence of Barnsley schoolmaster Maurice Firth who trained the boys' side and was also on the coaching staff at Oakwell. Pat was appreciative of the guidance he'd received from Firth and knew it would be to his advantage if it continued to be available to him.

The game on 5th November 1965 was his only outing in the first team that season and another single appearance came in the next. However, things altered dramatically in 1967/68. Twin centre halves had just become the vogue and in pre-season training the coaches were trying out players to share the role with Eric Winstanley. On seeing Pat in action they looked no further. He was in the side from the start and played in all 46 games – at the end of which the Reds were promoted to the Third Division. In fact, it was Pat's first League goal – at Chesterfield on 20th January 1968 – which equalized the score and enabled Barnsley to win 3 – 2 and get into the promotion places where they stayed for the remainder of the season.

He was a good listener, eager to learn. He considers himself fortunate in having such an excellent tutor as Eric Winstanley and the good understanding which they developed enabled the latter to move into the attack in the sure knowledge that his young partner would look after things at the back.

Pat's hard, accurate kicking of a dead ball resulted in him taking free kicks anywhere within reach of the opponents' goal. In March 1969 he scored the winner in a victory at Barrow; later in the year his free kick from outside the penalty-area secured a draw at Luton Town and in December 1970 his 25-yard drive clinched victory against Bradford City. But his most significant goal came in August 1971 in a replayed League Cup-tie at Hartlepool when, 10 minutes into extra time, he forced his way through a ruck of defenders to put the ball into the net. It gave the team a dream second round tie against Arsenal who, only three months earlier, had won the League championship and FA Cup.

That goal proved to be his last for the club. Already on the transfer list, there had long been rumours that he and Winstanley were to be transferred. As early as the spring of 1969 the board had received an 800-signature petition urging that the players be kept at Oakwell and there were frequent letters in the *Green 'Un* prophesying disaster if they were allowed to leave. But Pat, an ambitious young man, felt that if he was to remain at Barnsley he should at least be paid his worth. When his contract was due for renewal in the summer of 1971 – after he'd played in every one of the previous season's 55 League and Cup games and was undoubtedly one of the team's few star players – he asked that his wage be increased by seven pounds to £35 per week. This was refused. Consequently he asked to be transferred.

Early interest came from Rotherham United who offered their Neil Hague and £13,000. Barnsley were willing to accept and Pat, having formed favourable impressions of the Millers' manager, Jim McAnearney, was prepared to consider it. But discussions came to a halt when McAnearney, who must have known what the player was being paid at Barnsley, offered only the same amount.

Two weeks later a fee of £21,000 took him into the First Division with Newcastle United for him to make his debut on 18th September 1971 in a 2 – 0 win over Wolves. He had been signed as a stand-in for injured skipper and Scottish international Bob Moncur, but his displays in central defence were such that the captain had to be accommodated elsewhere when he regained fitness.

Pat held a first team place throughout five seasons in the North-East, and for this young man from Dodworth, Barnsley, playing at such grounds as Anfield, Highbury and Old Trafford was nothing less than a boyhood dream come true.

Those seasons included two appearances at Wembley Stadium – although neither had the result for which he had hoped. In 1974 the FA Cup final saw Newcastle lose 3 – 0 to Liverpool, and two years later in the League Cup final they lost by a single goal to Manchester City. On the way to the first of those finals, in a sixth round tie against Nottingham Forest, Pat was the central figure in a St James' Park flare-up in which hundreds of home supporters invaded the pitch, following his sending off for disputing a penalty decision. When play eventually resumed the spot-kick provided Forest with a 3 – 1 lead but, amazingly, 10-man Newcastle fought back to win 4 – 3. However, Forest protested that their players had been attacked by some supporters and their confidence had been thus undermined; Newcastle argued that Forest had accepted the decision to continue and should abide by the consequences. In the event, the FA wiped the match from the records and ordered the tie to be replayed. Two such games were necessary before Newcastle went through to the semi-finals.

Soon afterwards the Forest manager, Brian Clough, said in the *Daily Mirror* that he rated Pat among the five best central defenders in the country. It was a high opinion long held, for Clough later told Pat that while he had been in charge at Derby County he had been so impressed by his display for Barnsley in a private practice that he had tried to obtain him as a replacement for Dave Mackay, his captain, who was then nearing retirement.

In September 1976, after nearly 200 games for Newcastle United, Pat was transferred to Arsenal. Twelve months later he moved to Birmingham City for two final seasons in the First Division. In the intervening summer he was loaned to Portland Timbers in the North American Soccer League. The team created a record of 12 consecutive wins and reached the semi-finals of the league play-offs before losing to the eventual champions, New York Cosmos.

In July 1979 he joined Bury – in October scoring the goal which enabled his team to share the points at Oakwell. Remaining with the club for three years, he rarely missed a game and played 44 times in his final season, by which time he was nearly 35. He'd then had a surfeit of football. He felt completely drained and declined several invitations to move into non-League soccer, and two years elapsed before he even watched a game on TV.

It was 1984 before he experienced any inclination to involve himself, and he then took part in a pilot scheme for what is now the national Football in the Community programme. It was sponsored jointly by the PFA and the Manpower Services Commission, and Pat was one of half-a-dozen ex-pros who linked senior clubs within Greater Manchester to their local communities by making facilities available to the public, giving conducted tours of grounds, arranging courses and giving talks to organisations and schools.

In mid-1988 he was appointed Football Administrator in Salford Council's Recreation Department. The role requires him to promote the game within the city and provide courses for youngsters aged 10–16 years. He also conducts a School of Soccer Excellence on behalf of the FA. This has links with Manchester United: his best students are recommended to the club and periodically he takes a group to watch a game at Old Trafford and demonstrate their skills on the pitch before the start.

Pat Howard's ambitions were fixed firmly in his mind before he left school. He knew what he wanted and was determined to get it – leading the kind of life that suited a career in professional football and always making sure he was in good physical condition. At Oakwell he captained the youth team, the reserves and occasionally the first team and went on to captain Newcastle United in Division One. He was a hard man – uncompromising and unafraid of anyone or anything. In the air he was brilliant. On the ground he was exceptionally fast over the first few yards and, therefore, strong into the tackle. At Newcastle, where on his First Division debut he completely subdued Wolves' international centre forward Derek Dougan, he blossomed from a destroyer to a complete defender. On returning to Oakwell in the spring of 1977 to play in John Steele's testimonial game he lined-up again alongside Eric Winstanley. And the latter, at first dismayed and then, as the game progressed, with a sense of pride, realized their original roles had been reversed: his protégé was marshalling the defence and putting *him* in a supporting role!

Winstanley is a friend of long standing. Opponents – usually virtual strangers – experienced almost equal surprise on finding that this handsome, hard-as-nails defender who had taken every opportunity to exercise his great physical strength at their expense and sometimes seemed to walk all over them was, after the game, as pleasant and friendly a chap as ever they could hope to meet.

Dave Booth: Time On His Side

As a Queen Elizabeth Grammar School pupil in the mid-1960s, Dave Booth had lessons on Saturday mornings and in the afternoons he was an unwilling stand-off half in one of the school's rugby teams. The reluctance stemmed from an ambition to have a career in football's other code, hopefully with Barnsley FC. Indeed, a love of soccer propelled him into Saturday-morning truancy which might have continued longer than it did but for a Kexborough neighbour's chance remark to his father. 'Your lad scored a fine goal at New Lodge yesterday' brought, 'Not our David, he was at school at Wakefield.' But parental suspicion had been aroused and retribution was heaped rapidly upon an only and normally much-favoured son.

A year later, then 15 and less easily coerced into a rugby involvement, he was centre forward for Higham Rovers in a men's league. On completion of his schooling he took the first step towards becoming a professional footballer by knocking on Norman Rimmington's front door at Linton Place, Darton, and asking for a trial at Oakwell. Told to be there on the following Tuesday evening, he found teams were being chosen from the 50 or so youngsters present – and when someone asked, 'Who plays left back?' he held up his hand. Less than three years later, a former Higham Rovers centre forward was the left full back in Barnsley's first team.

Initially an amateur, he became a part-timer in 1967 while working at Bullcliffe Colliery. In the following year he was in the junior side which had an 11-match unbeaten spell, during which their victims included Wolves and Leeds United, and played in an international tournament in Germany. There the young Reds ended as runners-up and Dave was adjudged the second most outstanding player in the competition.

His first team debut was in a League Cup victory at York City in August 1968 and he retained a place throughout his remaining years at the club. Although almost always at full back, in his opening season he also played in midfield, at inside left and on the left wing, and at the season's end *Shoot* chose him in its Third Division side at left half.

His normal role meant he was rarely among the goals – eight in nearly 200 appearances – yet three times he got two in a single game. The first occasion was within a month of his debut, in a 4 – 0 success against Brighton & Hove

Albion. Then his second goal came five minutes from the end after racing almost half the length of the pitch with four defenders in his wake. Afterwards manager John McSeveney said he couldn't believe how Dave had been able to summon up the energy for such a run after the way he'd grafted in midfield throughout the previous 85 minutes.

January 1969 saw Leicester City at Oakwell in the FA Cup. The tie ended in a draw, but not before Dave had kicked off the line a goal-bound shot from Allan Clarke. But the replay score of 2 – 1 in favour of the First Division side rather flattered the Reds, for at one point Dave was on the goal-line when a shot from the home team's John Sjoberg flashed into the net to hit a stanchion and ricochet out again – and the referee waved play on!

Later in the same year the *Barnsley Chronicle* had a 'Booth the hero' headline to its report of a 1 – 0 success at Tranmere when he fastened onto a pass from George Boardman and unleashed a 30-yard swerving drive into a top corner of the net. Six months later, in a game at Mansfield Town, he had a brief to mark their midfield general, Jim Goodfellow. Not only did he completely subdue the other, but he was the one who made Barnsley's best scoring efforts and rounded off with a last-gasp equalizer.

In the spring of 1971 there was a dearth of goals, only two being scored in a six-match spell. In an effort to remedy the situation in the seventh game, against Reading on 24th April, Dave and Eric Winstanley were switched from defence into the attack; the result was a 3 – 0 success, Eric scoring one goal and Dave getting the other two – and in its match-report, *The Star* gave him Star Player rating and said he looked as though he'd been a front-runner all his life.

On the opening day of the following season, 14th August 1971, Dave got two more goals, this time from his customary left back position, but they were his last in what proved to be a final season at Oakwell.

In June 1972 he was transferred to Grimsby Town. The Mariners were newly promoted as Fourth Division champions, in effect replacing Barnsley in Division Three. The Reds were in desperate need of the £6,000 fee and, most important from Dave's point of view, manager Lawrie McMenemy seemed really keen to have him.

Thus began the most successful and rewarding period of his career. In the first four years he rarely missed a game; he was voted Player of the Year at the end of his first season and became captain in 1974. However, the 1976/77 campaign had barely begun when serious damage to knee ligaments put him out of the side. And apart from a brief return in the spring, he was sidelined until mid-March 1978. A return was then forced upon him by the unavailability of others, but he knew the knee wasn't up to it. He played in the final 12 games, but in the last, on 12th April against Brentford, the suspect joint collapsed and he was carried from the pitch, not to play again in a competitive game.

As soon as it became apparent that Dave's playing days were over he was appointed youth team coach. A year later, in the summer of 1979, new manager George Kerr promoted him to first team coach and he retained the role for two-and-a-half years, during which time the club was promoted from Fourth to Second Division.

In January 1982 Kerr was dismissed. It had been on the cards for some time and, realizing the likely consequences for himself, Dave had applied for an advertised coaching position at Watford. However, on Kerr's departure he took over as caretaker manager – and then he was offered the Watford job. But he decided to take his chance at Grimsby; he'd been a team-mate of some of the players, they were in bottom place in the division and he felt he couldn't desert them. A few weeks later he was appointed manager and the season ended with the team three places clear of relegation.

Dave remained at Grimsby for almost four years, and was Bell's Manager of the Month on three occasions. His first full season in charge was a continual struggle but 1983/84 ended with the team in fifth position in Division Two – on equal points with Manchester City and but two places from promotion into the First Division. It was, in fact, their highest League position since 1947.

The following season was another of comparative success, and in the Milk Cup the team dispatched Everton – at Goodison Park – before going out in the quarter-finals to Norwich City, the eventual winners. Yet six months later, in November 1985, he resigned to take up a business opportunity which arose in Tenerife.

Although the Grimsby board tried to get him to stay by offering a two-year extension of his existing contract, he thought a chance of a partnership in a cousin's property developing business was too good to miss. But a year later almost to the day he was back in England, a sadder and wiser man, living proof of the old adage that relationship can be one of the worst ships in which to sail.

Five months later, in April 1987, he was appointed manager at Darlington when the team were at the bottom of the Third Division. There was insufficient time for him to remedy a desperate situation, but in the following March they were in fourth place in Division Four, only to drop back in the season's final weeks. However, Dave's first rejection in more than 20 years was on the horizon. While at the club he'd turned down an invitation to take charge at Hull City, but in the second week of November 1988 and while a new two-year contract was on his desk awaiting his signature, he was told that a defeat in the next game, at Carlisle United, would bring about his dismissal. Consequently he travelled to the match in his own car in order to avoid the embarrassment of returning in the team coach if the worst happened. But Darlington won. And they won the next game too, but Dave's almost inevitable dismissal came on 12th February 1989.

Within a month he accepted an invitation to become coach-assistant manager at Peterborough United. On manager Mick Jones's departure a few weeks later he took over as caretaker manager until the appointment of the former Oxford United manager, Mark Lawrenson, at the end of the season.

With the Darlington experience still fresh in his mind, Dave was concerned how the new and, to him, unknown manager would view his own position. It was, therefore, with considerable relief that he heard him say, 'The only way we won't work together is if you don't want to.' He now enjoys working alongside a man used to the international scene and the Liverpool way of doing things; in Fourth Division terms, Peterborough United is a big club and the present managerial team seems well qualified to realize its full potential.

While he was at Oakwell, Dave Booth was noted for the strength of his tackle, speed of recovery and willingness to go forward for a crack at goal. He regards it as a compliment that two managers noted for their emphasis on coaching – John Steele and Lawrie McMenemy – never tried to influence his style, allowing him to do things in the way he thought best. John McSeveney went so far as to say that Dave was not only the best full back in the Third Division but better than many in the Second, and if with a bigger club he'd be in line for international honours.

As manager of Grimsby Town he wasn't far away from the First Division in 1984, but four years earlier it was only loyalty to former team-mates which kept him at the club. The irony of that situation is that John Ward, the man who took the coaching job at Watford which Dave was offered by manager Graham Taylor and declined, is now Taylor's assistant at Aston Villa. But, with time still on his side, it may be that Barnsley's Dave Booth will yet be part of a management team in the First Division.

Bob Earnshaw: One to be Envied

Sport in its various forms is Bob Earnshaw's whole life. As a boy he played cricket for his village team in a men's league when 11 years old and represented Rotherham at both cricket and football in addition to playing cricket for Yorkshire Boys. Indeed, he could have pursued a career in either game, and in every aspect of running, from sprints to cross-country events, he was so fleet of foot that all the indications were that he would compete in athletics at international level.

Football became a professional involvement at Barnsley, with whom he played 246 games between 1962 and 1973, and to this day he remains at Oakwell as a coach with the junior sides. Now in his mid-forties, he is as committed to football and fitness as he ever was. He conducts a School of Soccer Excellence on behalf of the Football Association, his responsibilities with Rotherham Boys have enabled him to take a team into Europe every summer for more than 20 years and he has coached his daughter, Susan, to membership of England's youth athletics squad.

Born at Scholes, at 11 he won a scholarship to Oakwood Technical High School at Rotherham where his sporting skills were as much to the fore as his academic abilities. On one occasion he *bowled out* 10 batsmen in an inter-schools game, and as a 15-year-old he was in Rotherham Town's first XI, opening the innings with the future Yorkshire and England batsman, John Hampshire. He was a wing half and centre forward in the Rotherham Boys football team and recorded some exceptionally fast times in track events at inter-schools athletics meetings.

For several years he was an almost fanatical Rotherham United supporter and followed them throughout the north of England, but by 1960 he'd started to outgrow that infatuation. One of his masters who was friendly with John Steele then arranged for him to have trials at Oakwell, the result of which was that he joined the club as an amateur.

In his final year at Oakwood School he had sufficient qualifications to enter university. Keen to pursue a career in Physical Education, he had the choice of Loughborough or Carnegie College and opted for the latter in view of its proximity to home and Oakwell, becoming one of an intake of 40 from more than 3,000 applicants. Three years later he had a teacher's certificate with distinction, a diploma in Physical Education and offers of three jobs. He chose

Kimberworth Comprehensive School because it had a brand-new gymnasium, and 12 months later he was appointed head of the Physical Education Department.

The athletics involvement of early teenage was given up in favour of Saturday afternoons with Rotherham Town. While at Carnegie he stayed there on Saturdays to play for the college cricket team, but returned home on winter weekends to pursue the football interest at Oakwell. His first game in the Northern Intermediate League was against Bradford City. He was at left half, and 20 minutes from the end Bradford were leading 1 – 0. John Steele was the coach and, seeing how things were going, ordered Bob into the attack. Immediately the pattern of the game changed; Bob scored three goals and his strong running created so much havoc among the opposition that Barnsley won 6 – 1.

During his time at college he graduated to the Central League side and, as a 19-year-old amateur, made his Division Four debut at Swindon Town in December 1962. On completing his college studies he became a part-time professional at Oakwell. It was a situation of his own choosing, principally because he knew he was capable of doing something more than just playing football.

A regular place in the team came in the 1965/66 season, in the course of which he got the winning goal at Notts County on 5th March and three days later he scored twice in a 5 – 0 beating of Rochdale. Speed was the essence of his game, and over the following five seasons he turned in some superb performances. In February 1967 a 3 – 1 success at Bradford Park Avenue was the Reds' first win in more than two months and Bob was the mainspring of the revival; he scored the second goal, hit the bar, and gave the home defence a terrible time. In April, in reporting a 1 – 0 success over Crewe Alexandra, Max Jessop of the *Daily Mail* said that Bob embarked on a mazey dribble, beating man after man before racing to the dead-ball line to put over an inch-perfect centre from which John Evans scored the winning goal. Jessop described it as a gem of a goal which he had not seen bettered in any division that season.

Divisional leaders Aldershot visited Oakwell in October 1966 and Bob scored in a manner which defied the theorists. Collecting a loose ball, he raced towards goal, twice losing control briefly and holding when it seemed wiser to part, and drove it into the net despite three burly defenders and the 'keeper breathing down his neck. In February 1968, following a 4 – 0 win over Hartlepools United, Keith Lodge's report in the *Barnsley Chronicle* described Bob as being at his exciting, spectacular, 'run-em-into-the-ground' best – scoring with a blistering left foot shot into the roof of the net and laying-on goals for Robson and Evans. Eighteen months later Lodge was equally rapturous about a display against Stockport County, saying he had one of those games when his tremendous speed created havoc in the opposing defence and his winning goal would be talked about for years to come. It followed a splendid 40-yard run in which he weaved past two defenders and the goalkeeper before sliding the ball into the untenanted net.

But that was to be his last season of regular first team football. He remained on the playing staff for a further three years but, perhaps without realizing it, he'd lost some of his appetite for the game. The demands made of a part-timer in a full-time game are not widely appreciated. Already qualified as an FA coach, he'd taken on duties with the club's junior sides and had to do his own training each week; there were out-of-hours responsibilities with the Rotherham Boys team and he had feelings of guilt about the time he wasn't spending with his family. When he sat down to analyse what he was doing, the only period in each year when he wasn't fully committed was the Spring Bank Holiday. The football season and its ancillary activities continued up to the holiday; after it he was arranging a school tour into Europe, and when that was over it was time to begin pre-season training. Add all that to the demands of a teaching career, and there's little wonder some of the edge had gone from his game.

With hindsight he knew he should have given himself an occasional summer of inactivity – then he'd doubtless have regained all his drive and purpose. But he didn't, and his final three seasons until ceasing to play in 1973 were in the reserves with only occasional appearances in the first team.

He had been fortunate in having headmasters who were accommodating regarding time needed to travel to away games. Nevertheless, there were occasions when he was unable to leave school in time to travel with the team. One journey to Stockport was with friends in their car which broke down at Woodhead – and few professional footballers can have arrived at a League ground in the cab of a petrol tanker. And after the Reds' FA Cup-tie at Cardiff City in 1967 he began the return journey, alone, at 11.15pm and arrived in Sheffield at 7.15am – just in time to get home for breakfast and be at school for 9 o'clock.

At Kimberworth Comprehensive he is now in charge of the Lower School and head of Physical Education with a staff of four teachers. The school has had exceptional success in football competitions. In 1988 it won its 50th trophy – far more than any other school, yet in terms of student numbers it is one of the smallest in the area. There was a year when Kimberworth won the inter-schools championships of the first, second, third and fourth years, and that is the only occasion any school has had that achievement. Perhaps not surprisingly, in that same year it provided *eight* players for the Rotherham Boys team, and they all became apprentices with League clubs.

The cricket team has had almost equal success. In 1970 their Steve Nicholson captained England Boys and he and three schoolmates were in the Yorkshire team during a five-year period when Kimberworth School didn't lose a single game.

It was at Bob's instigation that the school began to participate in European junior football, visiting Germany and Holland in alternate years. The German trip takes in a tournament involving teams from almost every country in Western Europe – and Kimberworth has carried off the trophy four times. The visit to Holland is to play against junior sides of some of the most prestigious clubs in the world, and many of his students can rightly claim, for the rest of their lives, to have played football in the stadiums of Feyenoord, Ajax, and Sparta Rotterdam.

As a player at Oakwell, Bob was one of the attractions of the place – a man who excited and often inspired with his great pace and individualism. John Steele maintains he was the fastest in professional football and there were managers who, on seeing him for the first time, couldn't believe he was a part-timer. The sight of him heading goalwards always created a buzz of excitement on the terraces and there is no doubt that with the crowd behind him he could be a real match-winner. In his main career he's achieved everything he set out to do and he still loves doing it. And with a lifetime in sport, years in League football with the only club he ever wanted to be with and putting a variety of skills to the benefit of young people, Bob Earnshaw has the kind of life that many will envy.

Bob Parker: Eminently Satisfactory

Bob Parker was a full back throughout 15 years as a professional footballer with Huddersfield Town and Barnsley. He joined Huddersfield as an 18-year-old in 1954 at a time when the club had had long membership of the First Division and its young players were required to undergo a lengthy and meaningful apprenticeship. Indeed, they were made very aware of their lowly place in the pecking order. Even reserve players, as Bob soon was, did not have ready access to the first team dressing room: they had to knock on the door and await an invitation to enter. Progression within the game was much slower than it was to become and, in common with many of that era, he didn't sample first team football until he was 24 years old.

A Durham boy, born at Seaham Harbour, he represented Sunderland and Durham boys and in 1949 had trials with All-England Schools. Huddersfield Town signed him from Murton Colliery Welfare. He was then apprenticed to his father, a painter and decorator, and joined the club as a part-time professional in order to complete the apprenticeship on reaching 21.

At the end of his first season, as a reward for the way he had applied himself, he was included in the club's summer tour of the USA and Canada. The journey included crossings of the Atlantic in the luxury of SS Empress of Scotland and further pleasures came when he played in two games during the tour.

Introduction into the first team came at Leyton Orient in January 1960, following which the *Huddersfield Daily Examiner* said that his positioning and distribution were excellent and he could look back on his debut with supreme satisfaction. He played regularly during 1960/61 and was in the side which knocked holders Wolverhampton Wanderers out of the FA Cup. Later in the season the local newspaper acclaimed his display against Stoke City, rating him the team's most consistently reliable performer who had proved himself equal in tackling and positional play to the England full backs on view – team-mate Ray Wilson and the opposition's Tony Allen.

The years at Huddersfield ended in 1965. Barnsley manager John Steele was then intent on strengthening the team for a quick elevation from Division Four, and Bob was one of several experienced free transfer men whom he obtained.

His opening Oakwell season saw him in the team on 43 occasions. In the following campaign he played in all the 52 League and Cup games and, but for a pre-season injury in a friendly at Barnet, he might have had the same high level of participation in 1967/68. Nevertheless, he returned in mid-season and shared in the euphoria of promotion into the Third Division.

That successful period proved to be his last in the first team. During the following season he put his wide experience to good use in the reserves and qualified as an FA coach. He then ended his playing career and joined the Oakwell coaching staff.

Throwing himself wholeheartedly into the new role, daytime duties with full-time players continued in the evenings with part-timers and amateurs; come Saturday mornings he was at the juniors' game, and usually in the afternoons he assisted with the first team. Over four seasons his working week was of 60–70 hours – and he loved every minute of it. He was therefore saddened and bitterly disappointed when in July 1973, in the wake of Jim Iley becoming manager, he was told his services were no longer required. He later received a letter of apology from the club in relation to the way the matter had been handled, but the circumstances were so hurtful that he severed his connection with the game and has not visited Oakwell since his employment there was terminated.

Despite having in his hands the trade which was learned as a young man, he decided he wanted some other line of work and obtained employment with BXL Plastics as a machine operator at the Darton factory. In 1985 he qualified as a fitter and now works in the maintenance section. Joining the company was forced upon him by circumstances outside his control but he now thinks it was the best thing that could have happened; it enables his family to have a settled way of life and provides a level of financial security which was never available to him within professional football.

Sportswise, he has recently again taken up golf. It was a game learned at Huddersfield and allowed to lapse, but buying a set of clubs for his son Shaun – a Cambridge MA – rekindled the interest and he now has a weekly round at Staincross. On the social scene he and his wife, Rena, have been dancing partners since before their marriage. Their speciality is sequence dancing and, although not ones for competitions, they have considerable expertise and are well known at dance clubs in the Barnsley area. Yet Oakwell supporters of the mid-1960s may have some difficulty in equating the rugged, hard-tackling Bob Parker with the grace and style of the Empress Tango!

Bob entered professional football at a time when clubs had large playing staffs and retained reliable men for long periods for them to be available for the first team as and when required. He was one such player. In 11 years with Huddersfield Town he played in the League side on only 65 occasions, yet was regarded as a valuable part of the club's resources.

He was a strong, powerful defender, and when he shook up an opponent he liked to think he'd done it fairly. He took pride in his distribution and a big part of his game was overlapping down the flank to cross the ball into the goal-area. One such foray occurred during the Reds' replayed FA Cup-tie at Port Vale in 1966; the cross went into the net, producing the one and only goal of his career and putting the team on course for a 3 – 1 success.

After so many in-and-out years at Huddersfield, from teenage to nearly 30, the move to Oakwell was eminently satisfactory to both parties. It allowed the player to have continuous first team football and provided Barnsley FC with Bob Parker – a man whose experience and total commitment was part of the foundation upon which the team made their successful push for promotion in 1968.

George Boardman: The Nicest Compliment

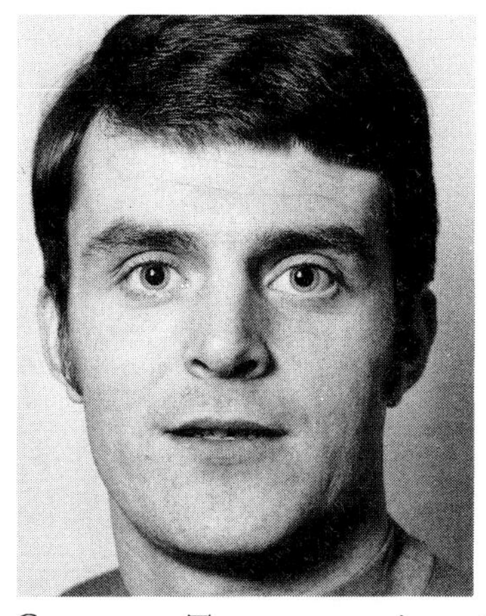

George Boardman was an amateur international who followed in father's footsteps by beginning a football career in his native Scotland and continuing it in Yorkshire. In the 1930s George senior was a centre half with Partick Thistle and Bradford Park Avenue: George junior was with the most successful amateur side of modern times, Queen's Park, and had been at Shrewsbury Town before joining the Oakwell staff in 1969. It was while playing in the Scottish Second Division with Queen's Park that he won amateur international honours, scoring a hat-trick in his first game and being top scorer in the English FA Centenary Tournament in 1963.

He had played in the same Glasgow City Boys team as the present Manchester United manager, Alex Ferguson, later joining local side St Rollox Amateurs. The Queen's Park interest arose after he played against one of their junior sides at Hampden Park; he joined them at 15, making his first team debut on the day after his 17th birthday to score in a 3 – 0 win over Dumbarton. From January 1962 he had a regular place in the side, in April 1963 scoring a hat-trick in a 4 – 0 win at Forfar Athletic.

The English FA Centenary Tournament was held in the following month and involved the UK sides, Eire, and three other European countries. Scotland were the eventual winners, and in beating Eire in the opening game George scored a hat-trick which included a goal after only 90 seconds. And finishing on an almost equally high note, he got two when West Germany were beaten 5 – 2 in the final.

Opportunity then arose for him to become a professional with either Airdrieonians or Third Lanark. However, word had got around that he was keen to move to England and he had other offers from Watford, Blackpool and Shrewsbury Town. George's dad was involved in the choosing process and he thought Shrewsbury boss Arthur Rowley seemed a genuine sort of chap, consequently it was Rowley's club that George joined.

His debut was three weeks into the 1963/64 season when he scored in a defeat of Bradford City, and in the following week he scored two in three minutes against Walsall. By then he'd decided that dad's assessment of the manager had been absolutely correct and he went on to have six thoroughly happy years at Shrewsbury. He was particularly to the fore in the Cup competitions, beginning in January 1965 against Manchester City. Then, in the FA Cup at Maine Road, the home side scrambled an equalizer in the 88th minute but were beaten 3 – 1 in the replay with George getting one of the goals. In the next round at Millwall he steered his side from the brink of defeat to victory with a fine equalizer and the success enabled Shrewsbury to make a first-ever appearance in the fifth round. And they did it again in the following year after his magnificent winning goal in extra-time of a second replay put paid to Second Division Carlisle United. In 1966/67 he scored the only hat-trick in the FA Cup's second round when Wrexham were beaten 5 – 1, and in the League Cup he got the equalizer when First Division leaders Burnley were held to a draw at Shrewsbury.

During that time Sheffield Wednesday and Sunderland tried to sign him but manager Rowley refused to let him leave. Yet George wasn't in the least bothered, for he liked everything about the club and was content to remain there. But nothing lasts for ever: Rowley moved on and things weren't the same under new manager Harry Gregg, and George felt the time had come to take on a new challenge.

In June 1969 he joined Barnsley. On 13th September he scored in a 2 – 1 success at Bury and in October he had a tremendous week when he scored the winner against Barrow, the second in a 2 – 0 win over Bristol Rovers and a point-producing goal at Bradford City. Indeed, his performances were so impressive that in November he was chosen by the *Football League Review* as their Third Division Sportsman of the Month.

Until this point George had always been an attacking player, but the move to Barnsley was not long after midfielders came into fashion. It was a role for which he was ideally suited and which he had from January 1970, thereafter being used in a mainly defensive capacity. In March 1971 he was in the side which recorded a 2 – 1 success over his previous club. Then he gave a vivid reminder of his capabilities, playing a big part in both goals, hitting the bar with a viciously dipping shot and seemingly treading every square inch of the pitch. In April 1972 he scored the winner against Bolton Wanderers, but later in the year disaster struck at Mansfield Town. There he went awkwardly into a tackle and stretched the ligaments in his right knee, and although he finished the game he realized he'd damaged himself quite seriously. The injury didn't respond to treatment, so in February 1973 a cartilage was removed – and in April he was given a free transfer. He was taken aback by not being allowed time to rehabilitate, but now regards it as 'one of those things'.

In the summer he returned to Scotland and signed for St Johnstone. In the light of the recent injury the club insisted on a week-to-week arrangement and, therefore, his family remained in Barnsley. However, by Christmas it was apparent the knee wasn't able to cope with the demands made upon it so he returned to Barnsley and sought other employment. Starting by selling insurance, he soon found that while forcefulness on the playing pitch had come naturally to him, it wasn't part of his make-up to be vigorous in getting people to spend money on life insurance. He then got a driving job with Curry's Group

Services transporting merchandise throughout Yorkshire and returned to professional football with Buxton Town.

Each involvement lasted about the same length of time – four months. Then he took employment with the Housing Department of Barnsley Metropolitan Borough Council and, 16 years on, is still there. The major part of the time has been at Wombwell where, after working initially as a rent collector, he moved into the Estate Management Office to deal with every aspect of housing activity. In the autumn of 1987 he made a sideways move to Barnsley and now deals with lettings of Council properties throughout the Metropolitan Borough.

Sportswise, he has a variety of interests which still include football. Golf has been one of his favourite activities since boyhood. At 11 he was a junior member of Glasgow's Bishopbriggs Golf Club, having an 18 handicap by the time he left school, and he now plays at Staincross. He has had membership of Brook Squash Club since it opened in the late 1970s, playing there twice-weekly with friend and former Oakwell team-mate Barry Murphy. He is a keen distance runner; he has two five-mile training runs each week and has participated in four Barnsley Six races and several half marathons, but doesn't really run to win – just to keep fit and raise funds for charity. And as an indication of what a genuine all-rounder he is, in order to fill what he regarded as a gap in his capabilities he learned to swim when 34 years old.

While he'd been incapacitated in the winter of 1972 manager Jim Iley used him in a scouting role. Two years later, on leaving Buxton Town, he resumed the Oakwell connection under manager Allan Clarke and was used for assessing and reporting upon the first team's future opponents. In 1981 he was appointed to coach one of the junior sides and retained that responsibility for the following five years. During that time his son, Craig, played for one of the teams but there was never any suggestion that the club intended to sign him. In the summer of 1986, Alan Hill, a former Oakwell goalkeeper and now Youth Development Officer at Nottingham Forest, approached George with an invitation for Craig to spend a few weeks training with Forest. In the absence of a similar offer from Barnsley, George agreed. The result was that Craig signed schoolboy forms and later, on leaving school, joined the club as an apprentice under the Government's Youth Training Scheme. Progress was all that father and son could have hoped for: Craig's first season saw him the Colts' Player of the Year and in his next he had several games in the Central League side – and present indications are that he is likely to make the grade in professional football.

Unfortunately for George, things didn't work out so well for *him* because Craig joining Forest resulted in his own services no longer being required at Oakwell. Having then to seek another appointment he decided he might as well try to get in at the top and offered his services to Spurs' manager David Pleat. He and Pleat had been team-mates at Shrewsbury and the latter had good cause to want George on his side – for while with Luton Town he'd been at the receiving end of a 7 – 2 home defeat when Shrewsbury's George Boardman scored four times! George is now thoroughly enjoying working for Spurs, and on their behalf sees at least one game each week – yet he would still rather be with Barnsley, for not only had he been player, scout and coach, for 18 years he'd also been a supporter.

His all-time favourite footballer is Pelé, who played in World Cup-winning teams in 1958 and 1970 – and there were occasions when aspects of his own play were likened to the brilliant Brazilian. Alan Hoby, reporting a Shrewsbury game at Millwall in the *Daily Express*, said that George flicked the ball over a defender and volleyed it into the net past the outstretched Alex Stepney for a goal even Pelé would have been proud to score. And at Oakwell on 1st November 1969 – a day when Halifax manager Alan Ball's life had been threatened and he was provided with a police escort throughout the time the visiting party was in the town – he scored with a 25-yard swerving volley which the *Morning Telegraph* described as being of lasting memory, worthy of a far more momentous occasion and of which Pelé himself would have been proud. For George Boardman, a man whose English career took him no higher than the Third Division, being mentioned in the same breath as one of the greatest players the game has known was the nicest compliment he could ever have.

Brian Arblaster: No Prizes – Lots of Praise

Immediately after Brian Arblaster's second game in goal for Barnsley he had the distressing experience of being told by the manager that it had been a mistake to sign him. John Steele's remarks followed a game against Luton Town in which Brian had been beaten five times, yet after a period of apparent disgrace he redeemed himself and in the 1970/71 season he was one of only two men to play in all the 51 League and Cup games.

Born in London during the Second World War, Brian was evacuated to Killamarsh and has lived in the area ever since. In schoolboy football he was a full back and a centre forward before becoming a goalkeeper – once losing his place in the team when the games master considered him to be too spectacular.

On leaving school he worked underground at West-thorpe Colliery and football was with a local side, Mosboro' Trinity, from where he joined Sheffield United as an amateur. Two years later, seeing little chance of progression for a fourth-choice goalkeeper while English international Alan Hodgkinson was a fixture in the first team, he responded to a newspaper advertisement regarding trials at Chesterfield FC. Reg Whittaker, Chesterfield correspondent for the *Green 'Un*, was at the trials and recognized Brian as a Sheffield United player. His telephone call to Bramall Lane resulted in the youngster being called to the ground on the following day to receive a dressing-down and an offer of part-time professional terms. He accepted both – one with some embarrassment and the other with a great deal of pleasure – and intentionally retained part-time status with his next two clubs.

Over the following 12 months he graduated to the Central League side and became Hodgkinson's deputy, and then fate took a hand in him joining the club he'd begun trials with in the previous year. In December 1964 he was transferred to Chesterfield to help out in an emergency when several of their players had been injured in a road accident. At that time men could not be loaned by one club to another and the arrangement was that Brian would be transferred back to Bramall Lane when the injury position improved. His debut was in a 2 – 1 defeat of Wrexham, when the same Reg Whittaker who had been instrumental in curtailing the earlier stay at Chesterfield described him as 'the hero of this victory who has come to stay in the side'. The correspondent was not only observant, he was also perceptive, for Brian did stay in the side despite having moved to the club only to provide cover for the first-choice goalkeeper.

Later in the season he gave a masterful display in a League Cup replay at Stoke City. After the game the players went into the Stoke City Supporters' Club and were recognized after only a few minutes; almost everyone then began chanting, 'We want the goalkeeper . . . We want the goalkeeper . . . ' It continued until Brian went onto the stage to acknowledge the applause – and while he was there they got him to present the bingo prize. A more significant consequence of his display was that Stoke tried to obtain his transfer. However, Chesterfield wouldn't agree and, instead, transferred John Osborne, the man he'd replaced, to West Bromwich Albion.

The determination to remain a part-time player was prompted solely by financial considerations. The combined income was appreciably more than full-time football could provide, even though on one Friday in four he had to work two shifts in order to qualify for bonus and be free for the Saturday game. It was the refusal to become a full-time player which brought about his departure from Chesterfield in 1967. He joined Scunthorpe United in preference to Barnsley and Halifax Town because they were in a higher division than the others. He started in the first team, but Keith Burkinshaw, the future Spurs' manager who had signed him, soon made way for a man who didn't want part-timers . . . so in the following spring he was on the move again.

Recalling Barnsley's interest of the previous year, he contacted John Steele. But the Oakwell boss couldn't take him and expressed disappointment that the call hadn't come a week earlier, he having just taken on trial a goalkeeper from another club. Yet within a month Steele came back to him. The other hadn't been satisfactory; Brian was signed until the end of the season, making his debut a few days later on 15th April 1968 in a 3 – 0 win over Brentford.

In the summer he was offered full-time terms and, well knowing the dangers inherent in refusal, accepted them. He'd decided he was going to enjoy being at Oakwell, but such thoughts were soon to receive a severe jolt. On 28th August he deputized for Roy Ironside at Luton Town – and picked the ball out of the net five times. In every respect it was a miserable evening and at the end of the game Brian was cold, wet and thoroughly dejected. But worse was to come. Next morning John Steele discussed his performance and concluded he'd made a mistake in signing him. No longer was Brian to train with the first team and the one consoling feature of the situation was that coach Norman Rimmington – himself a former goalkeeper – hadn't lost faith in him. Rimmington realized the player's confidence was at risk, and coached him in every aspect of goalkeeping. During that anxious time, while playing in a reserve game at Oakwell, he threw the ball from the edge of the penalty-area to a young trialist standing in the centre-circle. The other promptly volleyed it back over Brian's head and into the empty net – an action hardly likely to help restore a goalkeeper's sagging self-esteem!

After a month Rimmington perhaps felt the sins of Luton had been purged, for he arranged shooting practice for the first team and put Brian in goal. Seeing how well things were going, he brought John Steele to watch – and from that moment the player's career never faltered. He returned immediately to the first team squad and played at Bristol Rovers on 4th November. During the 4 – 2 defeat a finger on his right hand was almost severed in a compound dislocation, yet because no-one else was available he had to play in the next game and wore a heavily padded glove for protection. Again the Reds lost, this time 1 – 0, and Keith Lodge, writing in the *Barnsley Chronicle*, said that the second half was mainly a case of Southport *versus* Arblaster, and Brian had given one of the most magnificent displays of goalkeeping he had ever seen.

He succeeded Roy Ironside on the latter's retirement in 1969. After a 1 – 1 draw at Plymouth Argyle in September the home chairman was yet another to rate one of Brian's performances among the best he'd seen. A month later in a goal-less draw with a Fulham side destined for promotion, the visitors' former England star, Johnny Haynes, unleashed a series of blistering drives which were blocked by a string of spectacular saves. It was another display which prompted an opposing club to try to secure him – and instilled in Brian a belief that 'when you're doing well they won't let you go, and if you play badly no-one wants to know you!'

An injury which necessitated two operations on the same knee kept him out of the side for the whole of season 1971/72, and other absences were caused by fractures of an ankle, a cheekbone and an arm. Indeed, it was a broken bone which brought about his departure from Oakwell in 1974. In a practice match he was exercising goalkeepers' usual liking for outfield roles when a tackle from a groundstaff boy fractured his ankle. For months afterwards the joint became swollen and painful during training and, as he'd feared, at the season's end his contract was not renewed.

After a summer of inactivity the ankle was more tolerable and he became a part-timer with Boston United under the management of former team-mate in Sheffield United juniors and present Leeds United manager, Howard Wilkinson. In 1975 he moved to Matlock Town and in the following season the FA Cup competition took them onto a Football League ground for the first time in their history. They were drawn at Mansfield Town, and a historic occasion developed into a delightful event as they beat the Third Division side quite decisively 5 – 2. He remained with Matlock for six years until retiring from the game in 1981 when he was 38 years old.

On leaving Barnsley in 1974 he again took employment with the NCB. Having earlier qualified as a Class I HGV driver he worked in the Board's transport department, remaining when it became privatized as National Plant Transport. As the name suggests, his work requires him to transport heavy machinery and plant between coalfields throughout the country.

Of Brian's 17 seasons in professional football, the six spent at Barnsley were by far the happiest. Yet he retains an element of bitterness that his years of total commitment, during which he received some serious injuries and returned to the side on occasions when not fully fit simply because there wasn't anyone else available, were not acknowledged by way of a benefit. An instance of such hasty return was a goal-less draw at Reading in February 1973. It was within days of plaster being removed from a damaged ankle – and he proceeded to steal the show. Afterwards, Reading manager Charlie Hurley said, 'If he can play as well as that with a half-healed ankle I should hate us to face him when he's fit!' John Steele replied, 'He may not be the best goalkeeper in the Football League but he's certainly the bravest.' Those comments perhaps summed up Brian Arblaster's career, for while he never collected any trophies he won praise and admiration all along the way.

Mick Butler: The Three-Shift Goalscorer

At 22, Mick Butler was a comparatively late entrant into senior professional football. His goalscoring feats with Worsbrough Bridge Miners' Welfare Athletic and Ward Green Working Men's Club – with whom he played on Saturdays and Sundays respectively – caused Barnsley FC to look at him again in 1972 after he'd trained at Oakwell as a 15-year-old and been allowed to drift away. Yet there was no great hurry to sign him, for he had 14 games in the Fourth Division as an amateur and became second-top scorer before being offered professional terms. That was in May 1973, by which time there was perhaps a feeling within the club that if they didn't start to pay a man who was making that kind of contribution while working days, afternoons and nights at Dodworth Colliery then someone else would!

The belated entry into League football was perhaps in part due to his rather slow physical development. As a boy he was the smallest in St Edwin's School team at Athersley and in the Broadway Grammar School side, and he never caught the eye of the Barnsley Boys selectors.

At 16 he became an apprentice electrician at Dodworth Colliery. Football was then as a wing half with Athersley Youth Club, and in 1971 he helped them win the Barnsley & District FA Challenge Cup and reach an Oakwell final of the Beckett Hospital Cup.

A striking role came in the following season when he joined Worsbrough Bridge MW, by which time he'd grown to 5′ 9″ and weighed all of 10 stones. The club won promotion within the Yorkshire League in each of his two seasons with them but, in the second, 1972/73, it was a close-run thing. From February Mick had a place in the Barnsley first team, at which time Worsbrough Bridge had a four-point lead in Division Two. By mid-April the lead had been lost, and when the Oakwell programme ended Mick again turned out for Worsbrough Bridge. And in true story book fashion, his two goals against Scarborough in the season's final game helped them secure a place in the Yorkshire League's top division.

The trial with Barnsley had come in the form of a reserve game at Bradford City towards the end of 1972. A feeling that he hadn't done particularly well was, he thought, confirmed by the 'don't ring us – we'll ring you' attitude of the trainer. It was therefore with some surprise, soon after Christmas, that he received an invitation to play in a reserve game at York City and he retained a place in the side for the following six weeks.

Eighteen months earlier he had begun playing Sunday League football with Ward Green WMC with whom, on one occasion, he scored eight goals in a single game. Therefore, from the beginning of January 1973 until winning a place in the Barnsley first team on 17th February he played for Worsbrough Bridge on Saturdays, Ward Green on Sundays, and Barnsley reserves on Wednesday evenings!

Unknown to the Oakwell management, the few days prior to 17th February were being spent by Mick and his wife, Lynn, at the home of Lynn's parents at Royston. Consequently, to the consternation of those at the club, he could not be contacted and he learned of his selection on the Friday from a 'Reds draft local star into Derby game' headline on the sports page of the *Barnsley Chronicle*. His reaction was one of disbelief and he rang manager John Steele from a nearby 'phone box. Confirmation was quickly forthcoming, together with a lecture on the responsibilities of players – even amateurs receiving £5 expenses!

Coincidentally, his introduction into the first team was against Bradford City. The Reds lost 2 – 1, and Mick scored their goal with the last kick of the match. He played in each of the season's remaining 13 games and a further eight goals included those which secured vital points at the expense of Newport County and Exeter City, and a rare League hat-trick from an amateur in the first 45 minutes of a 4 – 1 success at Hartlepool in mid-April.

Mick was top scorer in each of the following two seasons. At Hartlepool in December 1973 he went part-way towards repeating his personal success there earlier in the year by scoring the winning goal. A fortnight later the *News of the World* carried a 'Brilliant Butler' headline when reporting his two goals which beat Brentford and the New Year was opened in celebratory fashion with a hat-trick against Scunthorpe United. Other special goals were winners against Swansea City and Rotherham United and, exceptionally for a man in his first season as a professional, he was awarded the accolade of Player of the Year.

Early in December 1974 he broke a small bone in his leg and at Christmas he had to undergo a cartilage operation, yet five weeks later he came back into the side in remarkable fashion. Two goals were scored against Bradford City on the day of his return and in March he got hat-tricks in consecutive games against Newport County and Rochdale. Such torrent of goals from a Barnsley player was quite uncommon, for consecutive hat-tricks had not occurred since Lol Chappell put Darlington and Crewe Alexandra on the rack exactly 20 years previously. But in mid-April he broke a leg for the second time in five months. He was out of the side for the rest of the season but was leading scorer – despite having played in only 28 games.

Earlier, at the end of the 1973/74 season, he had been placed on the transfer list. It was at his insistence after a promise of a pay increase after a year, made when he became a professional, was not kept. A transfer seemed on the cards soon after pre-season training began when Luton Town, newly promoted to the First Division, contacted manager Jim Iley with a request to borrow Mick for a tour of Belgium. He had to be at Luton that evening, and Iley drove him home to pack a bag and then the two returned to Oakwell prior to going on to Sheffield Midland Station. Iley was then told he had to telephone chairman Ernest Dennis at his office and, on doing so, was instructed that the player was not to be loaned to Luton Town. It was the most disappointing moment of Mick's whole career.

The pay dispute was resolved a few weeks into the new season when he received an increase of £10 on the basic rate. He therefore came off the list, but in March 1976 he was transferred without being on it. Some time previously the club had entered into an agreement to sell its Grove Street car park to a development company and had received an initial payment of £30,000. However, the deal fell through and the money had to be repaid. Jim Iley told Mick that it could only be done by transferring him. Consequently, with considerable reluctance, he joined Huddersfield Town.

His new club was in the same division as Barnsley, yet his pay increased by £30 per week. He scored on his debut in a 2 – 0 win over Swansea City and six months later he was back at Oakwell to score against the Reds when they beat his side 2 – 1. In 1977/78 his 19 goals included two hat-tricks and no doubt contributed towards the Player of the Year award which he received.

July 1978 saw him transferred to Bournemouth. In manager John Benson he found one of the nicest men he ever met and, with a club house on the sea-front, the Butlers' stay on the South Coast was, at least for a time, idyllic. Again he led the scorers in each of two seasons but the happy relationship with management ended when Benson made way for Alec Stock. The new man seemed to have little time for Northerners. Mick couldn't please no matter what he did, and it was principally that factor which decided him to leave the club.

By then he and Lynn had taken a liking to a new housing development at Royston. They bought a house there, and Mick contacted Jim Iley who was then at Bury. The former boss was glad to have him and he had two final League seasons with the Lancashire club until being given a free transfer in 1982. Even then he could have gone back, for in the summer Iley got in touch to say he couldn't find a striker as good as him who wasn't going to cost money, and he offered a new contract. But Mick knew he couldn't last much longer and he had a trade in his hands, so he declined and returned to his former work as a Class I Electrical Engineer in the mining industry. He started at Woolley Colliery and when that closed in 1988 he moved to his present job at the Riccall Mine in Selby Coalfield.

On leaving Bury he resumed the former association with Ward Green WMC in the Barnsley Premier League. He remained with them for three seasons, during which they were Sunday League champions and winners of the Sunday Cup and the Barnsley Challenge Cup. For the following 18 months he was out of the game until 1987 when he formed a team at the Cross Inn, Royston, which plays in the Barnsley League. Now nearly 40, he is player-manager, and regular football and the training sessions which he conducts at Royston Comprehensive School keep him physically fit and not noticeably heavier than when he became one of the very few amateurs to have played in the first team at Oakwell.

The three years at Barnsley were his happiest in football. The fans loved him because he was a goal-grabber, a quicksilver, darting player who thrived on the action inside a penalty-area. To score regularly in the Fourth Division as he did – 57 goals in 118 games for Barnsley – usually requires skill to be allied to the build of a boxer and heart of a lion. And although Mick Butler didn't give the impression of great physical strength, the other requirements were his in abundance and continually on display.

Leslie Lea: Mixing With The Finest

Seventeen-year-old Les Lea fulfilled the dreams of three generations of schoolboys by making his debut in the First Division as wing partner to the legendary Stanley Matthews. Their pairing, at Blackpool, was remarkable in that 45-year-old Matthews began playing League football 10 years before Les was born! Les later played in European Cup-winners' competitions with Cardiff City, and joining Barnsley in 1970 was his first experience of football at a lower level than Division Two.

Born at Urmston, Lancashire, he played in the same Stretford Boys team as actor Ian McShane and joined the Blackpool groundstaff at 16. His First Division debut on the opening day of the 1960/61 season resulted from having travelled to Leicester as 12th man and Scottish international Jackie Mudie being taken ill there on the Friday night. On the next day he played inside right to his hero in a 1 – 1 draw, their pairing allegedly creating the biggest-ever age gap between players in those positions in a senior team. Yet it wasn't the first occasion he'd been Matthews' partner; in the previous season the England star had a game in the reserves after an injury absence – an occasion which provided young Les with his biggest thrill in nearly 20 years' professional football.

Over the following two seasons his appearances were infrequent until winning a regular place at outside right in September 1962. Thereafter, his years at Blackpool were almost entirely in the First Division – and he had some memorable games. In May 1963 he scored in a 3 – 0 success at Manchester City; in September 1964 the *Blackpool Evening Gazette* described him as the mainspring of a 4 – 0 beating of Leeds United; six months later he scored twice in a 4 – 2 win at Blackburn Rovers and in March 1966 he got both goals in a 2 – 1 victory at Leeds United – then one of the top teams in Europe. In-between-times he was among the goals when Blackpool inflicted a rare 5 – 1 humiliation on Manchester United in the Football League Cup.

His seasons at the seaside ended in November 1967. Ironically, he had moved into a club house only three months earlier and had spent every evening of the last three weeks on hands and knees, laying a parquet floor. Having just applied the final seal, he was admiring his handiwork while massaging an aching back when manager Stan Mortensen brought news of his impending departure to Cardiff City. He had had no prior warning of the transfer, but Blackpool had dropped into the Second Division six months earlier and the recently-appointed manager was wanting fresh faces in his team.

The move to South Wales and Cardiff's success in the Welsh Cup put Les into European Cup-winners' Cup football in each of his three seasons there. In 1968 the team reached the semi-finals against S V Hamburg – drawing in Germany before losing by a single goal at Ninian Park in front of 55,000 roaring Welshmen.

Les's transfer to Barnsley came in the summer of 1970. At first he was reluctant to sign – in comparison with Blackpool and Cardiff City, Barnsley seemed such a small club and he wasn't at all sure it was the right move for him. The deal included team-mate Frank Sharpe; the fee of £20,000 would be the highest Barnsley had ever paid and Sharpe was enthusiastic about the transfer. Eventually the deciding factor so far as Les was concerned was John Steele – for he'd never previously met such a gentlemanly manager.

His debut was on 22nd August at Bradford City, and that first season at Oakwell was all he could have hoped for. He didn't miss a game, was leading scorer and was voted Player of the Year. Surprisingly, because he considered his strengths to be in areas other than the scoring of goals, he was again top scorer in season 1972/73. Then his tally included two at Hereford – the first in 72 seconds – two at Workington Town and two which beat Newport County.

In 1973 he was switched to midfield and held a regular place until late 1975 when injury put him out of the side. Its effects were such that he didn't play again and he was released at the end of the season after 220 first team games.

For the following two years he had no football involvement of any kind but in 1978, at the age of 35, the old urge returned. He then joined Redfearns' Sports in the Barnsley Premier League. Two years later he moved to Ardsley House FC in the Barnsley Sunday League, remaining with them for his final two seasons in active football.

Since then he has been a regular visitor to Oakwell where he gets a lot of pleasure from seeing how young players develop in the first team. He never asks for a ticket, being glad to make a small contribution to the club which provided the happiest years of his career.

Whereas the spectator-interest in football is of fairly recent origin, a similar attraction to cricket is of longer standing. It began at Blackpool where he liked watching Lancashire League cricket and county games at Stanley Park. Now he is an avid viewer of televised Test cricket and gets maximum enjoyment by turning off the sound and listening to ball-by-ball commentaries from Brian Johnston and other masters of their craft on BBC Radio 3's *Test Match Special.*

On joining Blackpool as a 16-year-old he was in the unusual situation of being a groundstaff boy who didn't work at the ground. He trained with the others in mornings, and each afternoon he was in employment which the club had arranged with a market gardener at Marton Moss. He learned to cultivate flowers and salad crops in the summer and chrysanthemums in the winter. Although he didn't realize it at the time, he was developing skills which were to stand him in good stead in future years. On leaving Oakwell he obtained employment as a gardener with Barnsley Council and is involved in all aspects of the maintenance of 21 cemeteries within the metropolitan borough.

His years with Blackpool and Cardiff City enabled him to travel extensively throughout western Europe and North America and twice he travelled around the world. Such journeys were not without an occasional mishap. In 1961 Blackpool went on tour with Sheffield United, and while the party changed flights at JF Kennedy Airport, New York, Les and a team-mate went onto the spectators' terraces in order to photograph incoming and outgoing air-traffic with Les's new cine-camera. Engrossed in what they were doing, they suddenly noticed that all the passengers on a DC10 which was taxiing towards take-off were waving frantically at them. . . . and the awful realization dawned. Hurrying to the departure area, worst fears were confirmed. There was an eight-hour delay and a joint outlay of some 400 dollars before two embarrassed young men rejoined highly amused colleagues on the other side of the continent in San Francisco.

Those same years put him in the company of some of the world's greatest players. In the summer of 1963 he played in a club competition in Malaga against a Real Madrid side containing such legends as Puskas, Di Stefano and Santamaria. In five First Division seasons he mixed with the best in England and his Blackpool team-mates included famous names from the 1953 FA Cup-winning side, and youngsters Emlyn Hughes, Alan Ball and Jimmy Armfield who were destined to become as renowned as their predecessors.

Les Lea arrived at Oakwell with the status of a successful, experienced winger. His quick bursts to the line more often than not ended with a low, dangerous ball into the goal-area; he never claimed nor even tried to be a striker – he preferred to set up chances for others. He was consistent, he loved to take people on and could hit a good ball with either foot, and the polished way he went about things generally was clear evidence of seasons spent in the First Division.

Kenny Brown: Sherry and Eggs – To No Avail!

When Kenny Brown first appeared in the Barnsley side he was a most unlikely looking footballer. Of above average height but weighing a mere eight and a half stones, he seemed so under nourished that the manager insisted he drank a bottle of Guinness and a glass of sherry and eggs every day. Two years later he weighed. ... eight and a half stones, and it was really nothing more than natural physical development which, during his remaining six years with the club, gradually put another stone onto his frame.

A pupil at Broadway Grammar School and a member of the school side and the Barnsley Boys team, he became an apprentice at Oakwell in 1967. His debut was in a 2 – 0 success at Halifax Town in April 1970 while still an apprentice, and he became a professional two years later.

He won a regular place in the 1971/72 season, but he'd already been given a rough time by some of the spectators. There was an element among them who looked for scapegoats during a depressing sequence of results and Kenny was one who was subjected to vociferous and unkind criticism from so-called supporters. It was a distressing experience for a teenager striving to make a career in the game, but he ignored the comments as best he could and continued to give his utmost. The tide turned for him in January 1971 when Wrexham were beaten 3 – 1 and he had his best game since first appearing in the side. On leaving the pitch he was rewarded by a round of warm applause, and he'd won over his detractors by a combination of skill and grit which could, with a little luck, have brought him a hat-trick. Indeed, if he needed an assurance of the way the crowd's attitude had changed it was provided soon afterwards in an early round of the Football League Cup. With the Reds trailing 1 – 0 and Kenny nursing an ankle injury, a chorus of booing rang out when it seemed he might be the one to be substituted – which showed the degree to which he had convinced his critics.

Thereafter his displays regularly won the Star Player rating in Barnsley's match-report in *The Star* – one of which occasions was in February 1973 when he dominated midfield in what was the team's first-ever win at Colchester. And in the following April at Crewe he contrived and executed a well deserved victory by forcing a free kick and being on the spot to ram the ball into the roof of the net for the only goal of the game.

The accolade of Player of the Year bestowed upon him in 1976 was the high point of his career. It was appropriate acknowledgement of constant, non-stop, one hundred per-cent commitment to the team cause – and it was pleasing to him that his sometimes unobtrusive work had been preferred to that of colleagues whose responsibilities within the side put them more readily into spectator view.

After almost 300 games, Kenny's years at Oakwell ended with a free transfer in May 1978. He had offers from Chesterfield and Bournemouth, and he chose the South Coast club. He and his wife, Iris – their marriage blossomed from a first meeting at Oakwell when she was a 'Golden Girl' selling the club's Golden Goal lottery tickets – were provided with a home in Poole in a luxury residential area where a boy from Athersley Estate could never had dreamed of living. Almost every house had a yacht in its front garden; Poole Marina was two minutes' walk away, as was the beautiful Sandbanks beach.

Socially and domestically the Browns had two enjoyable years but, footballwise, the pleasure ended after the first season. Then the manager who signed him departed and the new boss brought in two midfielders from his previous club, and Kenny spent almost the whole of the following season in the reserves. He was then given a free transfer and was offered the post of player-manager of Poole Town FC. It was a job he would have loved to have had but the area was, without the benefit of the subsidized club house no longer available to him, too expensive for him to continue living there.

Consequently he and Iris, together with two-year-old Sarah, resumed occupation of their detached house at Ardsley which had been let during the sojourn in the South and Kenny took employment as a caretaker at the Barnsley College of Technology.

He is still there but has an underlying feeling of regret that having had the ability to win a place at grammar school, he allowed too great an imbalance to develop between the time he devoted to football and that allocated to his studies.

He continued in the professional game by joining Frickley Athletic in the Central Alliance. After a season there he moved into local football and had two seasons with Worsbrough Bridge, followed by two with Ward Green – in the first of which the team won the championship of Division One of the Barnsley and District League and were winners of the league's Sunday Cup.

He ceased to play in 1984, since which time he has not had any involvement in the game. He was then 32, and injuries sustained during his career had taken a yard off his pace and youngsters in the Barnsley League had started to catch him. There have always been some in local football who relish taking a kick at an ex-pro: it was bad enough being deliberately kicked when he was being paid to play, but he didn't fancy the prospect of a broken leg when he was supposed to be enjoying himself!

The majority of Kenny's seasons in the Barnsley first team were in Division Four during the darkest period in club history. Those were difficult times for all the players but particularly so for him – the division's midfielders were generally in excess of 12 stones and against such opposition a lightweight was greatly disadvantaged. Yet whereas the sheer bulk of an opponent could cause him problems, he used his own physical and mental attributes to maximum advantage. He could think quickly, had sound positional sense, was supremely fit and was a good all-round player. His constant value to the team is encapsulated in an unusual item of memorabilia he has from 1975: a poster from a *Green 'Un* bill-board which proclaimed 'BROWN'S SAVER FOR BARNSLEY' to the town's Saturday night community. He was what is known within the game as a Player's Player – one whom colleagues want in the side because of his industry, all-round value and ability to always be on hand to help out in difficult situations – and manager Jim Iley is on record as saying that at a time when the club was really struggling for survival, Kenny Brown was a vital cog in the team's midfield machinery.

Barry Murphy: Records Beyond Reach

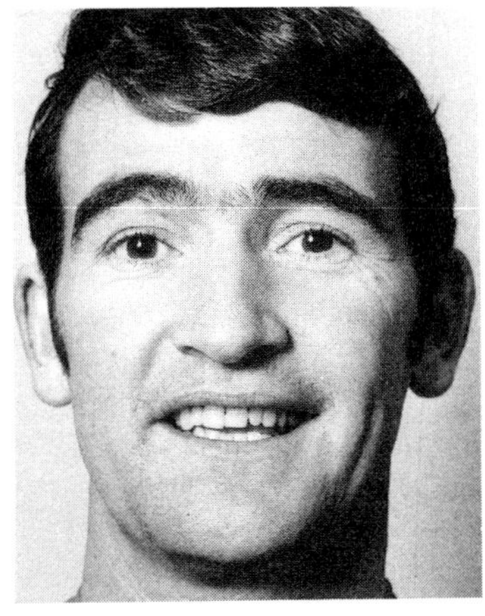

Barry Murphy holds the Barnsley club records in respect of total and consecutive games played – which have stood for 12 and 20 years respectively. His total of 564 is impressive in itself, but quite remarkable when one takes account of him not having a regular place in the side until he was 27 years old.

Born near Consett, he played school football at county level and then joined a colliery welfare team with the unlikely name of Morrison Busty. From there he moved to South Shields in the Northern Counties League to become the only amateur in a semi-professional side. His status enabled him to represent Durham in the Northern amateur championship and he helped them win the title in 1962.

In July of that year he became a professional with Barnsley and at that time he was a centre half. However, he was switched to full back almost immediately and in that position made his debut in September at Halifax Town. He played in about half of the games in that season but totalled only four in the next and for the following three years his appearances were spasmodic. Throughout almost all that time he captained the reserves. There were often as many as nine teenagers in the side, and manager John Steele was full of praise for the way in which Barry, by encouragement and cajolery, got the best out of them. At 27 he had almost come to accept that a regular place in the first team wasn't for him, but the breakthrough came on 18th May 1967. On that day against Notts County he began to string together his remarkable record of consecutive games.

On 7th April 1970 he bettered Harry Hough's record sequence of 176 appearances. By October he had totalled 199 – and with the magical double century available to him he was dropped in favour of a 17-year-old who hadn't previously played in the first team. He was not one who bothered about records and others had had to tell him when Hough's total was within reach. However, once that had been passed he naturally wanted to play as many more as he could and was particularly keen to reach 200. The disappointment of his omission against Doncaster Rovers on 31st October – incidentally, a home game which the Reds lost – was slightly lessened when Rovers' manager Laurie McMenemy walked past the trainer's bench and said, 'I'll tell you what, lad, I'm bloody glad you're sat here and aren't out there on the pitch!'

The highlight of Barry's 16 seasons at Oakwell was membership of the 1968 promotion side. That was the first occasion when he played in every game of a season – something he was to do a further four times.

As he approached his mid-thirties he had to accept that his days in the team might be numbered. Yet in August 1975, for the second time in consecutive seasons, after thinking he would be on the sidelines, he started the season in the side and played in almost every game. Indeed, he was an ever-present in 1976/77 and in the next, which saw his 38th birthday and the last of him as a player, he missed only three games in the whole campaign.

Barry was essentially a defensive player and, consequently, goals from him were few and far between. In fact, they averaged slightly less than one every five seasons! The first was against Luton Town in 1966. He had been chosen at outside right – his only appearance in the forward line – but moved to centre forward after an injury reshuffle and scored the opening goal in a 2 – 1 success. Three years later he was among the scorers in a 3 – 3 draw at Bristol Rovers and in February 1976 he scored from a penalty in a 3 – 1 win against Hartlepool. A month later his tally might have increased by more than 30 per-cent, but against Newport County a powerful spot-kick thundered against the bar – and rebounded almost to the half-way line!

In November 1975 he was appointed player-coach. Duties with reserves and juniors and playing in the first team gave him the best of both worlds, and under his direction the juniors were Northern Intermediate League champions and Cup-winners, and won a European knock-out competition in Germany. Later he took over as first team coach and retained the role for the remainder of his time at Oakwell.

The most significant happening of his career took place in October 1980. Then, Barnsley manager Allan Clarke was appointed to Leeds United and invited Barry to move there with him as coach. At first he couldn't believe it – and, having spent a playing career in the lower divisions, it was the nicest thing that had ever happened to him.

As he walked into the Elland Road ground he felt ten feet tall and that feeling of well-being remained with him throughout his years at the club. At his first training session there were 12 full internationals – and the whole squad did everything he asked of them. When he and Clarke arrived at Leeds the team were at the bottom of the First Division, yet at the season's end they were in a respectable ninth position. So far as Barry was concerned, just being involved at that level was an absolute joy for him. As coach he mixed with the highest in the game; he was in the dug-out at the most famous grounds in the land and saw his team draw at Anfield, Highbury and White Hart Lane, and win at Old Trafford and Goodison Park.

However, things didn't go as well in the following season, at the end of which Leeds were relegated and Clarke was dismissed. But Barry stayed. Indeed, he had created such good impressions that three directors sought his view on who should be the next manager. It had to be someone within the club and he recommended Eddie Gray – the man who got the job – and he continued as first team coach until the spring of 1984. Then his contract was about to expire and on 27th April Gray told him it would not be renewed. Going to Leeds had been his happiest day in football – this was the saddest. But he didn't regret anything. He'd had almost four years in soccer's big-time and had met everyone who was anyone in the game, and it had been the most enjoyable period of his professional life.

Having been with one of the biggest clubs in the land he couldn't bring himself to drop down again to football's more humdrum levels. He therefore decided to make a clean break and look for something outside the game. Ten weeks later he obtained employment with Barnsley Metropolitan Borough Council as Sports Development Officer at Penistone. There he organized coaching for every sporting interest, and among those who gave their services for the benefit of local young people were his former Elland Road club-mates Peter Barnes and Trevor Cherry, and Yorkshire cricketer Arnie Sidebottom. He generated such interest within the town that whereas he had started with a working week of 24 hours, when he moved on the Centre was operating a 13-hour day on six days each week. In 1988 he was promoted within the Council's Amenities and Recreation Department and is now required to maximize the use of all Community Centres within the Metropolitan Borough. Activities include sequence dancing, keep-fit classes and coaching in badminton, golf, and football. During each week of schools' annual summer holiday he arranges for a coach-load of older children to have a conducted tour of one of the major Football League grounds – and his influence is such that the conducting is usually done by the club manager.

Whilst his original intention was not to be again involved in football and he turned down offers of coaching jobs with Blackburn Rovers and Huddersfield Town, old habits die hard. After 12 months his resolve had weakened sufficiently for him to accept an opponent assessing/scouting role with Blackburn which was retained for three years. Then followed a year in the same capacity with York City until 1988 when he joined Nottingham Forest. Their first approach was for him to organize a School of Soccer Excellence in the Barnsley area. It meant, in effect, that he would have been running a Forest nursery side – something right up his street but which, after considering all the implications, he decided would require almost as much involvement as he'd previously had and which he had decided he no longer wanted. Instead he settled for a scouting role and now, every Saturday in the season, he attends a League game with a brief to identify players suitable for Nottingham Forest.

Despite having lived in Barnsley continuously for nearly 30 years he has retained his membership of Consett Victoria Working Men's Club. Recently he was there when someone who had known him since his boyhood said, 'You know, Barry, you're no different from when you lived here.' That really is Barry Murphy. An honest, genuine nature and infectious enthusiasm helped him become as popular in the First Division as he had been in the Third and Fourth – and native characteristics were apparent in his coaching, for he told players the truth and treated them all the same. As a member of an often struggling side at Oakwell he was not excluded from the sarcasm which was, at times, directed at almost everyone on the pitch. But doubtless the supporters had attitude as much as ability in mind when he became Oakwell's Player of the Year in 1972 – for in winning the accolade he received the highest number of votes ever recorded.

Resilience and supreme fitness contributed towards Barry's remarkable achievement of never missing a single game through injury in his entire career. Almost six feet tall and hefty with it, he was a natural defender who knew his limitations; he never over-elaborated and was fast enough to catch any winger he played against. It has now long been financially advantageous for players to move regularly between clubs and, consequently, there is little likelihood of his total games for Barnsley being improved upon. So far as the long consecutive run is concerned, the irony of being omitted from the side on 31st October 1970 is that he was brought back for the next game and made a further 95 consecutive appearances – missing only that single game in five-and-a-half years. Even so, his 199 consecutive games are almost unassailable and surely no man was every more deserving of being a record holder than Barry Murphy.

Brian Joicey: Highest Since The Record

Despite playing in the First Division with Coventry City and having some memorable moments with Sheffield Wednesday and Barnsley, Brian Joicey considers the high-point of his years in football came while he was an amateur with North Shields. That is understandable, for to be the match-winner in a team success at Wembley Stadium – as he was in the 1969 Amateur Cup final – must be the peak of every footballer's ambition.

Brian was born in the Durham village of Winlaton and as a schoolboy centre half he represented Blaydon Boys. From the age of 15 he had three seasons with Clara Vale – a local under-18 side which had produced such distinguished players as 'Pop' Robson, Frank Clark and Howard Kendall. It was while with Clara Vale that he became a centre forward and thereafter, except for a brief period during his time with Sheffield Wednesday, he had a striker's role in every team in which he played. Between the ages of 18 and 21 his several clubs included Ashington, Blyth Spartans and Tow Law, and in 1967 he joined North Shields whose manager, Frank Brennan, had been centre half in Newcastle United's FA Cup-winning teams of 1951 and 1952.

The second season with North Shields was particularly successful: the club won a league championship and three cups, and Brian's name was on the score-sheet on 44 occasions. In the Amateur Cup, his two goals against Skelmersdale United in a replayed semi-final took the side to Wembley on 12th April 1969. In that impressive arena, with 10 minutes of the game remaining, he rounded two defenders and hit the winning goal, and the Newcastle-upon-Tyne *Journal* said it was appropriate that the goal came from the game's outstanding player.

But North Shields' season was by no means over. They still had eight games to play in the Northern League; all were won, and they ended the season as Amateur Cup winners, League champions, and winners of the Northern League Cup and Northumberland Senior Cup.

After the Amateur Cup final he had offers from half-a-dozen clubs. Eventually he decided on Coventry City and remained with them for two years and, although he never commanded a regular place, he scored some important goals. In December 1969 he netted twice in a win at Crystal Palace; in the following April he got the winning goal at Wolves; another winner came in January 1971 against Ipswich Town and in Coventry's first experience of European football he scored in a 2 – 0 win against a Bulgarian side, Trakia Plovdiv.

In August 1971 Sheffield Wednesday obtained him for £55,000. Although the move took him out of the First Division he saw it as an opportunity for regular first team football with an even bigger club. At Hillsborough he was top-scorer in three consecutive seasons. Memorable moments in the first campaign were his 30-yard drive into the top of the net against Fulham, winning goals against Burnley and Watford, and a hat-trick against Orient.

In the 1973 FA Cup a fourth round second replay against First Division Crystal Palace took place at Villa Park, where Brian's hat-trick included the winning goal in extra time. However, the season ended with Wednesday escaping relegation by but a single point. In the following year they weren't so lucky, and there was further personal disappointment in that, for the first time since joining the club, he no longer had a regular place in the side. After appearing spasmodically at the beginning of 1975/76 he played at centre half in the reserves, making only one first team appearance in the second half of the season.

In the spring he was given a free transfer and had offers from Bristol City, Hartlepool and Barnsley. Barnsley's wasn't the best, but moving to Oakwell had the advantage of enabling him to remain in the area.

In his first season his 25 League goals made him the highest scorer in the Fourth Division and he did the hat-trick against Boston United in the FA Cup. Yet to this day he maintains the total should have been higher. He didn't get his name on the score-sheet until the seventh game, during which time manager Jim Iley, perhaps trying to prevent his new signing becoming depressed by the number of shots which weren't finding the net, wagered £50 that he wouldn't score 20 goals in the season. It was the kind of challenge that no striker worth his salt could ignore, and by the third week in January he had scored 18. Then Rochdale came to Oakwell. In the 15th minute he scored the first goal; on its way into the net the ball struck a defender on the line but there was no doubt in the minds of the Barnsley team that it was Brian's goal and he gleefully accepted their congratulations. However, when it was mentioned at the post-match press briefing, Iley, for whatever reason, said, 'Put it down as an own goal.' And that's how it appears in League records. Brian was a long time in forgiving Iley for what seemed an unthinking response, yet there was no ill-will on the manager's part when, four days later, he handed over what was, in effect, an extra week's wage after Brian had scored his second goal in a 3 – 1 defeat of Bournemouth.

He was again top scorer in 1977/78, but in the following season there occurred one of the saddest happenings in the club's history. On 11th November 1978 Barnsley visited York City – the venue of Brian's debut three years earlier and, sadly, where he was to play his last game. Immediately prior to half-time he was tackled in the York penalty-area and sustained a violent blow over the kidneys. The pain was excruciating and during the interval he passed blood. The club doctor was present and gave him some pain-killing tablets; he took no further part in the game and was ordered to go to bed on arriving home.

By Wednesday his condition had, in every respect, worsened. He telephoned the doctor and within the hour had been admitted to hospital, and he remained there for the following 10 days. Two weeks later, on 6th December, he was in the Mothercare store in Sheffield with his wife and child when he suddenly had the frightening realization that he couldn't speak. Ushering the surprised Sue and 18-month-old Philippa outside, his frantic thoughts were to reach his parked car. Sue tried to get him to sit down in the shop next-door, but he wouldn't – all he could think of was getting to the car and the security it seemed to offer. But two hundred yards up the road he lost the use of his limbs and collapsed onto the pavement outside, ironically, the Gateway to Health Club.

An ambulance was summoned and he was taken to the Royal Hallamshire Hospital. He had had a stroke, and medical opinion was that it had been caused by blood from damaged kidneys reaching the brain. The use returned to his limbs after a few hours, but almost two months elapsed before his speech improved sufficiently to be understood. Therapy continued for almost a year, and now no-one would know that speaking had been a problem. But he says that as a Geordie in Yorkshire, no-one had ever understood him very well, anyway!

Eighteen months after onset of the illness he asked the consultant if he could start footballing again. He didn't hope to play professionally but was delighted to be told the risk was minimal and if he wanted to play he should do so, with the proviso that he didn't overdo it.

He began with a pub team, the Royal Oak at Coal Aston, and later had part-time professional spells with Frickley Athletic and Matlock Town. His final club was Bakewell FC in the Hope Valley League, and while with them he was sent off for the first time in his career. It happened, of all places, at Dronfield where he lives and resulted from a comment to the referee. He felt the latter over-reacted, and there seemed to be sympathy for him at the disciplinary hearing but the chairman said they had to back their referees and imposed a £20 fine and a one-month suspension. The injustice of it all upset him so much that he told them he would never play in their league again – and he didn't. Present involvements are at lower levels but, at times, equally as competitive. He is centre half in the John Quinn All-Stars and plays in a weekly seven-a-side competition at Dronfield – and, as his long-time pal Peter Springett says, 'He still kicks lumps off everybody in sight!' Yet, proving he can adapt to whatever present company requires, he spends one evening each week coaching the 4th Dronfield Cubs. He impresses on them the importance of working hard at everything they want to be good at, and a one-pound coin is the reward for every boy who can tap a ball into the air 20 consecutive times.

Brian's recovery from his illness was so remarkable that the hospital arranged for him to write about his experience in the Chest, Heart and Stroke Association's quarterly publication *Hope – a magazine of optimism*. As the title indicates, its aim is to encourage patients to strive for as complete a recovery as possible, and contributors recount their own experience as an example of what can be accomplished. Brian's considerable achievement came from an absolute determination to recover for the sake of Sue and their two children.

A year before leaving Oakwell and with an eye to the future, he bought a partnership in a car sales business in Middlewood Road, Sheffield. There were obvious advantages in promoting a man who was so well known in local sporting circles and, renamed Brian Joicey Motors, the company flourished for a further two-and-a-half years until the national steelworkers' strike in 1981. In a district heavily populated by employees of BSC's Stocksbridge Works, the company was one of many which were unable to survive 14 weeks' unemployment. But the expertise he'd acquired was to stand him in good stead. He joined the staff of GT Cars in Suffolk Road, Sheffield and, starting in second-hand sales, he progressed to new cars and then to management of the Fleet Department. He is responsible for sales to business users; promoted in 1986 to what was a new department, in four years he has seen sales grow to 400 units per year.

After Brian's lean spell at Hillsborough it was a delight for him to find in Jim Iley another manager who had confidence in him. He responded magnificently. The 28 goals in his opening Oakwell season was not only the highest individual total in the division but is the most from any Barnsley player since Cecil McCormack created the club record in 1951. It was befitting that he became Player of the Year and was chosen by his fellow-professionals for the PFA Fourth Division side, and another achievement within that personally very successful first season was his hat-trick in the FA Cup – which became the third such event in club history and the only one within the last 60 years.

Alan Little: A Phrase Which Said It All

Alan Little's football career began as an Aston Villa apprentice in 1970. Twenty years and seven clubs on he is chief coach at York City and the high-point of his career to date is membership of Barnsley's 1979 promotion side. His wholehearted, no-quarter-asked-nor-given style made him a favourite at all his clubs and nowhere more than at Barnsley where he was the Supporters' Club Player of the Year when the Reds crossed the first hurdle on the way to their present position within the Football League.

Born at Newbiggin, Northumberland – where the Milburns and Charltons were raised – the place is a hotbed of football and Alan was steeped in it from boyhood. He and elder brother Brian were destined for Villa Park at an early age and trained there during every school holiday from reaching 13. His schooling ended on a Friday afternoon in July 1970, and on the Monday morning he was an apprentice professional footballer sharing digs with his brother near Villa Park. Four years later he won a place in the first team, but whereas Brian spent more than 10 years with Villa, Alan was less fortunate. He played only a handful of games but it fell to him to score the goal which put the team into the semi-final of the 1975 Football League Cup, from which they went on to win the trophy.

He had a lot of respect for manager Ron Saunders and, although it came as a great disappointment, he accepted his judgement that he wasn't going to become a First Division footballer. In late December – only three weeks after his success in the League Cup quarter-final – he was transferred to Southend United. He looked upon the move as a challenge and, hopefully, a stepping-stone back into Division One.

Memories of the first week at Southend will always remain with him. He began it by playing a vital part in the team's drawn FA Cup-tie at Queen's Park Rangers. Two days later he dashed to Birmingham to be married. On the following day he was in London for the Cup replay, and on the Saturday he gave Southend victory over Brighton with a fine left-foot shot from the edge of the penalty-area.

By then the surging runs and all-round aggression which were to delight the

Oakwell crowds featured prominently in his play. And events proved he could take what he handed out. In a game at Grimsby in March 1976 his nose was broken only seconds before half-time and at the interval he left the field with blood streaming from the injury. Ten minutes later almost everyone was surprised to see him reappear with the rest of the team. Afterwards manager Arthur Rowley said, 'He's a tough lad, he just pushed his nose back into place and carried on!'

Alan arrived at Oakwell in the summer of 1978 in exchange for a modest fee of £6,000. His first games were League Cup-ties which the Reds lost on aggregate to Chesterfield, but on the opening of the League programme he was quickly on the mark with the first goal in a 4 – 0 beating of Rochdale. However, it took some time for him to get properly into his stride. At first he was used wide in midfield where he was not seen at his best, and he was left out of the side for a couple of games in October. He returned at the end of the month for a 3 – 2 win over Hartlepool United, and in a more favoured central midfield role he played with an authority and conviction which immediately earned the fans' esteem. A few weeks later the match-report in *The Star* on a 4 – 1 win against Reading referred to him striding through the game like a colossus, scoring twice, making the final goal and tackling with a ferocity which had the visitors in a continual state of shock.

The following season, that of 1978/79, proved to be the best of all his years in the game. He was among the scorers on the opening day in a 4 – 0 victory over Halifax Town. Three weeks later he gave the team their fifth successive win with a 30-yard goal against Scunthorpe United which the *Barnsley Chronicle* described as 'fitting reward for a magnificent display of midfield power and aggression'.

On the last day of September Reading were beaten 3 – 1 and Brian opened the scoring with a tremendous goal from a free-kick outside the penalty-area, the sheer power of the shot leaving the goalkeeper groping hopelessly at thin air. His displays continued at that level throughout the season, and at the end of it Barnsley were promoted; Alan was voted the Supporters' Club Player of the Year and his fellow professionals allocated him a place in the PFA Fourth Division side.

He played in the first six matches in Division Three, the last of which was a 2 – 0 defeat at Bramall Lane. The game attracted a deluge of letters to *The Star* from annoyed Sheffield United supporters who had taken exception to what they regarded as Barnsley's overly robust style of play. At that time manager Allan Clarke had a weekly column in the newspaper in which, in referring to the game at Bramall Lane and the fans' reaction, he said, ' . . . I have a player called Alan Little whose strength is going in hard but fair for the ball. I wish all my players were like him . . . I'd like to see all my back four and midfield more like Alan Little . . . '

Yet on the night of that same edition of *The Star*, in speaking to the press after Barnsley's win at Blackburn Rovers, Clarke announced that Alan would be leaving the club! The player had been told earlier in the day that he no longer figured in the manager's plans; the intention was to replace him with Ian Banks and the midfield would be completed by an incoming player – in the event, Mike Lester – whose signing was imminent. Alan was absolutely shattered, the possibility of having to leave so quickly after two such good seasons had been the last thing on his mind. On the Friday the manager expounded further in the *Barnsley Chronicle*: 'Alan Little did a tremendous job for us last season and I am the first to acknowledge the part he played in winning promotion. But he no longer figures in my plans.' Yet Alan bore no ill-will and, looking back from the level of the game at which he now operates, he knows it is the kind of judgement that managers have to be continually making. Nevertheless, it was a wrench to leave Oakwell.

In the following week he had talks at Aldershot but at the last minute decided against going there. A few days later Frank Burrows, manager of Fourth Division leaders Portsmouth, rang him with an offer of a three-year contract and a wage double what he was receiving at Barnsley. He set off for Portsmouth to discuss the matter in detail but turned round at Birmingham and returned home – he liked living in the North and having already sampled the South he didn't fancy going there again. Not unexpectedly, on the following day he received a 250-mile verbal assault from a very annoyed football manager!

In December a fee of £30,000 took him to Doncaster Rovers. There manager Billy Bremner had assembled a young, quick team who made up in fitness for what they might have lacked in skill. The training was harder than anything Alan had experienced; although only 24 he was behind the others at almost everything – and he suffered. But he gave everything he'd got and was eventually able to do all that was expected of him.

In his second season at Doncaster he was again a member of a side which won promotion into the Third Division. However, a badly damaged left knee kept him out of the team for much of season 1981/82 and at one stage there were fears that his playing days were over. Six months elapsed before he could begin light training and his absence was a major factor in Rovers making a quick return to Division Four.

He returned to the side in April 1982, in October being part of a player-exchange deal which took him to Torquay United where manager Bruce Rioch – an Aston Villa player when Alan was an apprentice – appointed him captain. He loved being there. It was a delightful place in which to live; he had a good social life and the team did well, having a spell in the top three and a good run in the FA Cup. But the stay in the South-West was shorter than he'd hoped. At the start of the following season the club was desperately short of cash and Rioch insisted Alan had to be transferred. At first he refused – and the manager applied the ultimate sanction: 'You've got to go. If you don't, I shan't play you, anyway!'

Therefore, in November 1983 Torquay recouped £12,000 by transferring him to Halifax Town. Two years later he was on the move again, having been given the first free transfer of his career. He agreed terms with Peterborough United. The local press anticipated the signing and carried a feature on him, but he was then told there had to be an outgoing transfer before he could be taken on and he'd have to wait a month for things to be finalized. Having been in the game too long to take anything for granted, he returned to his native North-East and signed for Hartlepool United.

But he had a disastrous start. In August a broken leg put him out of the side until mid-March, yet the mishap provided an unexpected opportunity to continue in the game in another capacity. While rehabilitating from the injury he assumed responsibility for the apprentices. It gave him something to think about other than himself and lightened the load of coach John Bird. Not having previously considered a coaching role, he found he liked it. At the season's end he was appointed to assist Bird, and when the latter became manager in October 1986 Alan succeeded him as first team coach.

In November two years later the two of them moved, as manager and coach, to York City. The club then held 91st position in the Football League, but things soon started to improve. The team's resurgence included an away victory over the eventual champions, Rotherham United, and they ended the season in the top half of the table. The wide ranging responsibilities of management have been an eye opener for Alan but he relishes every moment of his new challenge. York City is a club with lots of potential and it's not all that long since it moved from Fourth to Second Division within four seasons – an objective which the Bird/Little partnership is now working towards.

Alan Little's attributes were the accuracy of his passing and great physical strength, in which respect he reckoned he could get the better of any opponent. On realizing his career was likely to be in the lower divisions he knew it would be to his advantage to move between clubs frequently – and although that in itself brought no great financial reward it enables him and his family to live exceptionally well. His style was admired at all his clubs and being a Player of the Year with five consecutive teams – Southend, Barnsley, Doncaster, Torquay and Halifax – must be something of a record.

At Oakwell his dominant, take-no-prisoners approach was ideal for the needs of the time. The supporters loved it, and the *Barnsley Chronicle* report of his eventual transfer contained an action picture of him with a caption, 'Thanks for the Memory, Alan' – a phrase which echoed the thoughts of thousands who had been excited by his commitment and saddened by his departure.

Peter Springett: A Triple Celebration

The annals of our national game make special reference to Peter and Ron Springett as the only brothers ever to form an exchange transfer between League clubs. The switch took Peter into the First Division with Sheffield Wednesday and to England under-23 honours, and his class was always apparent during his stay at Barnsley when he missed only two games in four seasons. In fact, manager Allan Clarke – not a man to give praise lightly – said during the push towards promotion in 1974 that he was one of the finest goalkeepers in the country.

A Londoner and the youngest of six children, as a boy he had no aspirations to be a goalkeeper and represented West London schools as a winger and a centre forward. It was in a schools training session that he deputized in goal and thus started on the road which led to 17 seasons in professional football.

Becoming an apprentice with Queen's Park Rangers at 15, in the following year he won English youth international honours and made his debut in the first team. At 18 he had a regular place and every encouragement to do well, for brother Ron had earlier moved from Rangers to Sheffield Wednesday but continued to live and train in London. It was an arrangement beneficial to Peter, for it allowed him – a young man filled with enthusiasm and ambition – to train in the company of the then England goalkeeper.

Even though he later played regularly in the First Division, season 1966/67 with QPR in Division Three was the highpoint of his long career. He played in every game and the team won the championship by 12 points. And at Wembley Stadium on 4th March, in front of nearly 100,000 spectators, they beat West Bromwich Albion to become the first Third Division side to win the Football League Cup.

The close-season saw the unique exchange of goalkeeping brothers when Wednesday, paying for potential as well as skill, swapped £26,000 and a former England player for a man who showed every indication of soon becoming one. For Peter it became a particularly memorable summer: not only did he join a First Division club but he visited Mexico with his new colleagues and toured Bulgaria, Turkey and Greece with the England under-23 party.

In December of that year he won his first under-23 cap and, in all, represented his country on six occasions. At that time he was senior to both Ray Clemence and Peter Shilton who later shared the goalkeeping position in the full international side, yet Clemence's first appearance at under-23 level only came about because Peter wasn't available for one particular game.

With Sheffield Wednesday he went straight into the first team and held his place continuously for two-and-a-half seasons, quickly overcoming the challenge of succeeding a man whom the supporters had idolized. Then came Scunthorpe United. In January 1970 the FA Cup took the Fourth Division side to Hillsborough and it would have been unrealistic if the Wednesday players hadn't been optimistic about the outcome. So much so that Peter, in anticipation of a £50 win bonus, visited Cole Brothers' department store and laid aside an expensive safari jacket that he'd had his eye on for some time. In the event he didn't get the jacket nor did he keep his place, for after a surprise 2 – 1 defeat his club paid a big fee to obtain Peter Grummitt from Nottingham Forest.

It marked the beginning of a long, and sometimes dispiriting spell of reserve team football. From being an ever-present in his first two-and-a-half seasons, in the next two-and-a-half he played only seven times. Frustrations came to a head in a Central League game against Everton when he was sent off for arguing with the referee – something he thought goalkeepers could get away with but, to his cost, found they couldn't.

But better times were on the horizon. He deputized for Grummitt in four games at the end of 1972 and again in the final four games of the season, following which the other was transferred. Therefore, at the start of the 1973/74 season Peter was back in the team, but a self-inflicted absence came in January when, after a 3 – 3 draw at Carlisle, the referee took exception to something he said as the teams were leaving the pitch. The result was a three-match suspension, during which the club borrowed former Scottish international Bob Ferguson from West Ham. When Peter was again available, much to his dismay, Ferguson remained in the team – a situation which angered some supporters who bombarded *The Star* with letters urging his reinstatement. That took place at Notts County on 9th March, and Wednesday won 5 – 1 after he had saved a penalty at a crucial stage of the game. He remained in the side until the end of the year, but he'd had feelings of uncertainty ever since Steve Burtenshaw became manager in January. Peter just couldn't get on with him; he didn't again play in the first team and in the following summer – that of 1975 – he was given a free transfer. His departure signalled the end of an era for Sheffield Wednesday, as for the first time in more than 17 years there was not a Springett at Hillsborough.

It was surprising that a fee wasn't required for a 29-year-old goalkeeper of his ability. However, Barnsley managers have never looked gift horses in the mouth and Jim Iley quickly used the situation to his advantage. Peter's first game was a friendly at Oakwell on 11th August against a Maltese side, Gudja United, which the Reds won 16 – 0. His League debut came five days later in the season's opening game when Watford were beaten 1 – 0, and he went on to make 125 appearances. Reporting the Watford game in *The Star*, Brian Steer said Peter turned in a magnificent display with three saves right out of the top drawer and immaculate timing to cut out a succession of dangerous centres.

Thereafter he regularly had headlines in the sporting press. Steer again awarded him 'Star' rating in a 1 – 1 game at Cambridge when a penalty save was supplemented by two others of the highest class, and he was *Daily Mirror* Man of the Match against Southend United when the reporter said that but for his splendid goalkeeping the visitors would have built up an unassailable lead by the time Barnsley realized they had a game on their hands. Similarly, in a *Barnsley Chronicle* report on a 2 – 0 victory at Darlington, Keith Lodge said that only a series of super saves by Peter prevented the home side being four up before the Reds started to play.

Season 1978/79 was his happiest since leaving London. A crucial moment in what became a promotion campaign was his 85th minute penalty save at Huddersfield Town which helped provide Barnsley with maximum points. That was doubtless one of the incidents behind comments which Brian Steer had in mind when he said in his column in the *Green 'Un* that, wherever he went in connection with Barnsley's matches, other reporters were continually telling him that Peter was the best goalkeeper in the lower divisions. Manager Allan Clarke went even further, and Clarke's predecessor Jim Iley, in explaining the absence of experienced goalkeeping cover to an Annual General Meeting, said Peter was so consistently good that it was impossible to find a mature goalkeeper prepared to come to Oakwell to play in his shadow.

Promotion was secured by victory over Grimsby Town on 8th May 1979. So far as Peter was concerned, the celebration couldn't have come on a more appropriate day, for it was the occasion of his 500th League game and also his birthday – an anniversary which he stoutly maintained was his twenty-eighth but, in reality, was his thirty-third.

In the summer Barnsley signed goalkeeper Gary Pierce from Wolves and Peter knew they wouldn't have paid £35,000 for someone they intended to use in the reserves. He was quite right, and for the first time since joining the club he found himself in the second team. In Pierce's injury-absence he returned to the side at the beginning of November and had considerable joy from being part of the Reds' 2 – 0 success at Hillsborough, and he kept his place until the end of December.

Peter's career saw several exceptionally high scoring games, not all of which were in his team's favour. He was in a QPR side which won 7 – 1 at Mansfield Town and in a Barnsley team which recorded an identical score at Darlington. On the other side of the coin, there was an occasion when he picked the ball out of the QPR net *eight* times in a League Cup match at Middlesbrough. Shortly before his transfer to Sheffield Wednesday he was drafted into an England team for what was then an annual eve-of-FA Cup final game against Young England. The senior side were beaten 5 – 0, and the Wednesday manager, Alan Brown, watched the game and still signed him!

Yet it was a heavy defeat which effectively terminated his stay at Oakwell. His spell in the first team ended with a 7 – 0 debacle at Reading on 29th December 1979. The manager held him responsible for two of the goals and promptly excluded him from the first team squad. Thereafter he trained with the juniors and, knowing full well that the season's end would not bring a renewal of his contract, he made enquiries about moving elsewhere. Eventually he provisionally agreed to join a club in Sweden. He would have lived in Stockholm and, with a house and car provided, he and his family would have had a higher standard of living than ever before. But on informing Allan Clarke what he had in mind he was told that the club was to exercise an option on his contract and had no intention of releasing him. He therefore gave back word to the Swedes – and three days later, by which time it was too late to resurrect the earlier arrangement, he was given a free transfer. And it wasn't the first time he'd been disadvantaged by a transfer that didn't reach fruition. In 1972, during the long, lean spell with Sheffield Wednesday, the manager told him he was to be transferred to Aston Villa. He put the family home – a detached residence overlooking Dore and Totley golf course – on the market and when the sale had reached a point of no return he was told the transfer had been called off.

On leaving Oakwell he joined Scarborough in the Alliance Premier League, but he was already considering a career outside football. His father-in-law and step-mother-in-law had been police officers and for some time there had been family encouragement to begin that kind of career. Consequently he applied to the South Yorkshire Police and was appointed constable in December 1981. Yet his previous occupation is constantly in view for, as a Community Constable patrolling the Highfields district of Sheffield, he works from a police station situated inside Bramall Lane football ground. It goes almost without saying that he has duties there on match days, but his responsibilities extend much further afield than that. There is an arrangement between the club and the chief constable that local officers travel to away games to assist the host force in identifying possible trouble-causers among the visiting supporters, and it is a duty which Peter regularly performs. It has proved a worthwhile exercise, for the fans are aware of the police presence and the good rapport which has been established has helped towards there now rarely being any trouble from them.

His own football involvement is limited to Sunday games with the John Quinn All-Stars and a weekly seven-a-side game at Dronfield in a team which includes his former team-mate Brian Joicey and former Rotherham United manager Emlyn Hughes. Squash also forms part of his keep-fit routine, and for the last 20 years summertime Saturday afternoons have been spent keeping wicket for the cricket team at his local pub – the Green Dragon at Dronfield.

He thinks joining the South Yorkshire Police is the best thing he has ever done. He enjoys the work so much that he looks forward to starting each day and his only regret is that he didn't join until he was 34 years old. Yet he wouldn't have wanted to miss the years spent in football. Although he didn't achieve full international status he reckons, philosophically, that it was no disgrace to be kept out of the national side by Gordon Banks, and the game took him all over Europe and into South America – and a week in Acapulco has, apparently, to be experienced to be believed. It also provided representative honours, membership of promotion-winning teams, seasons in the First Division and the euphoria of being in a Cup-winning team at Wembley Stadium. With that kind of background and still under 30, Peter Springett may well have been the best free transfer player that Barnsley has ever had.

Alistair Millar: The Headline Maker

Ali Millar is a Glaswegian and throughout his formative years his ambition was to play football for Rangers. At 17 he joined a local side, Benburb; his only reason for doing so was that their ground was adjacent to Ibrox Park – yet he had to travel on three buses to get there. He later had more than nine seasons with Barnsley, but it took the persuasions of another Glaswegian and the realization that Rangers weren't going to have him before he finally agreed to move to Oakwell. As an attacking midfielder his style was reminiscent of another homesick Scot, Jimmy Baxter, and, like Baxter who once couldn't get back to Scotland quickly enough, he gives every indication that he will spend the rest of his life in Barnsley.

As a pupil at East Bank Academy he played football for Glasgow Boys. On leaving school he became an apprentice electrician with Glasgow Corporation, but he hated it – all he could think of was footballing with Rangers. Post-school Saturday afternoons were with Eastcraig, one of the best amateur clubs on Clydeside, and at 17 he was a part-time professional with Benburb.

While with the club he had offers from Airdrieonians and Clyde and he trained on two evenings each week with Kilmarnock. All were in the First Division but were part-time clubs – and he was determined to be a full-time player. In January 1971 he had a trial in the Second Division with Hamilton Academical, scoring one goal and making another in a 2 – 2 draw with Stenhousemuir. After the game he almost allowed himself to accept part-time terms when Hamilton manager Bobby Shearer – himself a former Rangers' player – said he would get him transferred to Rangers within six months. It was only when the Benburb manager interposed with, 'Don't listen to him, he says that to them all' that Ali remembered his resolve to await an offer of full-time terms.

A step towards eventual fulfilment of his hopes came a few weeks later when a Barnsley scout watched Benburb's success in the quarter-finals of the Scottish Junior Cup. Trials were arranged at Oakwell, and Ali travelled from Glasgow by train. At a point in the journey when he knew he was nearing his destination, the train reached a large built-up area which he thought was big enough to be Barnsley, but then he discovered he was at Leeds. On arriving in Barnsley he just couldn't believe the town had only a two-platform railway station. He compared it with the big and busy Glasgow Central which he knew well, and he wondered where on earth he'd come to.

He stayed at the Rockingham Villa Hotel near Oakwell, and two days later he played in a reserve game – then promptly returned to Glasgow. Manager John Steele was soon on the 'phone to him and, with a great deal of reluctance, he returned to Barnsley. But he hated the place. He was lonely and could hardly understand a word of what anyone said. And no-one seemed to understand him, either. So, after one more reserve game, back he went to Scotland. This time Steele travelled to the Millar family home and, relating his own experience, was able to convince dad that his only son would not only be well cared for in Barnsley but, eventually, might even like being there. Once dad was on the manager's side, Alistair couldn't hold out much longer. On that day, Sunday 28th February 1971, he became a full-time professional footballer with Barnsley. Two days later he returned to the town and in the evening made the short journey with the first team to Rotherham and a final of the Sheffield and Hallamshire County Cup. He was a revelation. Playing as though he'd been in Barnsley's midfield for years, he was always available in space, he was eager for the ball, he covered in defence and was frequently up having a crack at goal, he sprayed accurate passes all over the pitch and never put a foot wrong. After the game Steele enthused to the press, 'Now you can see why I raced to Scotland to sign him before anyone else snapped him up.' On the Saturday he made his home debut in a 2 – 2 draw with Rochdale. Again his performance delighted the fans and he was applauded off the pitch at half-time and again at the end of the game.

A month into the next season, in reporting another draw with Rochdale, the *Morning Telegraph* likened Ali's attacking flair to such immortals as Danny Blanchflower and George Best. And during the following seven years there were many occasions when 'Millar Magic' headlined the Reds' match reports. In December 1972, in a beating of Hartlepool, he dispossessed a defender, slipped a tackle and beat the goalkeeper with a spectacular 20-yard drive into the top of the net. His 100th game was in March 1974 in a 3 – 1 win against Gillingham when Michael Morgan wrote in the *Daily Express* that Ali had given one of the finest midfield displays that he had seen in any division that season. And in April – again against Hartlepool – he provided the game's one moment of real class by slipping past two defenders with a cheeky hip waggle and blasting in a spectacular opening goal. Yet in the following year Keith Lodge of the *Barnsley Chronicle* was perhaps reflecting the supporters' frustrations when, referring to a Boxing Day victory over Rochdale, he described him as 'the enigmatic Scot who could be the most exciting player in the division if only he would add a touch of steely consistency to his undoubted but wayward talents'. Lodge went on to say that Ali had produced a Christmas parcel of sheer magic and delighted the crowd with a superb winning goal by wriggling past two defenders and screwing the ball into the net like an expert snooker player triumphantly potting the final black. Another year on, at Brentford, he made the winning goal out of nothing by robbing a defender, rolling the ball back with the sole of his boot to evade a retrieving challenge, doing a little shuffle to send another defender the wrong way and slotting the ball ever so neatly past the advancing goalkeeper. And at Halifax Town two months later he had the home defence almost continually at panic stations as he carved out opening after opening – one of which provided John Peachey with the winning goal.

The biggest disappointment he ever had was when manager Allan Clarke broke up the 1979 promotion side. In October after more than 300 first team games he was replaced by an incomer, although it must be said that by then he'd put on about a stone-and-a-half in weight and wasn't as mobile as he'd previously been.

In the spring of 1980 he was given a free transfer and the first approach he received was from Hull City. Their assistant manager watched him in a reserve game and invited him and his wife, Jackie, to visit Boothferry Park to talk terms with manager Mike Smith. They did so, and the manager couldn't have been more hospitable. A two-year contract and top wages were agreed, and Smith was to bring the contract to Oakwell for signature after the game which Hull were to play there on the following Saturday. Before the Millars left the manager's office they were handed a copy of a local newspaper on which Smith had marked properties which were for sale in areas where he thought they would like to live. At the end of the match at Oakwell Ali went to the visitors' tea room but there was no sign of Smith. He hung about for an hour but the manager was nowhere to be found and, despite contract and terms being agreed and desirable residences recommended, Ali never heard another word from him.

In July he turned down an opportunity to play in Australia and, instead, joined York City. But he couldn't have made a worse start. In a pre-season practice he damaged ankle ligaments, the results of which were as bad as if he'd broken a leg. He was out of the side until Christmas, but the effects of the injury were such that he couldn't hold a place in the team and in February his contract was cancelled.

Thereafter his football involvements were brief in the extreme. He spent the spring of 1981 playing indoor soccer in the United States with Phoenix Inferno and Baltimore Blast. When the domestic season began he had spells with Matlock and Worksop Town, but these were curtailed by the old ankle injury. In the following season he went into local football with Ward Green FC, but his system was geared to kicking-off at three o'clock on Saturday afternoons and somehow he couldn't come to terms with Sunday morning football. That could have been overcome if the will had been there, but he wasn't prepared to tolerate the 'nut cases' who go out of their way to inflict verbal and physical abuse on anyone whose abilities they can never hope to equal. Therefore his stay at Ward Green, Barnsley, was as brief as the time spent in Phoenix, Arizona!

In August 1985 he began another association with Barnsley FC. His pal, Ronnie Glavin, had been appointed youth team coach and he invited Ali to be his assistant. The arrangement lasted for seven months until Glavin's unexpected dismissal brought his own involvement to an end. But their partnership continues. Ronnie now works for Port Vale, scouting and reporting on future opponents, and Ali accompanies him on weekly journeys throughout the country. He also shares Glavin's involvement with soccer camps, coaching at weekends at towns in northern England and Scotland.

Alistair Millar was a player with tremendous natural ability. He had good control and vision, and the merest flick of the hips slipped him almost nonchalantly past defenders. But by his own admission he hadn't much of a right foot and his heading did leave something to be desired. Those deficiencies must be the reason why his career was spent almost entirely in the Fourth Division – a level at which a talented left foot such as his can rarely have been seen. With hindsight he regrets not having worked harder to bring other skills up to the standard of those which nature bestowed upon him, and John Steele is in no doubt that a little more dedication would have taken Ali Millar to one of the country's leading clubs and into the Scottish international side.

Trevor Aylott: The Goal Of The Century

As a member of the Barnsley team which won promotion in 1981 and ended the following season in sixth place in the Second Division, Trevor Aylott was a leading figure in the club's most successful side of the last 60 years. In 1982 they beat three First Division teams to reach the quarter-finals of the Football League Cup, en route to which Trevor's 35-yard shot against Brighton & Hove Albion produced what the *Barnsley Chronicle* described as 'Oakwell's goal of the century.' He had played in the First Division before joining Barnsley and did so again afterwards and he has been in another promotion-winning team, but he considers the Barnsley side to have been the best in which he has played.

A Bermondsey boy, in schools football he was in the South London team which reached the quarter-finals of the 1972 English Cup, and he won representative honours with the school teams of Surrey, London, and South of England. With such impressive credentials it was surprising that he reached the age of 15 without having had a single approach from a professional club. That changed when he played for a local side, Dickens Estate, against a Chelsea under-15 team and he was offered, and accepted, an apprenticeship at Stamford Bridge.

Chelsea had about 40 professionals and a dozen apprentices. In fact they had so many on the staff that professionals played regularly in a junior side. Consequently, much to young Trevor's dismay, he found that his first game was to be in the juniors' second team. In his own mind he felt he'd already been rejected: of course he hadn't, and a hat-trick in that first game was sufficient to get him into the other team from where he progressed to a place in the reserves. In schoolboy football he had been an averaged sized lad and joined Chelsea as a midfielder. However, full-time training put several inches and a couple of stones onto his frame and by the time he appeared in the first team he was the 6′ 1″, 12-stones plus young man who was eventually to become a firm favourite at Oakwell.

He entered the First Division scene in October 1977 in the second half of a game against Bristol City and made a story book beginning to his career by scoring the winning goal – a happening which the supporters hadn't had an opportunity to celebrate in any of the previous five home games. He did it again in the following week against eventual League champions Nottingham Forest and, co-incidentally, his winning goals on consecutive Saturdays each came in the 55th minute. Over the following two years he made 26 appearances in the first team but he realized that his opportunities with Chelsea were always going to be limited and his career would be furthered by moving elsewhere.

In mid-November 1979 Barnsley manager Allan Clarke paid £50,000 to bring him to Oakwell. A fortnight earlier he had watched the Reds' home game against Chester when there were nearly 10,000 spectators and lots of enthusiasm within the crowd; he was impressed by the overall team performance and knew that the proposed move would be good for him.

He and his fiancée, Liz, had already arranged to be married in London in the following June, but the transfer prompted them to fix an earlier date. It was hurriedly rearranged for Monday, 26th November – Trevor's 22nd birthday – but being unfamiliar with the Third Division calendar, he had lost sight of the fact that lesser clubs have FA Cup commitments at that time of year. On the Saturday prior to the wedding the Reds had a first round tie against Hartlepool United. Allan Clarke, on hearing of the intended nuptials, made it clear to Trevor that in the event of a Tuesday replay, wedding or no wedding, he wouldn't allow him to leave Barnsley on the Monday – yet arrangements for the ceremony and reception had been finalized. At Oakwell on the Saturday the score was 2 – 2 at the three-quarter stage and a replay looked almost certain. In a state of great agitation Liz watched from a seat in the stand – her mind racing through all the long distance cancellations she would have to make on returning home. She was on the verge of tears when her hero came to the rescue, breaking the deadlock and enabling the Reds to go on to a 5 – 2 victory. For the player it was an impressive debut. He won nearly everything in the air; his control was first-class; he held and laid the ball off with the style of a quality player and took his goal superbly, volleying home first time. Of equal importance to him personally, two days later the wedding went ahead as planned.

But, for Trevor, the following season opened on anything but a happy note. On 16th August 1980 he was substituted mid-way through the second half. He knew he hadn't played well. As he walked towards the touch-line he was annoyed at his level of performance and disappointed at being brought off. And, on approaching the dug-out, emotion overcame common sense and he pulled off his shirt and threw it at the manager. He continued walking until he reached the dressing room. A few moments later he realized how foolish he'd been, and he knew his recklessness would cost him dearly. He was soon joined by a furious Allan Clarke who laid into him at length about his irresponsibility – ending with, 'You'll never play for this club again, son!' At 9 o'clock on Monday morning Trevor presented himself at the manager's office to give a heartfelt apology, details of which appeared in the next edition of the *Barnsley Chronicle*. For the following six weeks he played in the reserves, on 24th September scoring five goals when Middlesbrough were beaten 10 – 2. Earlier in that week Clarke had departed for Leeds United, thus paving the way for

Trevor's reinstatement in the first team. The season saw the Reds win promotion, during the course of which his goals included a hat-trick against Hull City and two in a fine 3 – 2 success at Fulham.

The new season at the higher level exceeded everyone's expectations. For the first time the Reds reached the fifth round of the Football League Cup. In so doing they beat three sides from Division One – Swansea City, Brighton, and Manchester City – and went out to the eventual winners, Liverpool, only after a commendable draw at Anfield when the *Barnsley Chronicle* said Trevor was the most accomplished player on the field. The earlier tie against Manchester City, played in front of 33,792 spectators, ended in Barnsley's favour when Trevor scored with a superb header in the 52nd minute. But of all the goals he scored, the first of his two against Brighton in the third round is of everlasting memory. Then, after dispossessing centre half Steve Foster – a man who played for England three months later – he sent a remarkable 35-yard swerving shot curling sweetly into a top corner of the net to help towards a 4 – 1 scoreline against a team placed seventh in the First Division.

The Second Division programme was almost equally fruitful, and the final sixth position was the club's highest League placing since 1922.

But the end of that exceptional season also saw Trevor's time at Oakwell drawing to a close. Reports in the national press that he had asked to be transferred because his wife couldn't settle in the town and wished to return to London were totally untrue. Liz was perfectly happy in Barnsley. Living in a modern detached house at Monk Bretton, she mixed well and often with the other Oakwell wives and, nearly 10 years and four clubs on, considers them to be the friendliest football group she has ever met. Then, as now, she sees her home to be where her husband's career takes them. Trevor's departure stemmed solely from his contract having expired and the club refusing to offer terms which he found sufficiently attractive. Everton, Aston Villa and Luton Town were among the half-dozen clubs which enquired about him and backed away on being quoted a fee of £400,000. In the event he joined Millwall after a Football League tribunal had decided on a valuation of £150,000. Even at that late stage he was prepared to remain with Barnsley but they refused to match the terms he had been offered by Millwall – a club in the Third Division.

The stay in east London was fairly brief. In March 1983, on the last day for unrestricted transfers, he moved to Luton Town. He had, in fact, almost joined them from Barnsley and had even agreed terms, but they then declined to get involved in the lottery of a tribunal fixing the transfer fee.

In August 1984 he joined Crystal Palace – another club which had wanted him two years earlier. In his first season he was top scorer, but an injury in the summer put him on the sidelines at the start of the next campaign. He regained his place but wasn't at his best, and was again out of the side when Barnsley took him on loan in February 1986. Perhaps surprisingly in view of an earlier furious utterance, the loan was arranged at the instigation of Allan Clarke who had taken charge again some six months earlier. And despite the player's goal-touch having temporarily disappeared, Clarke tried to get him on a more permanent basis. A player-exchange deal was set up involving Larry May, but it foundered when, once again, Barnsley couldn't match the terms which Trevor had in London. On the expiry of the loan period he returned to Palace and was the substitute in their next game – at Barnsley. It just *had* to happen. Having failed to score in nine consecutive games for the Reds, he was on the spot to crack home the deciding goal as soon as he played against them!

In the following summer he joined AFC Bournemouth where he repeated the achievement he'd had at Barnsley by helping them win promotion into the Second Division. But this time his team topped the table from February and went up as champions with a record number of points.

In the opening season in Division Two he was Bournemouth's leading scorer, and the esteem in which he was held was evident when he was voted Player of the Year. The accolade carried with it a very acceptable prize of two weeks' holiday in Portugal for himself, Liz and two-year-old Nicola.

On 26th November 1988 Bournemouth were beaten 5 – 2 at Oakwell and rarely has the crowd given the biggest cheer of an afternoon to a goal by a visiting player. It was a game in which the Reds' David Currie did the hat-trick – and Trevor was the last Barnsley player to have scored three times in front of the home supporters. But perhaps the most satisfying moment of his season came 10 weeks later in the FA Cup. It was the day on which the Reds lost at home to Everton, but the fans had *some* enjoyment from that fifth round, for many would have been among the millions viewing *Match of the Day*. They then saw their former favourite score a great equalizing goal against Manchester United which took his side to a replay at Old Trafford.

At 32, Trevor is still knocking in the goals – one of which, in April 1990, provided Bournemouth with victory at Oakwell at a time when both teams were struggling desperately for Second Division survival. He freely admits that his career success owes much to the guidance of Allan Clarke. Without him it might have fizzled out in the early stages for, as a youngster at Chelsea, he did most of the wrong things and was rarely out of trouble – arguing with referees, regularly being sent off and spending too much time in West End night clubs. Clarke's advice was to look after himself and then football would give him a good life, otherwise he'd be out of the game by his mid-twenties. The aberration of August 1980 apart, he has followed the advice to the letter and even now, in preparing for a Saturday match, he never has an evening away from home after Wednesday.

Maybe he has not scored as many goals as he should have done, but for a big chap he has plenty of pace and is an ideal target-man, continually laying the ball off with skill and style. His best years were spent at Oakwell and, although the England manager has shown how naive it is to hope for a Barnsley player to be in the national side, few supporters who watched the two tremendous seasons when Trevor Aylott was at Oakwell would disagree that he was worthy of a place in England's World Cup squad of 1982.

Derrick Parker: The Best Of Reasons

Derrick Parker became Barnsley's record signing when he joined the club in exchange for £60,000 in February 1980. Manager Allan Clarke was then spending money in unprecedented amounts while building a team to challenge for promotion to the Second Division: the fee paid for Derrick beat the previous record created only 11 weeks earlier when Trevor Aylott was signed – and remained the highest for a whole month until an even larger sum obtained Ian Evans. Derrick's part in the promotion-winning season of 1980/81 and the following campaign which established the team at the forefront of the Second Division is part of Oakwell history – his pairing with Aylott developing into one of the most exciting and fruitful partnerships of the club's post-war years.

A Wallsend boy who represented town and county in school football, Derrick became a Burnley apprentice at 15. Opportunity was also present for him to join Newcastle United or Middlesbrough, but the deciding factor was that a school pal, Ray Hankin, was already at Burnley.

His Central League debut came while still 15 when he scored his side's goal in a 4 – 1 defeat by Sheffield United reserves. A few games later he reverted to the juniors but won a regular place in the reserves in 1973, when he scored four times in a 10-goal defeat of Bury and did the hat-trick against Bolton Wanderers reserves. Becoming a fully-fledged professional on his 17th birthday in February 1974, the following year had some significant happenings – not all of which were to his credit. In February, in an FA Youth Cup-tie against Spurs at White Hart Lane, he was sent off for the only time in his career. Six weeks later a much more memorable event was his First Division debut against Derby County, but the end of the year saw him again in trouble. Burnley's under-21-year-olds were forbidden to enter licensed premises, yet on Christmas Eve the reserve team trainer spotted four of his teenage players in a public house. The fact that Derrick was drinking lemonade was irrelevant: all were suspended for 14 days without pay and banned from playing, training, and even attending the

By the time Derrick was 19 he had played half-a-dozen games in the first team – and he wanted to be in it *all* the time. Impatient and headstrong, he was prepared to argue his claim for inclusion with the manager – yet now, with the wisdom of maturity, he regards Jimmy Adamson to be the most knowledgeable football man he ever met. And at that time at Burnley, anyone who didn't conform went further back in the queue. The crunch came when on again protesting about being in the reserves he was told, 'We want you to bring on the young lads.' He was 19 years old and responded by pointing out that he was still a young lad himself and asking for a transfer.

The result was that he joined Southend United early in 1977. Initially it wasn't a good move. The team were second-top in Division Four and the leading scorer, co-incidentally, also named Parker, was transferred on the day that Derrick arrived. The other was the supporters' favourite and they were, understandably, unhappy about losing him. And at the beginning when things didn't go well for Derrick and the team missed out on promotion he became a target for their annoyance. However, a turning-point came early in the next season when his four goals against Torquay United included a first-half hat-trick. Thereafter he scored consistently but, because of the bad start he'd had, he felt he had to do well all the time or the fans would be on his back again at the first opportunity.

It was his goal which enabled the team to take a point at Oakwell on the last day of 1977. During the season his goals won maximum points on seven occasions and went a long way towards the final runners-up position and promotion to the Third Division.

He was leading scorer in each of two completed seasons at Southend and also in 1979/80 when he had only 19 games prior to joining Barnsley. Perhaps the opening move in a transfer which wasn't even in his mind at the time was scoring the first goal when Southend won 2 – 1 at Oakwell in December 1979 – which was followed by a hat-trick against Chester in the next game. But within a matter of days, and as at Burnley three years earlier, an opinion expressed frankly to a manager put him on the transfer list.

Allan Clarke was quickly on the scene to bid £50,000 – which was increased fairly substantially in order to meet Southend's valuation. Then there was another stumbling block. Manager and player met but the latter wasn't inclined to accept the terms on offer. It seemed an impasse had been reached. Derrick returned to Southend and Clarke told the local press that he would not be joining the club. But over the following few days Derrick mulled over what the manager had discussed with him and he realized that Barnsley were going to be a really good side – and he wanted to be part of it. Consequently he got back in touch with Clarke and the transfer took place on 7th February.

Two days later Derrick and Trevor got the goals in a 2 – 2 draw at Millwall. Other goals from Derrick in what remained of the season were the winner against Brentford, one of the four which defeated Mansfield Town and one which clinched victory over Hull City.

He was to the fore during the promotion season of 1980/81, but his best was still to come. On 31st August 1981 the *Morning Telegraph* carried an action picture of his spectacular overhead kick which scored the second goal in a 4 – 0 victory over Shrewsbury Town on the opening of the Second Division programme. Against Oldham Athletic in November he seized upon a defensive error to score the second goal and three minutes from the end he burst through to chip the 'keeper and put the issue beyond doubt. Later in the month in a draw with Wrexham he scored the first goal with a 25-yard drive and the second with as cheeky a back-heel as anyone is likely to see. Three days afterwards more than 30,000 spectators attended the Reds' game at Hillsborough. The *Morning Telegraph* report on the 2 – 2 draw said Barnsley's performance was a joy to watch – pure First Division. It went on to say Wednesday were outclassed in every department and Derrick was yards faster than anything the home side could offer. On one occasion he beat three defenders before being fouled on the edge of the penalty-area; seconds later he left centre half Mick Pickering for dead and fired in a fierce 35-yard shot which flashed narrowly past a post – and soon afterwards he scored the first goal. Yet disaster was looming. In the dying seconds, with the Reds trailing, he layed the ball off to Ronnie Glavin who raced through to score the equalizer. But before the ball was in the net Derrick was on the ground in considerable pain, his right ankle having been damaged from a challenge by Pickering.

The injury was so severe that he was out of action, in and out of plaster casts, for months. He returned briefly in February 1982 but further prolonged treatment was necessary before he regained a place in the side at the beginning of the following season. But things weren't as good as they had previously been. Some of his pace had gone – as had Aylott and McHale with whom he had linked so effectively.

Nevertheless he produced some excellent performances. In September 1982 he scored the winner at Newcastle United, and other goals which made him second-leading scorer included one in a 3 – 0 win over Chelsea and winners against Wolves and Rotherham United. In reporting the latter game, the *Morning Telegraph* said that Derrick displayed the class which Rotherham lacked when, despite facing the wrong way, he produced a brilliant turn and shot to give his side the points.

In August 1983 a fee of £40,000 took him to Oldham Athletic. He had an awful start, being substituted in his first game – which annoyed him immensely – and dropped after the second. In the following week he was injured in training, and two months later manager Joe Royle said he'd made a mistake in signing him and put him on the transfer list. He returned to the side early in November, scored the winner against Cardiff City and kept a place for Barnsley's visit on 3rd December. On that day he had the saddest and most unexpected experience of his whole career. In the last minute of the game, in an off-the-ball incident involving Mick McCarthy, he sustained a fractured cheek-bone. He subsequently began legal action alleging assault by his former team-mate which, in the event, was settled out of court.

A year later he had a spell on loan at Doncaster Rovers, and in the summer of 1985 he was on the point of being transferred back to Barnsley in exchange for Ron Futcher when manager Bobby Collins was dismissed. Negotiations continued with Allan Clarke – again in charge at Oakwell – who disregarded the terms offered by Collins. Perhaps he recalled how keen Derrick had been to get to Barnsley on a previous occasion. Be that as it may, he offered less than the player was getting at Oldham. This time Derrick stood firm.

He joined another of his former clubs, Burnley, and remained there for two years. The summer of 1987 was spent footballing in Finland, following which he had three months as a non-contract player with Rochdale. During that time a game against Darlington enabled him to score his 100th League goal.

Then followed a spell with North Ferriby in the North-East Counties League, after which he joined Northwich Victoria in the GM Vauxhall Conference. Although the season was half over he ended as top scorer – an achievement repeated in the following season when he played in every game and scored 23 times.

On leaving full-time football Derrick began a career in Sales, starting in accident insurance and selling to commercial organisations in Huddersfield and Sheffield. In the autumn of 1988 he joined Nilfisk, a Danish company with a base in Suffolk which sells heavy duty, high powered suction equipment to industry. Customers include British Coal and British Steel, and Derrick's area of responsibility covers part of West and most of South Yorkshire.

Derrick's partnership at Oakwell with a man who became a good friend was one of the deadliest outside the First Division. The two complemented each other ideally: Aylott had height and weight and no mean sprinkling of skill, while Derrick contributed quickness off the mark, turning and dribbling skills and clinical finishing. The fact that Barnsley had him at his peak was largely fortuitous. Press reports of the initial breakdown of the transfer were specific about the cause – yet nothing was said later about why he had a change of heart. The money on offer held no particular attraction, and the reason why Derrick Parker joined the Oakwell staff was simply that he wanted to play for the club.

Ian Evans: A Misplaced Loyalty

In September 1974 Ian Evans and present Spurs manager Terry Venables were transferred from Queen's Park Rangers to Crystal Palace in exchange for the Palace winger, Don Rogers. Two years later Venables – older than Ian and an English international – told him he'd had doubts about going along with the proposed transfer and did so only because Ian seemed so excited about the prospect of joining Palace: if he'd dropped out the whole deal would have fallen through. That is one of several reasons why Ian holds the other in high regard, yet the move was beneficial to each of them. Venables was to become Crystal Palace manager and embark upon an extremely successful post-playing career. Ian became the club's most-capped player and had a leading role in Venables' first managerial success by captaining the Palace team which won promotion into the Second Division in 1977.

However, his elation was short lived. Five weeks into the new season he suffered grievous injury, and two years elapsed before he returned to competitive football. Indeed, he joined the Oakwell staff without having played a single first team game since the date of the injury and although a club record fee was paid in order to obtain him, it was then not possible to get him insured. Nevertheless, he had a major part in Barnsley's 1980/81 promotion season and also in the following campaign when they proved a force to be reckoned with in the Second Division.

Born in Woking of an English mother and a Welsh father, Ian was spotted by Queen's Park Rangers and trained with them weekly from being 12 years old. On leaving school he became an apprentice professional and played at full back in the junior side, yet he soon realized he wasn't doing too well. Tall, rather gangly and not very quick, he had such doubts about making the grade that he applied to the Metropolitan Police for an appointment as police cadet. But it was to be expected that others would be monitoring his football development and making adjustments in the light of what they saw. In the weeks during which his application to the police was being processed he was moved to centre half. There his height was used to best advantage and he had a natural spring which made him a commanding figure in central defence. An improvement in play and confidence was immediate; a professional contract was offered on the same day in January 1970 that he received a letter of acceptance from the Metropolitan Police – who consequently lost a young man who may well have had the same level of career success in law enforcement as he was to have in professional football.

His League debut was in the following April in a 1 – 0 win over Sheffield Wednesday. Two years later he was established in the side and played in the early part of a successful push to the First Division in 1973, but injury in a game against Millwall in November cost him his place.

It was because he was in the reserves that he was so keen to join Crystal Palace, even though it was a Third Division club. Having a first team place from the outset, it wasn't long before manager Malcolm Allison appointed him captain – and he must have been the only captain who refused to lead out his team. Because of a superstition about being first onto the pitch he insisted on a condition of his captaincy being that he never took to the field at the head of the Palace side.

In 1976 Palace reached the semi-finals of the FA Cup, during the course of which they had away victories over two First Division sides – Leeds United and Chelsea. At Elland Road he was *News of the World* Man of the Match, the report saying, 'He will never have a better game. In defence he was immaculate and his forays upfield were devastating.'

In that season Ian almost led Palace to promotion. He put them on course with a hat-trick in an early 3 – 2 win over Colchester United, and on 16th September his 89th-minute goal provided a three-point lead at the top of the division. That position was held until January, but in the end they missed out through inconsistency in the second half of the season. However, reward came in the following year. The captain played in all 46 games and, as if to make his name familiar in an area where he was to receive future acclaim, two of his goals came in victories over Rotherham United and Sheffield Wednesday.

He had already represented Wales at under-23 level and made his full international debut against Austria in 1975. He went on to play for Wales a further 12 times and, of all those memorable occasions, the most treasured is a 1 – 0 victory over England at Wembley in 1977.

The incident which put him out of football for two years and almost ended his career occurred in a game against Fulham on 1st October 1977. The irony of the situation was that it was his 100th consecutive game and should have been an occasion for celebration. However, shortly after the interval he was at the receiving end of a two-footed tackle from George Best which caused a compound fracture of his right leg. The referee didn't see anything amiss, but there must surely have been something unlawful about a tackle which fractured one leg and put a laceration in the other which required 12 stitches!

Treatment over the following year involved a spell in hospital, several operations, traction, insertion of a seven-inch plate and seven screws, and a bone-graft from his hip. But nothing worked. Even the metal plate broke and the fracture just would not heal. Terry Venables, to ensure his captain's recovery was not hindered by financial worries, gave him a new *five-year* contract within two weeks of him being injured, and physiotherapist Charlie Simpson was a continual support. It was he who learned of the treatment which eventually brought about Ian's recovery. An American technique, it involved the insertion of tiny electrodes around the fracture which then received constant mini-shocks from a battery encased within the plaster cast. The broken bone started to knit almost immediately and after three months the plaster was removed. A period at the RAF Rehabilitation Centre near Epsom followed and, almost two years to the day after the injury, he came through his first game in Palace's reserve side.

Further reserve games followed, but he could see that there was not an opening in the first team so he spoke to the manager about moving elsewhere. 'Right,' said Venables, 'I shall want £100,000 for you.' 'You must be joking,' replied Ian, 'I've only played a dozen games in two years.' 'No matter, I've been good to you and I now have to think about the club's interests. You can still play and that's what you're worth.'

A few months later, in January 1980, Ian joined Barnsley on loan as cover for the suspended Mick McCarthy. From the outset Clarke wanted his transfer but that was something the player wasn't certain about. Then came an offer from Hull City. He went there and agreed terms but the club doctor, after examining his right leg, couldn't believe he'd been playing football for the previous two months. Deciding he didn't want to be where there was any uncertainty, he accepted instead the offer from Barnsley. Signing on 6th March for a fee of £80,000, insurance cover could not be obtained until he had played a dozen first team games without any adverse reaction in the previously injured leg.

Over the following two seasons a feature of the Reds' play was the pairing in central defence of Ian and Mick McCarthy. Initially it wasn't an ideal partnership because their styles were identical – each attacked everything in the air. Ian decided that it would be better if he left it to Mick to do the attacking and he covered, tidied-up and set moves in motion. It worked to perfection, becoming part of the team's normal pattern of play and no doubt influencing the opinions of his peers when he won a place in the 1981 PFA Third Division side.

The goal-scoring flair which he had displayed as a central defender with Crystal Palace wasn't so much in evidence at Oakwell. In the League he got only three, but two of them won games against Sheffield United and Luton Town. And in October 1980 against West Ham in the League Cup, his goal held the scores level until the final seconds when the First Division side's David Cross was credited with the winner after putting the ball into the Barnsley net with his hand.

Some of the best football of Ian's career was played while he was at Oakwell and he was bitterly disappointed at not being recalled to the Welsh squad. Indeed, Barnsley's two most successful seasons for many years were while Ian was playing – throughout which time he was player-coach, having been appointed to that post by manager Hunter in September 1980. Injury kept him out of the side for almost all of 1982/83 but he retained the coaching role.

On taking up his duties he had been told, 'Move away from the players and regard yourself as being more with me.' It was a brief appropriate to the role and Ian complied as much as continuing as a player allowed. An intelligent, articulate man, he was in charge of training and travelled the country assessing players – something the manager was reluctant to do – and he sorted out problems and generally acted as buffer between players and manager. Yet in August 1983, after three years without any indication that he had ever given anything less than total satisfaction, Hunter sent for him and said, 'I don't think you're as close to me now as when you started. I want you to revert to being a player.' Ian was completely taken aback. He refused to remain in a playing-only role and within a couple of weeks had been loaned to Exeter City, later having a spell with Cambridge United until a knee injury brought that to an end in November.

At the end of the year his contract with Barnsley was cancelled and he was paid for the unexpired part of it. Over the following six months he kept fit by running in the lanes around his home at Silkstone and reducing his handicap on the local golf course. In the summer he was invited by the Crystal Palace chairman, Ron Noades, to be assistant to the newly appointed manager, Steve Coppell – a man whom he had never met. In the light of the Barnsley experience he was at pains to emphasize to Coppell that he did not, and would not, want his job. But, in any event, there was never any indication that insecurity was a characteristic of *this* manager. Ian's role provided free rein in training and tactics and he was involved in every aspect of management – and he loved every minute.

In February 1989 he was asked by Doug Sharpe, the chairman of Swansea City, to become manager there. Knowing it was time to progress further, he was glad to accept. Five years ago the club was on the brink of extinction, yet only a short time earlier it had been in the First Division. Despite the limited funds available, Ian was determined to do everything within his power to return the club to its former exalted position; certainly he has the necessary personal and professional qualities and, other things being equal, the task was within his capabilities. It was, therefore, a blow to both pride and ambition when on 13th March 1990 – after only a year and two weeks in post – he was dismissed.

It seemed an example of the worst that professional football can offer. His departure – with the team comfortably placed in the division – followed quickly upon his predecessor, Terry Yorath, being sacked by Bradford City. A little more than a year earlier Yorath had walked out on Swansea to manage the other club, so incensing the directors that they sought to stop him by way of High Court injunction. After all that, as soon as he was again available they dismissed Ian and reappointed him. Yet only three months earlier Ian had demonstrated *his* loyalty to Swansea City by declining an invitation to become manager at Oakwell.

Mick McCarthy: Fresh Fields To Conquer

Mick McCarthy was in the Barnsley first team at 18 and not only did he retain a place throughout six consecutive seasons but he never missed a match through injury. In fact, his only absences were brought about by suspensions – and there were quite a few of those. Starting at Oakwell in the Fourth Division, he later established himself in the English First and Scottish Premier Divisions and currently features on the international scene as captain of the Republic of Ireland team which, in 1989, qualified for the first time for World Cup Finals.

Mick was born in Barnsley on 7th February 1959, eligibility for the Eire side coming through his father, Charlie, a native of Waterford who came to Barnsley in 1947 to work in the mines and married a local girl, Josie Taylor. Always big for his age, at 15 Mick was in the Worsbrough Bridge Miners' Welfare Athletic first team and playing in four games each weekend; Saturday mornings with Worsbrough High School, afternoons with Worsbrough Bridge, and twice on Sundays – for Swaithe Main Athletic and Barnsley Boys Club.

A year later and while still at school he was in Barnsley reserves and keeping an apprentice out of the side, yet he wasn't at all sure that he wanted to be an apprentice himself. Schooldays were drawing to a close and he'd been offered a job as an apprentice electrician at Barrow Colliery. It had advantages over a position at Oakwell in that several of his pals were at the colliery and a wage of £25 was almost double what an apprentice footballer was paid.

In the end Mick was influenced by Norman Rimmington – a man whose guidance he has frequently sought – and the Boys Club leader, Keith Steele. Each, separately, convinced him that there was a better future available to him in football than in the mining industry. Keith Steele urged him to ask manager Jim Iley for an apprenticeship, saying, perhaps with some inside knowledge, that he knew Iley would agree.

That proved to be so, and Mick became an apprentice in December 1975. In the following season he captained the club's junior side which won the Northern Intermediate League title, the County FA Youth Cup and an Easter international tournament in Holland. Three months later, on 16th August 1977, he made his first team debut in a League Cup match with Chesterfield. The Reds faced a three-goal deficit from the first leg, but an opening goal from the new centre half put them on course for a 4 – 4 draw before going out in a replay.

From that day, throughout the following six years, Mick was never omitted from the side. He was an ever-present in his first two seasons, the second of which brought promotion into Division Three.

A significant happening in his development came when Ian Evans joined the side in the spring of 1980 to play alongside him in central defence. Evans was the senior by eight years and, as a Welsh international, had played against some of the best forwards in the world. He was a source of continual inspiration and with his encouragement, Mick – already a very good player – developed into one of the best centre halves in the country.

Their pairing was a major factor in the team's promotion to the Second Division in 1981, yet for Mick the start of the season was anything but auspicious. The opening game was lost; the second, at Hull City, was won but not before Mick had stroked the ball into the Barnsley net for an extraordinary own goal, and at Gillingham in the next game he was sent off in the third minute!

In the following season he was to the fore in a splendid run to the quarter-finals of the League Cup, during the course of which it became apparent that he could dominate players of the highest quality. In the third round Brighton & Hove Albion were beaten 4 – 1, Mick scoring an equalizing goal with what Keith Lodge described in the *Barnsley Chronicle* as 'one of the most powerful headers I have ever seen – a certainty for the goal of the month had the match been televised.' In the next round he made Manchester City's £1m-rated striker, Kevin Reeves, look a very ordinary player, and on a murky, memorable evening at Anfield when the home side must have counted themselves fortunate to get a replay, the renowned Kenny Dalglish was marked completely out of the game.

In September 1983 Mick was sidelined through suspension; when he was eventually available manager Hunter told him that his replacement, Nicky Law, had played too well to be dropped. It was at a time of press speculation that he was about to be the subject of a bid from Newcastle United and, never previously having been left out of the side, he responded with, 'If I can't be in the team, then sell me to Newcastle.' He was well aware that Newcastle United wanted him and that their manager, Arthur Cox, had tried to obtain him earlier while in charge at Chesterfield. In fact, he did so again, with an equal lack of success, when he was at Derby County.

It was therefore with considerable surprise that Mick learned that he was to be transferred to Manchester City. The move took place in mid-December, and although he'd always been happy at Oakwell he quickly came to love being at a really big club.

The impressions he created at Maine Road were such that after only 24 games he was voted Player of the Year, and in the following season, 1984/85, he captained the side into the First Division. And in October 1986 his awesome aerial power went nationwide when the several million viewers of *The Match* saw his splendid equalizing header against Manchester United.

At the end of the season and with a year of his contract remaining several clubs were wanting his services. Liverpool and Sheffield Wednesday were the front-runners and City manager Jimmy Frizzell told him that whatever Wednesday offered, Liverpool would outbid them. Nevertheless, Mick favoured a move to Sheffield, reasoning that he could be fairly certain of a first team place at Hillsborough, whereas at Anfield he was more than likely to be a squad player. At that point an offer came from Celtic – the terms of which he doubted even Liverpool could have improved upon.

The move to Glasgow took place on 20th May 1987 and the fee was £500,000. At that stage in his career, despite having been in three promotion-winning teams, Mick had never had a medal. But that soon altered. In his first season Celtic did the double by winning the Premier Division championship and Scottish Cup – and in the following year, 1989, they won the Cup again.

The Celtic connections also enhanced his standing with supporters of the Republic of Ireland team. There had been earlier occasions when he suspected they had difficulty in relating to a native South Yorkshireman, but there were no such problems once he was with a side which was highly regarded in Dublin. His international appearances began while with Manchester City in 1984, and over the next five years he represented his father's country on 36 occasions. In the light of a reply which Bobby Robson gave to John Steele in 1982, the game which no doubt gave him most satisfaction was a European championship victory over England in June 1988.

Club and international football has taken Mick to almost every part of the world and in the summer of 1989 he and his wife, Fiona, with their three children, set up home in the South of France. That came about through a half-million-pound transfer to the French club, Lyon, after the happiest and most successful two years he'd had in football. The Celtic manager, Billy McNeill, told him he was offering a new contract but felt obliged to give him an opportunity to earn the kind of money Lyon were offering. It was certainly too good to refuse, and Mick is contracted to the club until he is 33 with an option for a further year. Therefore, for the following three years at least, the McCarthys will be experiencing the delights of living in the Rhone Valley at Dardilly, less than an hour's drive from some of the finest beaches on the French Riviera.

There was a period in Mick's time at Oakwell when it would have been impossible to entice him away, and he knows full well that Allan Clarke was determined not to let that happen. Right from the start of his career, and even before he became an Oakwell apprentice, he was a man among boys. And from those early days stems an absolute determination to succeed. This is apparent in every aspect of his play and in the way in which he prepares for each game, for he's as committed in the five-a-sides in training as he is on the pitch – and that doesn't always endear him to his team-mates. He is appreciative of the advice and encouragement which was always available from Norman Rimmington; Norman is one of his greatest admirers and reckons he's as strong as a horse but a softy at heart – a view which strikers throughout England, Scotland and most of Europe will have difficulty in reconciling in total with their own impressions of this towering central defender.

In the air he is unbeatable and his style involves domination of an opponent to an extent that, until fairly recently, he couldn't bring himself to mix socially with the other team after a game – it was as though an opponent didn't cease being an opponent simply because the final whistle had blown. But he became less ill-disposed towards them after he'd been a while in the Eire side, perhaps because having established himself in the First Division and on the international scene, he'd achieved all that could be expected at that stage of his career. And anyway, at post-match get-togethers at national level, those he knows best are usually members of the other side.

So this Barnsley-born young man, having helped in his home town club's rise from Fourth to Second Division, played with distinction in the English First and Scottish Premier Divisions, in European Cup football and reached the 1990 World Cup Finals, now has fresh fields to conquer in French domestic football. But no matter what the future may hold, Mick McCarthy is already Barnsley's most successful footballing son.

Ronnie Glavin: A Most Memorable Man

The credentials which Ronnie Glavin presented on arriving at Oakwell from Glasgow in June 1979 were impressive in the extreme. A Scottish international, he won a League Cup medal with Partick Thistle whom he captained in the Premier Division when 20 years old. Later, with Celtic he won FA Cup and championship medals and played European Cup football for three consecutive seasons. Always a midfielder, he was a strong runner who scored a lot of goals – so many, in fact, that when Celtic won the Premier Division championship in 1977 he was leading scorer ahead of his redoubtable team-mate, Kenny Dalglish.

Ronnie's junior football was always in teams which were older than himself. Consequently he was usually the smallest on the pitch and only exceptional skill enabled him to compete with the others. At 15 he joined Lochend Rovers – an under-18 side – and within a few weeks he was capped for Scotland's under-18 amateur team. A year later he was training with Partick Thistle and playing in their reserve side, but he became somewhat disillusioned when neither Partick nor any other club seemed inclined to sign him.

However, in his second season he began to score a lot of goals and was invited to a trial for the Scottish junior side. He was chosen as a substitute forward and when the players reported it was discovered that the selected number 9 was ineligible. Consequently, Ronnie stepped in. At 16 he was still small compared with the others but he had a great game, getting a hat-trick in a 7 – 1 win. It was the breakthrough he needed. Earlier, no-one had seemed interested but now he had half-a-dozen clubs wanting him.

He signed for Partick because he knew everyone there, and thus began a professional career which, once he'd got into the first team, brought him success upon success. At the age of 18 he had a regular place in the side. In the following year, 1971, Partick won the Second Division championship and in the next they won the Scottish League Cup by beating Celtic 4 – 1.

Ronnie captained the side for two years until his transfer to Celtic in November 1974. At the end of that season he collected his second championship medal – this time for the Premier Division – and he had another when Celtic were again champions in 1977. In-between-times he had an FA Cup-winners' medal in 1975 and was involved in European Cup football in each of the following three seasons. During that time he attained what he regards as the pinnacle of his career by representing his country at Hampden Park in a 3 – 1 success against Denmark. There was, however, a downside in that he received an injury which kept him out of Celtic's Cup-winning side 10 days later.

In August 1978 he voluntarily took up the duties of reserve team player-coach while continuing in the first team. However, in mid-September he was injured in a match against Hibs and, thereafter, was unable to hold a regular place in the side.

In the following June he was asked to contact the Barnsley manager, Allan Clarke. He knew it could be for only one purpose and the prospect didn't attract him at all. He wasn't even sure where Barnsley was and the only thing he knew about the team was from football-talk in Glasgow which told him they had a player named Ali Millar.

Nevertheless, he got in touch. The purpose was what he knew it would be and Clarke asked to see him in Barnsley. Ronnie decided to test the manager straight away and if the answer wasn't the one he wanted he had no intention of making the journey. He pointed out that a strike of petrol tanker drivers prevented him from travelling by road, a train journey would take six hours but a flight from Glasgow to Leeds Airport took only 50 minutes. 'Right, get it then,' was the reply.

Clarke met him at the airport and they drove to Oakwell where Ronnie was shown around the ground. The manager exuded enthusiasm but his guest wasn't impressed, seeing nothing to compare with what was available to him at Celtic Park. He'd already decided on a ploy commonly used in such situations: when Clarke began to talk terms he asked for a wage which he thought the other would reject out of hand. It brought the response he'd anticipated and the discussions seemed at an end. A return flight to Glasgow was booked for the early afternoon and the two lunched together at Brooklands Motel. Talk didn't touch on monetary matters until they returned to Oakwell preparatory to driving to Leeds. Then Clarke suddenly said, 'Right, I want you at this club. You've got your money.' This put Ronnie on the spot. He didn't want to leave Celtic but he was being offered *three times* what they were paying him! He was allowed a week in which to accept. Reluctant as he was to make the move, he knew another such financial opportunity was unlikely to come his way. Consequently he accepted Clarke's offer and the transfer fee was a fairly modest £40,000.

By the time the season began Ronnie had learned that he'd been signed on the recommendation of assistant manager Martin Wilkinson – Clarke never having seen him play. And that was soon apparent. He was required to play wide on the left side, whereas his strength was in making runs from the centre of midfield and having a crack at goal. In the role which was thrust upon him he wasn't as involved as he liked to be and looked a very ordinary player.

Two of his first three games were lost and things came to a head in the fourth – at Chesterfield on 21st August 1979. At the pre-match briefing Clarke had a dossier from which he described the strengths and weaknesses of every opposing player. This was something quite new to Ronnie: he began to think he was in the wrong dressing room, about to play against England, not Chesterfield. But he came back to reality with a jolt when the manager said to him, 'You're wide left. The right back's your man. Stop him coming forward.' Ronnie couldn't believe what he was hearing – he was used to attacking at every opportunity and letting the opposition worry about stopping *him*!

Nevertheless, he did as he'd been told. He played wide on the left and by half-time he'd hardly had a kick. But he wasn't having any more of that. When the second half began he moved into the middle, collected the ball and raced through to send in a shot which was pushed out for a corner. Immediately a voice bellowed from the dug-out. 'What're you doing? Get back down here!' So back down there he went. But not for long. Soon he was up again, sending in a shot which flashed past the post. Response from the dug-out was to hold up the number 4 board and off Ronnie went, totally disillusioned.

Clarke didn't speak to him after the game but summoned him to his office on Monday morning.

'When I tell you to mark a right back, that's what you'll do.'

'You obviously don't know how I play. I score goals. I *don't* mark right backs.'

'You'll play how I want you to play or you won't play at all!'

Ronnie was dropped for the next game – a 2 – 0 defeat at Sheffield United – but returned in the following week at Blackburn Rovers. This time he received no specific instructions and, playing in his normal way, he scored the goal which enabled Barnsley to win 1 – 0. Thereafter no restraints were ever imposed upon him and he responded in a manner which was of tremendous value to the side and a continual delight to the supporters.

In fact, in that first season he pleased the supporters so much that they voted him their Player of the Year. The trophy was presented on 22nd April 1980 immediately prior to the kick-off against Hull City, Ronnie responding by scoring from the penalty-spot in a 3 – 1 success. In all he scored 23 goals – far more than anyone else.

By the start of the following season his surges from midfield were a feature of Barnsley's play and a buzz of expectancy rose from the terraces every time he set off for goal. On 30th August, on reporting a 2 – 1 win over Sheffield United under a 'Glavin masterminds Reds' power show' headline in *The Star*, Tony Pritchett said that on the day's form Ronnie was the best player in the Third Division. A few weeks later Keith Lodge had a 'Glavin star of top-level production' headline to his *Barnsley Chronicle* report on a 3 – 1 success against Carlisle United. *Match Weekly* had him as their Matchman of the Month for November and in December his two goals against Walsall – one from a move he started on the half-way line and the other a cracking shot from 30 yards – took him to a total of 100 in Scottish and English football.

It was a season which ended with Barnsley's elevation to the Second Division. Again Ronnie was top scorer and it was he who clinched promotion in front of nearly 26,000 spectators in a 1 – 0 success against Rotherham United, who were already assured of a place in Division Two. Which of the teams were to be champions was to be determined by the results of their final matches. Rotherham, two points ahead, were favourites: for Barnsley to be champions they had to beat Newport County by four clear goals while their rivals lost to Plymouth Argyle. In the event Rotherham won and took the title, but Barnsley gave a tremendous display and Ronnie was the star of a 4 – 1 success with a splendid 16-minute hat-trick.

Earlier, in March 1980 when Allan Clarke moved to Leeds United, there was speculation that he would seek Ronnie's transfer. To deter such an approach, the Barnsley board put a price-tag of £400,000 on him and this had the desired effect. However, over the following three years there were frequent reports that Ronnie was about to leave Oakwell. Two transfers which might have materialized involved Newcastle United and Sheffield Wednesday. Each would have paid the fee required but, despite being in the First Division, weren't prepared to match the wages which the player was getting at Barnsley.

Ronnie's contract expired in 1984 and he was taken aback when the new terms offered were appreciably less than he'd been receiving. Refusing to accept, he joined Belenenses in the Portuguese First Division.

He remained in Portugal for a year until August 1985. On returning to his Barnsley home he was contacted by Allan Clarke, recently reinstalled at Oakwell. Clarke asked him to be youth team coach, which was just the kind of opening he'd been hoping for. He revelled in the new responsibilities – for all of seven months. Then, without having had any indication that his job was insecure, he was dismissed as 'an economy measure' on 10th March 1986.

Even at 35 there were still clubs wanting him. Burnley and Doncaster Rovers were among them but he joined the former Belenenses manager, Jimmy Melia, at Stockport County. However, four months into the season, in November 1986, Melia was dismissed. Ronnie was asked to be caretaker manager but he'd already decided Stockport wasn't the place for him. Consequently, he signed for St Louis Steamers in the American Indoor Soccer League, remaining there until the following summer when he began a one-year engagement with Rochdale as reserve team player-coach.

Ronnie is an articulate, confident man, at ease with people and able to demonstrate soccer skills in a way which is easily understood. This has enabled him to pursue a new career in commercial coaching. In 1988 he joined the sportswear firm, Nike International, to conduct their two-day soccer camps. In the following year he branched out on his own. Ronnie Glavin Soccer Camps are now held at centres in northern England and Scotland, providing a valuable step in the development of many of the game's young hopefuls. A spin-off is an involvement in Canberra Football Cruises. Each summer he enjoys the luxury of a fortnight aboard the liner in the Mediterranean where he, Alan Mullery and Gordon Banks organize games for passengers and give talks on their playing experiences.

Ronnie was Allan Clarke's first major signing. On moving to Oakwell he joined a club whose players had, in the main, been raised in the Fourth Division. Their having a colleague with his level of achievement was a new experience and his presence gave the team both style and stature. He was someone who made things happen: in the dressing room he was a joker and on the pitch he could be quite magical. One-against-one situations with a goalkeeper were tailor-made for him, for he would always score and team-mates even forgave his reluctance to defend – a typical response being Ray McHale's 'I'll cover for you Ronnie, you just keep winning my bonus!' His electrifying bursts of speed and knack of being able to get into the penalty-area almost unnoticed made him an opponent to be feared. Indeed, he seemed to run faster with the ball than most ran without it and his scoring rate from midfield must have been the envy of many a striker. The fans loved him, and a hefty physique and the looks of a film star made him a special favourite of the female supporters. Two Player of the Year awards at Barnsley complement similar accolades while with Celtic and Partick Thistle, and his peers held him in equally high regard, voting him into the PFA Third Division side in 1981 and the Second Division side two years later.

Ronnie Glavin was the kind of footballer one doesn't forget. Supporters who savoured Barnsley's most recent promotion and the following three seasons in the Second Division will readily recall his electrifying acceleration from midfield, and the accompanying buzz of anticipation from the crowd and the roar that went up as he added another goal to his remarkable tally. And those who can recall the club's earlier seasons will undoubtedly place him among the most exciting players ever to grace Oakwell.

Phil Chambers: The Easiest Job In Football

As a 15-year-old, Phil Chambers could have joined almost any club in the land – Manchester United, Arsenal, Spurs and the two Sheffield clubs being among those who were keen to obtain his signature. But, being a Barnsley-born lad, he was receptive to an approach from John Steele. He remained at Oakwell for 17 seasons, during which he was a member of two promotion-winning teams and captain of that which reached the Second Division in 1981. In fact, he and McCarthy were the only players to hold regular places in those two sides. Therefore, after that level of involvement and having been with the club from leaving school until his early thirties, he was saddened by the insensitivity which thought it appropriate for notification of a free transfer to be sent by post to his home.

A Worsbrough High School pupil, Phil was a member of the Barnsley Boys side which won the 1969 Yorkshire Shield and reached the semi-finals of the English Trophy. It was a season in which he attained schoolboy international status, representing England on six occasions and playing in such prestigious arenas as Wembley Stadium and the Olympic Stadium in Berlin.

During the summer of that year he became a Barnsley apprentice, in which role he played in the first team in the last three games of the 1970/71 season, and again in the following August and early September. However, he was omitted from a League Cup-tie against Arsenal on 9th September but travelled with the team in order to experience the occasion. On arrival at Highbury he was detailed to help carry the kit to the dressing room; with boot bag on his shoulder he was walking in some awe through the famed marble hall when he was stopped by a commissionaire who pointed out, with some disdain, that the bag wasn't properly fastened and the visiting team's boots were strewn along 30 yards of highly polished floor!

Two months later, on his 18th birthday, he was a fully-fledged professional, on a path trodden by two older brothers – John, who had a career in Southern League football with Hereford, and David who was with Rotherham United and York City.

In August 1972 he became first-choice left full back. Thereafter, apart from occasional appearances on the other flank and in central defence, he was always a left-side defender. He went on to play 170 consecutive games, a sequence which ended abruptly in November 1975.

Over the following two-and-a-half years he was out of the side more often than in it, and he was most unhappy about the situation. Encouragement was not to be had from manager Jim Iley: enquiries about when he could hope for a regular place brought a non-committal reply and an expression of satisfaction with the existing side. He was reduced to filling-in for those absent through injury and was told not to bother asking for a transfer, nor was he to be loaned elsewhere. Whenever he did get a game he acquitted himself well – frequently earning Star Player ratings and celebrating his 200th appearance with an equalizing goal against Bournemouth. It became a totally frustrating period, the only time in all the years he was to spend at Oakwell that he wished he'd taken up one of the other options available to him when he left school.

He wasn't back in favour until April 1978 when he played in the season's last six matches, having managed only four in the preceding seven months. But the corner had been turned and he went on to play in all but one of the 46 games in the following promotion season. Soon after it began he secured maximum points at Bournemouth by driving the ball home from outside the penalty-area and in the final game, at Wimbledon on 14th May 1979, he ended a triumphant season on a personal high note by equalizing the score after the team had trailed at the interval.

Phil was sometimes switched to right full back for man-to-man marking on a left winger thought likely to cause problems, and in the autumn of 1979 he had an emergency spell in central defence. One of those occasions was a 2 – 0 success against Gillingham when the *Barnsley Chronicle* paid him the supreme compliment by saying that he even outshone Mick McCarthy.

One of the proudest moments of his career came in the aftermath of a depressing team performance at Reading on 29th December 1979. Following a 7 – 0 defeat, Allan Clarke called a meeting of the players at which he spoke some hometruths and said he intended to bring in new faces. Then, turning to Phil, he said, 'I want you to be captain. Will you do it?' 'Of course I will,' was the reply, and he felt it was the highest honour he could ever have.

Under Phil's captaincy the team were promoted 16 months later. The following season, 1981/82, exceeded everyone's expectations for not only did they attain the club's highest League position for 60 years, they also dispatched three First Division sides from the League Cup. Yet he reckons his job as captain was the easiest in football; the team had four others who had captained sides and every man knew exactly what was expected of him. Consequently, when playing at Oakwell the main thing he had to do was win the toss in order that they could kick towards their own supporters at the Pontefract Road end in the second-half – and in more than four seasons as captain there were only two occasions when he didn't win it.

He remained in the side until early in the 1984/85 season when, after a Milk Cup-tie against Grimsby Town and despite being the Sponsors' Man of the Match, he lost his place. He was recalled for a single game in February 1985 but was in the side on only four more occasions, his last appearance being in a

1 – 1 draw at Fulham on 4th May. From the turn of the year he'd been helping to coach the junior sides, and a few days before the season ended manager Bobby Collins told him he'd arranged with the directors for him to become youth team coach. In June he went on holiday, secure in the knowledge of continued employment, but while he was away Collins was dismissed and Allan Clarke returned as manager. When the latter next saw Phil he said he had no knowledge of him being youth team coach and it was not an appointment which figured in his own plans. And a few days later Phil received a letter stating that he had been given a free transfer.

He began the 1985/86 season as a non-contract player with Rochdale, but in October he was told the club could no longer afford to pay him. Moving to Hartlepool United, he stayed there for the remainder of the season and then joined Rotherham United as youth team coach. He was appointed by his former Barnsley boss, Norman Hunter, and remained at Millmoor on Hunter's dismissal in December 1987. However, he became a casualty of the second management change in three months, being required to leave in the following March when newly-appointed Billy McEwan brought in a coach of his own choosing.

Almost immediately he was appointed reserve and youth coach at Scarborough. He is still there, now working for former Oakwell team-mate Ray McHale. Responsibilities include recruitment of young players and he is already having the satisfaction of seeing some of his earlier signings progress to the first team squad.

He is an all-round sportsman and has been a club cricketer for more than 20 years. Much of that time was with Ward Green, but more recently he's played for the NCB, Manor House and Worsbrough Bridge, and for Kexborough in the Huddersfield League. His first game was when 14 years old, after having travelled to Hoylandswaine as scorer. On arrival the team were a man short so he was pressed into service – and he caught out three batsmen and threw down the wicket of the last, in so doing providing a win which took Ward Green to the top of Division One of the Barnsley League. Other notable occasions were when he was the Barnsley League's highest scorer; leading the league averages at batting and bowling; taking nine wickets for 12 runs against Central WMC and being Man of the Match when Kexborough won the Ted Gill Knock-out Trophy in 1988.

In the spring of 1981 there were perhaps some supporters who thought Phil Chambers might have difficulty in adjusting to the greater demands of higher level football. If so, they couldn't have been more wrong. He was a revelation, and speed of thought enabled him to continue in a style which could have suggested a lack of pace. He assessed situations instantly, and a great left foot enabled him to pick out whichever player could be used to best advantage. He seemed to find Trevor Aylott almost without looking, and many of Ronnie Glavin's surges stemmed from him having made space in the sure knowledge that Phil would pin-point a 40-yard pass to perfection. By allowing others to do the things they were good at he earned their continual appreciation, yet the greatest fulfilment he has so far achieved came from being a Barnsley-born man who captained his home town club into the Second Division.

Billy Ronson: An Astonishing Experience

Billy Ronson held a regular place in Barnsley's midfield in the early 1980s and his on-going career has taken him to three other clubs in the English Second Division and twice to America where he now plays indoor five-a-side soccer with Baltimore Blast. Not the tallest of players, he compensates by a tremendous work-rate and a never-say-die spirit. This regularly incurred the displeasure of referees, and when he thought he was the victim of a wrong decision he didn't hesitate to say so. It was an attitude which cost him a lot of money until he learned to keep his mouth shut.

Billy is the son of Percy Ronson, once a renowned winger in Lancashire Combination football who played more than 500 games for Fleetwood Town between 1947 and 1963 and won amateur representative honours at county level. Billy's own career began as a winger, and after playing for Blackpool Boys he joined the town's Second Division club as an apprentice in 1972.

His debut was against Nottingham Forest in March 1975 and it was the kind of introduction for which every young player hopes. Reporting in the *Daily Express* under a headline 'New Boy Billy is Everybody's Hero', Derek Hodgson said it was the most impressive debut he'd seen for years. In the following season Billy played 17 times and was being hailed in Blackpool as the new Alan Ball, and from August 1976 he had a regular place in the side.

Blackpool were relegated in 1978 and Billy spent the summer on loan to Fort Lauderdale Strikers in the North American Soccer League. Then 21, he couldn't believe what was happening to him: he played against the great Franz Beckenbauer and was a team-mate of Gordon Banks and George Best. Indeed, when Best was brought into the dressing room to be introduced Billy just looked at him in awe, for he still had a picture of the brilliant Irishman hanging on the bedroom wall at his home in Fleetwood. Another example of his non-stop love affair with football came later, on the day of his marriage to Miss Julie Neave at St Peter's Church, Fleetwood, when the happy couple walked down the isle to the strains of the theme-tune from BBC TV's *Match of the Day*.

He returned to Blackpool in August for the start of the new season, but he hated the Third Division. The assertive, argumentative style continued, as did the bookings, and in the preceding year manager Bob Stokoe had begun fining him £50 every time that happened. In the spring of 1979 there was a week when he was booked and fined three times, following which the club suspended him for a fortnight. During that time he read in a newspaper that they were having difficulty in fielding a team, so he went to Stokoe and offered to play without being paid. The manager had to refer this to the board – who responded by putting him on the transfer list. At this point Billy and Julie sat down together one evening to calculate what the bookings had cost them. And when they realized Billy's wages had been reduced by nearly *a thousand pounds* he knew he'd got to start keeping his mouth shut.

In July 1979 he became Cardiff City's record signing at £135,000. Again in the Second Division, he was back in his best form. Being appointed captain gave him a greater sense of responsibility: in two seasons he missed only one game and was a Player of the Year and winner of seven other trophies sponsored by various branches of the Supporters' Club.

Two years later he moved to Wrexham after a tribunal had halved Cardiff's asking price of £250,000. His one season in North Wales ended in relegation and, still having an aversion for the Third Division, he wanted to be away and signed for Barnsley in August 1982.

The first three seasons at Oakwell were the happiest of his whole career. Apart from an injury absence in the autumn of 1983 he was never omitted from the side, but that changed when Allan Clarke became manager in the summer of 1985. As men, he and Clarke like each other. However, right from the start Clarke made it clear that there was no place for Billy in his team.

From the time of Clarke's appointment he had only one first team game and a handful in the reserves – and he even lost his place in that side. Never one to boot the ball out of defence if it could be played in a more stylish way, in a reserve game at Bramall Lane on 18th September 1985 he relieved a situation by a piece of smart play which incurred the wrath of Kenny Burns, a player who was temporarily in charge of the team. Burns stepped from the dug-out and shouted to Billy to tell him, in thoroughly derogatory terms, how he should have cleared the ball. In the almost empty stadium everyone present must have heard – as they undoubtedly heard Billy's shouted reply which was couched in equally unflattering language. He didn't get another game until the visit of West Brom reserves three weeks later. Then he was involved in a quite amazing incident. In the second half, with Barnsley's substitute in use, Burns held up the number 10 board and shouted to Billy to leave the pitch. This immediately followed him having worked the ball out of defence and it inadvertently going out of play. The referee ran to the bench and Billy, standing nearby, heard him say, 'What are you doing? You've already used the sub.' Burns replied, 'I know I have. I still want him off.' The referee, looking puzzled, turned to Billy. 'What are you going to do?' Billy said, 'It's taken me long enough to get a game. There's no way I'm leaving now!'

He stayed on the pitch and he and Burns had no contact with each other after the game. However, at 9am next day Billy was at the manager's office demanding to know why Burns continued to humiliate him. Clarke denied knowledge of the incident and, leaving him in the office, went in search of Burns. On returning he said to forget about it as he'd spoken to Burns and there would be no repetition. Determined not to prolong the agony, Billy refused to talk to reporters who tried to interview him about the incident. Yet it was still apparent that he wasn't wanted. Twice he was chosen for the first team – once to play and once as sub – and his name was deleted while the players were changing in readiness for the game. He even got the cold shoulder at training sessions and finally resorted to keeping fit by running in the lanes around his home at Hoylandswaine. In November he was loaned to Birmingham City for a few games in the First Division and in mid-December Clarke sent for him to say he was to be transferred to Lincoln City. But that didn't figure in Billy's plans. He spoke to the Lincoln manager and asked for terms which he knew the other wouldn't be able to meet. Clarke was most displeased and said he'd never play in the first team again. Billy responded by asking for a free transfer. Clarke at first said this was out of the question but he relented and arranged it two weeks later, early in January 1986.

Billy was promptly in touch with Kenny Cooper, part-owner and head coach of Baltimore Blast in the US Major Indoor Soccer League. Five years earlier Cooper had said there was a contract for him whenever he could get his release from English football. While arrangements were being made to go to America he had a spell as a non-contract player with Blackpool. In early March he and Julie travelled to Baltimore where he signed a contract which provided an income 50 per-cent higher than what he had been getting at Oakwell.

The team's fixtures take them many thousands of miles from homes in the east to Tacoma near the Canadian border, to San Diego on the west coast and as far south as Dallas, Texas. The season is from November to April with as many as three games each week, and so much travel is involved that the players can be away from home for up to three weeks at a time. Billy's quick, all-action style is ideally suited to the indoor game. In his four seasons with Blast they have always reached the championship play-offs, once winning it and twice being runners-up. In 1989 he was their top scorer at that stage of the competition, scoring 17 goals in the 13 games. He is one of only four players contracted throughout the year and in close-seasons he coaches youngsters at the club's summer camps

Billy has applied to live permanently in the United States. If approved, that will allow him to continue working there after he ceases playing and he then intends to conduct his own training camps. Already he has been invited to take up, when circumstances permit, appointments as consultant at a high school and soccer director at the YMCA.

His career is now in its 18th year and still going strong, yet but for Bob Stokoe's firm action it might have fizzled out in his early twenties. The former Blackpool boss is one of five people to whom Billy owes a great deal. Another is Julie who has given continual support, not least in uprooting the matrimonial home and travelling 3,000 miles to enable her husband to start again in a new game, and the others are his brother, Peter, and his mother and father.

Percy Ronson is a living legend in Fleetwood. In 1963 international players took part in this non-League footballer's benefit match and more than a decade later, when Billy was firmly established in the Blackpool side, rarely a week passed without some knowledgeable old-timer saying to him, '. . . but you'll never be as good as your dad.' He visits the UK each year to have a few weeks at the family home and father and son spend a lot of time together. Wherever they go there are people giving a friendly acknowledgement to Percy, and Billy loves having a dad with whom he has so much in common and who is so well-known and respected within their home town.

Stuart Gray: Returning to the Top

Stuart Gray joined Nottingham Forest during the 1978/79 season, in the course of which they became champions of the First Division. His debut came three years later at a time when the club held the European Cup, and within a week he played in a match against a Uruguayan side, Nacional, in Tokyo to determine the 1980 World Club Championship. He joined Barnsley in August 1983 but, much as he liked the place, he always hankered to return to the First Division. In November 1987 a transfer to Aston Villa took him part-way there, and the objective was achieved less than six months later when Villa were promoted to the level at which most of their long history has been spent.

A Withernsea boy, Stuart was playing for a youth club side when Hull City had him for trials and then rejected him. Two years later and still with the youth club he trained with Forest's juniors for two months, during which time, and remarkably for a trialist, he got into the Central League side. Almost equally remarkably, for clubs don't normally commit themselves to 17-year-olds for that length of time, at the end of the trial he was given a two-year contract.

Introduction into the first team came in February 1981 at Maine Road, Manchester. The *Daily Express* referred to it as a debut of utter coolness and promise, Stuart making the kind of impression one would expect from a seasoned professional. The report went on to say he rarely wasted a ball or missed a tackle, and Gerry Gow, the home side's renowned midfield destroyer, had his most ineffective game since joining them in the previous November. A fortnight later, after his third game – a 3 – 1 win over Arsenal – Forest's assistant manager, Peter Taylor, was quoted in the national press as saying that Stuart had been 'head and shoulders' the best player on the pitch.

In-between-times he was at the National Stadium, Tokyo, as part of Forest's European Cup-winning team which played Nacional – winners of the South American Champions Cup – to decide the World Club Championship. The Uruguayans won 1 – 0, thus earning themselves a £5,000 per-man bonus, and it was Stuart who came nearest to scoring for Forest with a header which hit a post 12 minutes from the end.

For the remainder of the season he was part of the youngest midfield in the First Division, receiving such consistently good notices that he was disappointed at not getting under-23 honours. But that might well have happened. There was an occasion when Jock Stein, manager of the Scottish national team, whilst watching a game from the directors' box at the City Ground, Nottingham, remarked to one of his hosts on how well Stuart was playing and enquired about his nationality. He got the reply 'Oh, he's English through and through.' Yet Stuart's father was a Scot and he is therefore eligible for either England or Scotland.

He opened the following season at left full back before reverting to midfield, remaining in the side until Easter 1982 when injury put him on the side-lines.

A big disadvantage about losing one's place at such a club is that replacements are always available. Consequently, over the following year Stuart had more games on loan at Bolton Wanderers than in his own first team. But most of the time was spent in Forest's reserve side. Becoming fed up with that, in the summer of 1983 he asked to be transferred and, almost immediately, moved to Barnsley in exchange for a fee of £40,000.

The transfer was finalized within the day, and arranging a home in the area was done equally quickly. Never previously having been to Barnsley, on approaching the town through the village of Hickleton he saw a house for sale there. On the return journey he stopped at Hickleton and agreed to buy the house he'd passed only a couple of hours earlier.

His debut was in the season's opening game – a 3 – 0 beating of Fulham. He was among the scorers, as he was in three of the next four games. However, in December he sustained a serious spinal injury which wasn't correctly diagnosed until March. An operation to fuse three vertebra followed, and by the time he returned to the side in March 1985 he'd been out of action for 15 months.

Most of the following season was at left full back and, consequently, there were few goals from him. However, in November he scored a gem of a winning goal against Millwall by curling a 20-yard free kick delightfully into a top corner of the net.

The 1986/87 season opened disastrously and the first seven games were lost. With the team at the foot of the division, it was Stuart who provided the first success with a goal at Grimsby Town on 27th September. A fortnight later his two goals secured a win at the expense of Bradford City, and on 25th October two more produced a creditable draw against Sheffield United after the Reds had trailed 2 – 0.

During the earlier lean spell Spurs visited Oakwell in the Littlewoods Cup. Barnsley lost 3 – 2 but not before Stuart had equalized with a fine diving header and put them 2 – 1 ahead from the penalty-spot.

It was a season which emphasized Stuart's versatility, for by the end of February 1987 the only positions he hadn't filled during his time with the club were goalkeeper and right full back. But his preference was for the left side of midfield from where he could make late runs into the penalty-area – a ploy which brought most of his goals.

The season ended with the team in a mid-table place and Stuart's 13 goals put him at the head of the scorers. His popularity with the fans was such that when prizes were allocated he swept the board, becoming Player of the Year for the Supporters' Club, the Disabled Supporters, the Away Supporters and the Sponsors – Hennessy Cognac.

Perhaps it was his personal success during the previous 12 months which decided him to move to a club more likely to get into the First Division. When the 1987/88 season began he asked to be placed on the transfer list, and in November, for a fee of £175,000 he joined Aston Villa. He couldn't have had a better start. His first game was at Bradford City when he scored twice in a 4 – 2 success. Retaining a midfield role throughout the remainder of the season, he was among the scorers on three further occasions and in May the team were promoted to the First Division.

Stuart was one of only four players who had previously been at that level. Therefore the 1988/89 season was, in the main, a learning experience and, eventually, relegation became a close-run thing. In the event it was avoided by a single point, and Stuart's equalizer against Middlesbrough on 29th April ensured his team's survival and the visitors' relegation despite their having been in the lead until the dying seconds of the game.

The near escape was reflected in Villa's chances of winning the 1990 League championship being quoted at 500 to 1. Yet under Stuart's captaincy they were in the hunt from the start, and in late February replaced Liverpool as leaders of the First Division. It was a position held for several weeks until a couple of disappointing results enabled Liverpool to surge ahead. Nevertheless, Aston Villa finished in a commendable runners-up position.

On reflection, Stuart thinks he was perhaps too quick to join Barnsley; he was anxious to get fixed up, but if he'd waited he might have been able to spend all his career in the First Division. Certainly he is one of the best all-round left-sided players that Barnsley FC has had, and also one of the most versatile. In a 1 – 0 win at Hull City in March 1986 he played for the first time as a sweeper; the following week's *Barnsley Chronicle* said he'd excelled once again, was undoubtedly Man of the Match, and so complete and authoritative was his performance that it was as if he'd had the role throughout his career. Looking to the future, he is already a licensed FA coach and his ambition is to become a manager. In that respect he has worked for two of the best in the business – Brian Clough and Graham Taylor – and the knowledge thereby gained, together with his own abilities and experience, is ideal preparation for the kind of post-playing career he hopes to have.

Gwyn Thomas: Few of Them About!

Gwyn Thomas joined the Oakwell staff from Leeds United in 1984, but Barnsley connections had been building up over the preceding 12 years since his schooldays in South Wales. Then he captained the Swansea side which won the Welsh schools' trophy by beating Chester – a team containing Paul and Ron Futcher, later to be his team-mates at Oakwell. On becoming a Leeds United apprentice he was coached by Bobby Collins who, 10 years later, was the manager who signed him for Barnsley. And his introduction to the First Division was as a 17-year-old substitute in a game against Wolves in April 1975 when the man he replaced was another future Barnsley manager, Allan Clarke.

As a pupil at Gowerton Grammar School he was a schoolboy international soccer player and represented West Glamorgan at rugby, and on the athletics field in 1973 he created new schools' records for the long and triple jumps. His talents were such that there was often conflict between those who required his services. Indeed, he scored the goal which beat South London Schools to put Swansea into the quarter-finals of the English Trophy but he only played after a personal appeal by his father, Lawrence, secured his release from a schools' rugby seven-a-side tournament at Hereford.

All the indications were that he could become a top-level player in Rugby Union. Similarly, scholastic attainments were such that an opening in teaching was there to be worked for. But, having trained at Elland Road during holidays since he was 13, there was never much likelihood that on leaving school he would do anything other than become an apprentice with Leeds United. That proved to be the case and a year later, on his 17th birthday in September 1974, he was a full-time professional footballer.

Junior days at Elland Road saw him play three times for the Welsh junior side, the first of which was at Maine Road in March 1976. In the second-half of that game Wales trailed 2 – 0 and Gwyn had had an emergency spell in goal before returning to the attack; he then scored his side's first goal to put them on course for a quite remarkable 3 – 2 success.

In the following season he won the first of three Welsh under-21 caps. He also had a place in the Leeds United side for the season's final month, scoring in his first full game in a 2 – 1 win against Bristol City. However, appearances over the following four years were few and far between; he didn't come to the fore until the spring of 1982, by which time Leeds were on their way out of the First Division.

Until then Gwyn had always been a striker, but under the direction of new manager Eddie Gray he became a midfielder. In that role his ability to win the ball and set attacks in motion while still having sufficient energy to get into scoring positions was seen to best effect.

He held a regular place until injury at Carlisle in December 1983 put him out of the side. He was incapacitated for several weeks and, apart from a substitute appearance at Crystal Palace in early March, he didn't play in the first team again and was transferred later in the month to Barnsley. The fee was £40,000 and Gwyn was manager Bobby Collins' first signing for the club.

His impact on the Oakwell scene was such that, in March 1985, in contemplating the forthcoming Player of the Year award in his weekly column in the *Green 'Un*, Trevor Lovatt referred to the claims of various members of the team but was emphatic that, in the light of 100 per-cent commitment, home and away, throughout the season, the man most deserving of the accolade was Gwyn Thomas. As things turned out, it went to someone else but at least one experienced observer thought there had been a more appropriate recipient.

Perhaps surprisingly in view of the years he'd spent as a striker, his goal scoring was infrequent. But the first, on 13th November 1984, was sufficiently well timed to gain maximum points at the expense of local rivals Sheffield United. In the following season he scored twice to secure victory over Brighton & Hove Albion and three other goals enabled points to be shared with Norwich City, Bradford City and Oldham Athletic.

Soon after Gwyn's arrival at Oakwell the supporters became so impressed by his tremendous work-rate that they nicknamed him Thomas the Tank Engine. His displays were consistently worthy of such acknowledgement, and after a victory over Sunderland in December 1986 the *Barnsley Chronicle* said he seemed to cover every square inch of the pitch in ensuring the authority in midfield which helped towards what was only the team's third home win in a barren 12-month spell.

The season's final game was the return at Sunderland. Gwyn got the winner after the Reds had trailed 2 – 0, the goal being of historical significance in that it proved a major factor in the hosts' relegation to Division Three for the first time in their 108-year existence.

In November 1987 it seemed Gwyn was about to add full Welsh honours to those received at under-21 level. He was called into the international squad for a European Championship game against Czechoslovakia. In the event, although travelling to Prague, he didn't get onto the pitch but, nevertheless, there was satisfaction in knowing that the selectors hadn't lost sight of him.

January 1989 brought a traumatic period into his life. The season had begun well enough for him and in October in the final seconds of a game against West Brom he scored the winning goal after the Reds had trailed at the interval. On 2nd January his display against Hull City earned him a Star Player rating in *The Star*, but, five days later, disaster struck in a third round FA Cup-tie against Chelsea.

The Londoners arrived at Oakwell as joint leaders of the Second Division after an unbeaten run of 13 games. Yet Barnsley wiped the floor with them. Gwyn scored in the third minute and by the 39th the Reds had a three goal lead. Then Chelsea showed a cynical side. Two minutes later there was a fracas involving David Currie and their Joe McLaughlin, and immediately players started squaring up to each other. As the ball spun away from the main protagonists there was a tackle on Gwyn. He ended up on the ground in agony and, while lying there, another Chelsea player stamped on him, thus compounding the damage which the first contact had already done to his right knee.

It is the only injury of any significance that Gwyn has ever had, which is perhaps surprising because he's always in the thick of things, without shin-pads and wearing what can be best described as ankle socks. But it could hardly have been worse. He had four days in hospital where a cruciate ligament was found to be extensively damaged, and it was the kind of injury which, even a few years ago, would have put a player out of the game for good. The following 11 months were spent in and out of hospital, on crutches and on the treatment table, and in the gym driving himself through long, lonely hours of rebuilding exercises worked out for him at the FA rehabilitation centre at Lilleshall.

The first public sign of recovery came in late December in a reserve game at Scunthorpe, and three weeks later, exactly a year after the ill-fated visit of Chelsea, he was in the squad without getting into the game for a third round FA Cup-tie against Leicester City. Again in the squad for the fourth round tie, a fortnight later he received appreciative applause when the team ran onto the pitch in readiness for a game against Swindon Town – his first for more than 13 months. But it was to be his last. He made two further appearances as substitute without displaying his previous high standard, and a few weeks later on the transfer-deadline day he moved to Hull City.

When Mel Machin became Barnsley's manager in late December 1989 he promised to lead the club into the First Division within three years. Such confidence was not in keeping with the team's placing at that time, and supporters perhaps thought – mistakenly, in the event – that he was banking on being able to use Gwyn Thomas. Gwyn is a player in the mould of Spurs' Dave Mackay and Liverpool's Tommy Smith of bygone days – hard men whose determined aggression was not only an example to colleagues but continually inspired them to greater efforts themselves – and throughout the spring of 1989 when, without him, Barnsley narrowly missed the promotion play-offs, supporters continually pilloried Machin's predecessor for failing to replace him with a similar type of player. Yet one can sympathise with Allan Clarke, for much as he may have wanted another Gwyn Thomas, there were very few of them about.

Paul Futcher: A Forthright Perfectionist

Paul Futcher's years in football have involved him in some notable happenings. As captain of Cheshire Boys he was the first *Cheshire Observer* Schoolboy Footballer of the Year; in 1973 he became the youngest Chester footballer to appear in their League side and a year later, on moving into the First Division with Luton Town, he became the first £100,000 17-year-old. On a more personal note, he and his brother Ron – the elder by 20 minutes – were the first twins to play in the First Division and, 10 years later, were the first to play in Barnsley's side. Ron's stay at Oakwell was of short duration but Paul has now been with the club for six years and it may well be that his cultured style will be a feature of the Reds' defence throughout the remainder of his playing career.

Paul and Ron became apprentices with Chester, their home town club, on leaving school in 1970. They could have entered the game at a higher level but an older brother, Graham, was a professional with Chester and family thinking was that it would be no bad thing for him to keep an eye on them.

Paul's entry into the first team was at Cambridge in March 1973, when he was exactly 16½, and his appearance created much favourable press comment. The *Liverpool Echo* said Chester lost points but had found a star; the *News of the World* reported that Paul was Chester's hero, hardly putting a foot wrong and playing like a veteran; the *Sunday People* expressed an almost identical view and, nearer home, the *Chester Chronicle* said that with Paul on the books, the club was sitting on a gold mine. And that's what he proved to be.

Luton manager Harry Haslam had been alerted to the player through a chance conversation with a Chester supporter. Manchester City were also interested but dithered at the asking price. Their hesitation cost them dearly, for when they eventually signed him, four years later, his valuation had more than tripled.

Paul's elevation to the First Division came after only 21 games in the Fourth – and again the local press raved about him. His first game for Luton was in August 1974 as substitute in a Texaco Cup-tie against Southampton. Afterwards the *Luton News* referred to his cool head and skill in tight situations and said, at 17, he was the club's most valuable asset. Nevertheless, he didn't gain a place in the League side until a visit to Chelsea in December, Luton then being firmly fixed at the bottom of the table. Soon after signing Paul, Haslam had returned to Chester to obtain the other Futcher twin and the two were major factors in a team revival which turned despair into a glimmer of hope. Paul played as though he'd been in the First Division for years and Ron was to end the season as second-top scorer.

At that time there was rarely a Luton match report which didn't refer to Paul's quality and class. In February he trained for four days with the full England squad, yet, in a season when he received so much acclaim there were occasional black moments. He admitted responsibility for a vital point lost at Queen's Park Rangers in March when he allowed himself to be dispossessed on the half-way line, from which the home side scored the winning goal. And at White Hart Lane a month later, his indiscreet remarks to a linesman following the award of a goal to Spurs resulted in the first sending-off of his career.

Luton's results improved considerably soon after he and Ron went into the side. There were three consecutive wins on three occasions, but even that couldn't compensate for the poor run from August to December and, in the final analysis, the third-bottom place put the club into the Second Division.

There was a cash crisis during most of Paul's time at Luton – at one stage the overdraft was half-a-million pounds and increasing weekly. One influential view was that much of the problem could be resolved by Paul's transfer, but in September 1976 manager Haslam was quoted as saying, 'If he goes, I go too. A player like him is essential for the success of our club.' Haslam's view prevailed, and three months later Paul won the first of his 11 England under-21 caps.

But by the summer of 1978 Haslam had gone and the club weren't inclined to turn down Manchester City's offer of £350,000 for their star defender. Having paid their highest-ever fee to get him in the first place, they received a record amount when he moved on.

Over the following two years Paul played a further seven times in the under-21 side, but his situation at Maine Road wasn't as favourable. Having started in the first team, early in 1979 he began to have spells out of the side and didn't play after the middle of April. The uncertainties about his position stemmed from the time Malcolm Allison became coach in January and when pre-season training began in the following summer Paul sought him out and asked if he figured in future plans. He was assured that if he worked hard and showed what he could do, all would be well – and to enable him to prove his worth he was permitted 45 minutes football in four pre-season games! It therefore seemed a decision on his future had already been made. For a time he languished in the reserves and there was newspaper speculation that he was about to join Oldham Athletic. In fact, he did have talks with them following an approach by the England coach, Bill Taylor, who was at Oldham, but decided against moving there because he knew he was good enough for the First Division. In September he was recalled to the side against Coventry City and received Man of the Match ratings after a 3 – 0 victory, following which Allison said he would be staying at the club.

Nevertheless, nothing had changed and he became completely disillusioned.

He had gone to Maine Road as the young centre half who was regarded as the natural successor to Dave Watson in the England side, yet he was unable to hold a place in Manchester City's first team. The club was in the process of a massive upheaval in the wake of Allison's appointment; players valued at some £2m departed, to be replaced by others of similar valuation. After the announcement that Paul wouldn't be leaving he played a further dozen games over the remaining major part of the season and was then transferred to Oldham Athletic.

At Oldham he missed only a handful of games in two-and-a-half years and was ever-present in 1982/83 until his sudden transfer to Derby County at the end of January. It was a move he was reluctant to make. Perfectly happy at Oldham, a transfer was the last thing on his mind but Derby's offer was too good to refuse. They were in bottom place in Division Two when he went there but didn't lose another game until May and ended in a fairly respectable 13th position.

However, the improved form wasn't maintained when the next season began. Following a 5 – 1 defeat at Blackburn Rovers in September 1983, manager Peter Taylor put three of the back four, including Paul, on the transfer list. Later in the season he had a spell in the reserves and at one stage there were four players – internationals McFarland, Watson and Burns, and himself – competing for two positions in central defence. Still on the transfer list, a series of disagreements with Taylor worsened his situation. Yet he liked Derby; he thought it a great club and he got on well with the other players, but the antagonism between Taylor and himself was such that he knew he had to get away. Nevertheless, he refused an opportunity to join Norwich City but, eventually, an offer came from Barnsley. By then the ill-feeling between manager and player was such that as he was leaving the ground to travel to Oakwell, Taylor's parting shot was, 'And if you don't sign, don't come back!'

To the lasting benefit of both Paul and Barnsley FC he did sign and, from a personal point of view, the timing couldn't have been better. For his Oakwell debut, on 31st March 1984, ended in a 5 – 1 humiliation of the club he'd left only nine days earlier. Thus began the longest association and happiest years of Paul's whole career.

Even so, there have been some depressing moments. Against Huddersfield Town in March 1985 – with the Reds trailing 2 – 1 and pressing for an equalizer – he was caught in possession on the halfway-line and the visitors raced away to put the issue beyond doubt. It happened five minutes from the end – and on entering the dressing room manager Allan Clarke handed him a typewritten notice of the imposition of £50 fine for his mistake on the pitch. A prompt retort of, 'I'm not paying this' was countered with, 'It's a hundred pounds now!' His response, 'I don't care, I'm still not paying it' brought, 'Right, it's doubled again!' Wisely, Paul then shut up. But he referred the matter to the PFA and, in the event, the fine was not enforced and neither party mentioned it again.

There have been other occasions when tops have been blown – almost always because Paul is a perfectionist and hates criticism of his play. But such upsets became things of the past, principally because manager and player learned to be more understanding of each other and, anyway, Paul reckons he has mellowed and no longer has to make an instant response to annoying situations. Yet he is still a forthright man who speaks frankly at post-match inquests. And Allan Clarke was in good company, for the young Paul Futcher was inclined to speak first and think afterwards, and some of the best known managers in the game have been at the receiving end of his pointed observations.

A dispute over a new contract resulted in him missing the end of season 1985/86 and the first game of the next, and he had some games with the reserves in late 1989, but apart from those two short spells he has had a place in the side since joining the club. The supporters have always regarded him highly, voting him Player of the Year in 1985 and 1989.

Few would argue with an assertion that, even at 33, Paul is one of the finest centre halves in the Second Division and better than many in the First. One detects in him a barely concealed belief that his comparatively short time at the top level is through having a reputation of being hard to handle; certainly his performances for Barnsley have consistently been of First Division standard. In fact, when the Reds won 5 – 2 at West Ham in the Littlewoods Cup in 1987, Keith Lodge wrote in the *Barnsley Chronicle* that Paul was the classiest player on the pitch, turning in an immaculate performance which would have graced the international stage And 18 months later, at Oakwell in the fifth round of the FA Cup when Everton won by the narrowest margin, his faultless display resulted in the visitors' £2m striker Tony Cottee barely getting a kick.

He is training for the future in the same systematic manner that he prepares for each game of football. A fully licensed FA coach, he currently coaches schoolboys in Kirklees where he lives and has attended a football managers' course organized by the PFA. Keeping his options open, he has a qualification in recreation management and has received training in licensed house management – yet he intends to keep on playing football for as long as he can.

When the 1989/90 season began Paul had been at Barnsley much longer than at any of his previous clubs and he had a feeling that it was perhaps time for him to move elsewhere. On 17th October he was left out of the side to play against Sheffield United; he wasn't told until the last minute but expressed no ill-feeling, merely telling the manager that he'd been thinking about a transfer and this seemed as good a time as any. Consequently his availability was circulated and he spent several weeks in the reserves.

During that time there was an approach from Scarborough for him to become their player-coach – just the kind of opening for which he'd been hoping. Therefore he wasn't at all happy when nothing materialized because Barnsley priced him at £30,000 while Scarborough had been hoping to get him on a free transfer.

However, the outlook changed for the better when he was in the first side to be chosen by new manager Mel Machin which ended 1989 with a victory at the expense of Leeds United. He retained a place for the remainder of the season and press reports were as favourable as at any time in the preceding six years.

It is to Allan Clarke's credit that *he* never felt the need to get rid of this once hard-to-handle player and the resultant benefit to the club has been enormous. Mel Machin was quick to speak favourably of Paul's consistency and class, in the light of which it may well be that the cultured Futcher defensive style will remain an attraction of the Oakwell scene for several years to come.

Clive Baker: A Remarkable Achievement

Clive Baker is a goalkeeper who joined Norwich City straight from school at 18 and remained with them for seven seasons but, as understudy to the established Kevin Keelan and, later, Chris Woods who went on to play for England, he was in the First Division side on only 14 occasions. However, due to Keelan's summertime commitments in America, Clive deputized for him in pre-season games, thereby playing about 50 times in the first team. Yet on joining Barnsley in August 1984 it seemed he was to continue as an understudy, this time to Andy Rhodes. But the latter was injured three games into the season and Clive was given his chance – and results could hardly have been better, either for himself or the team.

Born at West Runton, near Cromer, he played for Sheringham reserves at 14 – once scoring by kicking the ball the full length of the pitch. A year later he was in the Norwich City junior side and could have joined the club as an apprentice. However, he decided to stay on at Paston Grammar School and two years later, with 'A' levels in maths, chemistry and physics, there was a place for him at university. But, despite the earlier rejection, Norwich were still keen to sign him and he agreed to join them, feeling that otherwise he might later regret not having done so.

His First Division debut was in April 1978 in a 2 – 2 draw against Newcastle United, following which the *Eastern Evening News* described him as 'a player of rich and precocious potential'. However, by the time Keelan retired a year later there was another goalkeeper on the scene. Clive didn't get into the side again until November 1980; he played 10 consecutive games but in the following March a fee of almost a quarter-of-a-million pounds took Woods to the club. The new man was in the side continuously throughout the following three-and-a-half seasons, and long before the end of that time Clive realized that the other's form was so good that he'd never be promoted, no matter how well he played.

Consequently, late in 1983 he asked to be transferred but was still at the club at the end of the season, at which stage he was given a free transfer. Cardiff City were interested in having him but he chose Barnsley, although manager Bobby Collins gave no assurance of a first team place.

At the start of the following season, in August 1984, he began to further his experience of reserve team football, but a breakthrough came in the fourth game. The first three had been lost and Clive made his debut on 4th September at Notts County, immediately impressing with impeccable handling and giving every indication that the Reds had secured a very competent goalkeeper.

Four days later at Portsmouth he was the one who stood between the home side and an emphatic victory, Barnsley being penned in their own half for most of the game and only his faultless display enabling them to share the points. And against Leeds United in October his two superb saves early in the second half seemed to cause the visitors to lose heart, following which the Reds went on to win 1 – 0. Throughout this period the new 'keeper had received consistently favourable press reports. After a victory over Sheffield United in November the *Green 'Un* awarded him Star Player rating, saying he appeared quite unbeatable, and at the post-match press conference Bobby Collins likened a point-blank save to one of Gordon Banks's in Mexico in 1970 which was supposedly featured by every TV station in the world. After their shaky start the Reds went 15 games without defeat, Clive keeping a clean sheet on 11 occasions.

Having spent most of the previous seven seasons as second-choice goalkeeper, he couldn't have had a better start to regular first team football – the icing on the cake coming in the spring when he was placed top in the voting for Player of the Year.

In August 1985 he was back at Carrow Road, Norwich, for the first time since leaving there a year earlier. It was a visit which must have given him much satisfaction, for the home side – who were destined to end the season as Second Division champions – only snatched an equalizer in the closing seconds after Clive had produced what the *Barnsley Chronicle* described as 'an inspired performance which included five top-quality saves'.

Similar press comment continued throughout the season, 'Bread-winner Baker' . . . 'Baker saves the day' . . . 'Baker wins – hands down', and 'Bold Baker lone hero' being but a small sample of the headlines he created. And it seems those sentiments were echoed by the supporters, for in March, for the second time in two years, he was Player of the Year.

He continues to give quality performances. After a 5 – 2 beating of Stoke City the *Barnsley Chronicle* said that but for excellent goalkeeping the visitors would have scored five themselves. In a Littlewoods Cup-tie at Wimbledon against the FA Cup holders he was quite unbeatable, at one stage drawing loud applause for the way he retrieved a situation by leaping first low and then high to turn the ball safely away. And as recently as March 1990 he helped towards three priceless points with a spectacular reflex save which thwarted Oldham Athletic who, earlier in the week, had knocked out Everton to reach the semi-finals of the FA Cup.

Having now completed five seasons at Oakwell, Clive is one of the most popular custodians the Reds have had and it is most unlikely that any other free transfer player in the Second Division has ever ended each of the next two seasons as winner of supporters' major accolade.

When he was a teenager in Norfolk there were indications that he could reach the top in cricket. He played for Sheringham at both cricket and football – as did his father before him. As a 12-year-old playing against local rivals Watton, his five wickets for 12 runs included those of three middle-order batsmen in one over, and a year later he scored 125 not out in the club's highest total since the Second World War. Soon afterwards he captained an England Schools under-15 side which contained present-day Yorkshire player Kevin Sharpe and Nottinghamshire's England batsman, Tim Robinson, and at 17 he led Norfolk Young Amateurs in their games against county clubs' colts' sides.

Later he was with Cromer CC for five years, during which time he was in a Norfolk Alliance championship side, topped the batting averages and was captain for two years before moving to Barnsley. He then joined Kexborough, and 10 wickets for 28 against Denby Dale was one of a string of impressive performances when they were the 1985 champions of Section A of the Huddersfield League's Central Division.

It is true to say that Clive Baker arrived at Oakwell as a player of unknown quality, but it was quickly apparent that he was an excellent acquisition – something for which two subsequent managers have had cause to be grateful to Bobby Collins. In fact, Allan Clarke was so impressed by Clive's display in a 1 – 1 draw with Blackburn Rovers that he presented him with a large glass of whisky while the players were still in the bath, saying, 'You were magnificent, Clive. This is only whisky but you really deserve champagne!' That wasn't the only time he was singled out for special praise. After a 2 – 1 defeat at Reading, Clarke answered an enquiry about injuries with, 'They didn't put themselves about enough to get injured, but our goalkeeper was magnificent.'

In training, Clive is a workaholic. Even on the players' day off his morning is usually spent on the training ground, defending the goal from shots bombed in from all angles by Eric Winstanley. Although a licensed FA coach and a member of the PFA management committee, his present intention is to leave the game when his time as a player comes to an end. Currently studying towards a BA degree from the Open University, he is attracted to a career in teaching. And preparations which have been long in the making will ensure that, in whichever direction Clive Baker's next career takes him, he will be as well qualified for that as he is to be Barnsley FC's first-choice goalkeeper.

Steve Agnew: A Stirring Prospect

A record for the briefest debut in League football was surely created at Oakwell on 14th April 1984 when Barnsley's substitute, 18-year-old Steve Agnew, entered the game against Charlton Athletic *15 seconds* before the final whistle!

Since then his career has been interrupted by serious injury, following which he was retained on a week-to-week basis. Yet he has fully retrieved the situation, having held a regular place since September 1986 and captaining the side at the highest level that Barnsley has so far attained.

Steve was born at Shipley where his father, Maurice, was serving in the West Riding Constabulary. The family moved to Barnsley in 1968 when Steve was two years old and later, as a pupil at Worsbrough High School, he played for the town's boys' team from the age of 11 to 15.

By that time offers of apprenticeships with Sheffield Wednesday and Leeds United had been declined in favour of joining what he has always regarded as his hometown club. At that early stage of his career he was a striker, his present midfield role being something he was pressed into several years later by manager Allan Clarke.

As an apprentice, Steve received much encouragement from coach Bobby Collins and he was a member of the junior side which, under Collins' direction, were Northern Intermediate League champions in 1983. In the following year the team had a successful run in the FA Youth Cup and Steve scored in every round. His goals included three against Wolves, two in a 3 – 1 beating of Manchester City, an equalizer against Manchester United which took the team to a triumphant replay at Old Trafford, and a penalty against Sunderland which put them into the quarter-finals. Then, against Everton, it was his splendid 30-yard shot which took the tie into extra time, only for the visitors to end the young Reds' longest-ever run in the competition with a goal three minutes from the end.

Steve's first full League appearance came later in the year of his 15-second debut, in September 1984, in a 5 – 1 success against Wolves. It was the team's biggest win and most encouraging performance of the season. He scored one of the goals and was given a hero's reception as he left the pitch, 10 minutes from the end, after sustaining an injured ankle. Afterwards, in a post-match press conference, Bobby Collins – by then the manager – said, 'Steve's a player with a tremendous amount of natural skill and he provided something we've been lacking – an ability to hold the ball while others get into position, and he's got some deft touches and speed as well.'

Steve also played in the next game, a 1 – 0 win at Crystal Palace, but by the time March arrived and the Reds were drawn at Southampton in the fifth round of the FA Cup he'd had only two further outings. Nevertheless, a *Daily Express* headline of 'Steve wonder sinks Saints' was an indication of the impact he made on the game. He was in the side only because others weren't available but, with the team trailing 1 – 0, he took a cross from the left and, on the turn, hit a splendid shot past England's Peter Shilton. And just before the interval he was brought down in the penalty-area, following which Gordon Owen struck home the winner from the spot.

In January 1986, and still without a regular place in the side, he sustained a broken leg while taking part in a five-a-side practice at Oakwell. The physical anguish was compounded by the worry of being out of action and his contract coming up for renewal without him having yet proved himself. Luckily, recovery was uncomplicated and he was able to have a couple of reserve games – with a 12-inch plate in his leg – before the season ended.

So far as a new contract was concerned, at that stage there wasn't one. Clarke's best offer was a week-to-week arrangement for three months, by the end of which Steve had got to have proved an ability to make the grade. The final blow came when the manager went on to say that, in any event, he was already satisfied that he hadn't a future as a striker.

Steve was then sure that Clarke was the most heartless man he'd ever met. But, looking back with the benefit of greater maturity, he now knows that the manager was throwing down a challenge in the hope that it would be taken up. And that's what happened. Within a year Clarke was talking to the press in the terms, 'Steve Agnew is one of the best young midfield players in the Second Division' ... 'Agnew is the sort we need to hang on to, he's not for sale.'

A month into the following season, in September 1986, Steve had a regular place in the side, in midfield, and a three-year contract. Since then he's gone from strength to strength. In September 1987 the *Morning Telegraph* had an 'Elegant Agnew' heading to its report on a victory over Plymouth Argyle which referred to Barnsley's scoring opportunities stemming from Steve's volleyed passes and him being the game's most elegant and determining influence.

Long-range shooting was by then a feature of his play. A few weeks later, in the second leg of a Littlewoods Cup-tie at West Ham, Barnsley were two goals down at the interval and seemingly out of the hunt, but hit back in a manner which reduced the home side to a shambles. The tide turned in the 54th minute when Steve hit home a penalty and he struck again with a ferocious free kick which took the tie into extra time – from which Barnsley emerged as 5 – 2 winners. In December another fiercely-struck kick smashed through West Brom's defensive wall to help towards a 3 – 1 success. And a fortnight later in a 4 – 1 defeat of Millwall his 25-yarder opened the scoring and he got a second from the penalty-spot.

In August 1988, only a matter of days into the season, there was press speculation that Steve was about to be the subject of a half-million-pound bid from Manchester United. Certainly their manager, Alex Ferguson, had been present at a Yorkshire and Humberside Cup-tie against Leeds United when he scored from a spectacular 35-yard free kick. Yet despite Clarke's continual assertions that the player wasn't for sale, it is hard to believe that an approach for him from that source, had it materialized, would have been rejected. However, only a few months later, in January 1990 after a third-round FA Cup win at Leicester City, new manager Mel Machin said Steve was in the same class as the home side's £1.3m rated striker Gary McAllister – and he pledged to keep him, saying, 'I like his attitude and I shall resist very forcibly any new interest in him that might arise.'

A significant milestone in Steve's career was reached on the evening of 17th October 1989. Then, with the Reds about to play Sheffield United, skipper Paul Futcher was unexpectedly omitted from the team and Steve took over his role. And just as he'd had a goal in his first full appearance in the side five-and-a-half years earlier, in his first game as captain he scored what seemed a point-saving equalizer. But it wasn't to be, for an injury-time penalty swung the result in the visitors' favour.

However, the next game brought a 3 – 2 success at Oxford United. The *Barnsley Chronicle* said Steve appeared to revel in his new responsibilities, carving out the opening for the first goal and generally providing the inspiration which enabled the team to achieve a greater ascendancy than was indicated by the score.

As a boy, Steve Agnew was always going to be a footballer. In fact, he was once sent out of a maths lesson at Worsbrough High School after telling the teacher that he believed his games with Barnsley Boys to be more important than his lessons. And from the time he became an Oakwell apprentice it was apparent that he was going to be a *good* footballer. Even the breaking of a leg, in time, seemed to have helped, rather than hindered, his progress. Previously he'd been a somewhat skinny lad, but the increase in weight which occurred while he was in plaster remained with him, in the form of muscle, when he regained fitness – ideally suiting the midfield role which was thrust upon him.

Captaincy was something he'd contemplated for some time and he really does revel in the responsibilities which go with the job. It was Allan Clarke who appointed him, and when the new manager's promotion-promise is fulfilled it may be that Steve Agnew's name will appear in League records again – as the first captain to lead a Barnsley side into the First Division.

Eric Winstanley: A Legend In The Making?

Apart from a period in the 1970s, Eric Winstanley has been at Oakwell continuously for the last 30 years. Now youth team manager-coach, he was first-choice centre half at 17 and later became the youngest captain in the Football League. Then he was one of the most talked about young players in the country – the *Morning Telegraph* describing him as 'a tough teenager with the skills of a veteran and the poise of a First Division player' – and but for serious injury he would undoubtedly have joined one of the game's leading clubs. Nevertheless, he captained Barnsley for a further seven seasons and led the side to promotion in 1968. This six-foot, 13-stone centre half's goal scoring abilities were as renowned as his defensive skills. In fact, in 1969 he was leading scorer, and a hat-trick against Watford which turned a two-goal deficit into a remarkable victory is an enjoyable memory for those who saw his inspiring display.

Schoolboy football at Longcar Central and with Barnsley Boys was as an outside left and he was in the town team which won the Yorkshire Shield in 1960. The summer of that year saw him on the Oakwell ground staff, and in 1962 he played four times for the England youth team – his introduction to the international scene being delayed for several weeks due to a need for him to deputize for Duncan Sharp at Brentford on 17th March.

Sharp retired unexpectedly at the end of the season, but it was not manager John Steele's intention that Eric should succeed him. Conscious of the lad's inexperience, he planned to bring him along gradually but a move to sign a centre half from Hibernian fell through when the player was injured in Canada in the summer. Consequently Eric had a place at the start of the 1962/63 season and if ever a youngster grabbed his chance it was him, with a record number of games, never being dropped and establishing himself as one of Oakwell's all-time greatest players.

In October 1964 he was appointed captain and, at 19, was by far the youngest in club history. The team weren't doing well and the manager's instructions were, 'I want you to make the others play. Don't bother about anything off the pitch – just give them the right spirit so we can get some better results.' It was an expression of confidence in him; equally it was a tribute to his ability and personality that older and more seasoned professionals accepted his leadership.

The appointment came at a time when the national sporting pages carried almost continual reports of other clubs' interest in him. On one occasion he left John Steele's office to be buttonholed by coach Norman Rimmington.

'Where are you going then, Eric?'

'What do you mean? I'm going into the bath.'

'I mean which club are you going to. They're all after you, you can take your pick.'

Certainly, leading clubs were represented at every game and Spurs' manager, Bill Nicholson, was in the directors' box at Luton on 7th April 1965 – a day which became the worst in all the years Eric was to spend in football. Then, 10 minutes before half-time, he twisted his left knee. The pain was severe but at the interval a doctor thought there was nothing seriously amiss. Substitutes were not then available and he played throughout the second-half, but two days later a cartilage was removed and more serious damage identified. The major problem was a torn cruciate ligament. At first it was decided to see what nature would do about it, but after three months' inactivity he broke down in pre-season training and the surgeon was again consulted. His view was that without further surgery Eric wouldn't play again, and the subsequent operation involved routing a thigh ligament through the knee.

The following three months were spent in plaster and on crutches and he was out of action until the spring of 1966. Then he had a few games in the 'A' team – and again the knee collapsed. At that stage even John Steele began to despair but, nevertheless, he arranged an appointment with a Harley Street specialist. There Eric was put through strenuous exercise and he denied the intense pain which this caused. The specialist then said that no-one had ever recovered sufficiently from this type of operation to play again, but, more hopefully, he went on to say that the surgeon – Mr Evan Price of Barnsley – had done a brilliant job and he'd wait a little longer before making a final decision.

That seemed to be the encouragement Eric needed. This time pre-season training was completed and he had a place in the side for the following seven years. Yet it was always a struggle to be fit enough to continue to play, and only the fact that those in charge understood what he'd been through enabled him to do so. He was allowed to decide when and how to train, and after almost every session he spent 15 minutes hosing cold water onto a swollen, inflamed left knee.

In 1968 he led the side into the Third Division and in the first season at the higher level his goal-scoring was, for a centre half, quite remarkable. Reporting in the *Barnsley Chronicle* on a defeat of Darlington, Keith Lodge said that the skipper had another splendid game, snatching a dramatic winner seven minutes from the end, and he posed the question, 'What would Barnsley do without Eric Winstanley?' It was a topic on which the *Green 'Un* received much correspondence from supporters, and several hundred signed a petition urging the board to reject offers for his transfer. It was also something uppermost in John Steele's mind; he was determined to do all in his power to keep his star player at Oakwell and he recommended to the board that any offer below £100,000 – a figure which would have created a Third Division record – should not be accepted. Consequently a bid from Norwich City was turned down, and the *Morning Telegraph* said that Sheffield United would have to substantially increase their £65,000 bid to have any hope of obtaining a player of Eric's goal-stopping, goal-scoring ability.

Many of his goals came after putting himself into attack when the team were trailing. Often he was able to retrieve a situation, and usually he did it in style. Towards the end of 1968 *The Star* had a 'Two-goal Eric is star of Oakwell show' introduction to its report of a 2 – 1 victory over Hartlepool; against Bournemouth a few weeks later he jumped head and shoulders above everyone else to score a great equalizer from a Hamstead corner; early in the 1969/70 season he got the winner against Stockport County by launching himself into a brilliant overhead kick which crashed the ball into goal before the 'keeper was able to move, and on a visit by Crewe Alexandra he scored an equalizer which paved the way for a 2 – 1 success. Of that game the *Daily Express* said that much of Barnsley's effort had come from their dynamic centre half and they would be in a sorry mess without him.

Although Eric was ambitious he felt indebted to the club for keeping faith with him during the long injury absence. His dearest wish was to win further promotion with them, and all his efforts were directed towards that objective. However, that was not to be. He now feels that two good signings could have provided success 10 years before it came in the early 1980s, but in 1972 the club dropped back into the Fourth Division.

Twelve months later he was Player of the Year by a mile, but a decade in which it had been almost impossible to imagine a Barnsley side without Eric Winstanley was about to end. In the summer of 1973 a fee of £15,000 transferred him to Chesterfield. He only moved because, with his best years behind him, he knew it would improve prospects of remaining in the game as a coach if he had had experience at more than one club. He stayed at Chesterfield for four years, playing exactly 100 games before a 14-year-old knee injury finally ended his playing career.

His coaching began almost as early as his captaincy and he was qualified by the time he was 22. A year later he was the youngest of a group of coaches sent by the FA to Zambia to further the game there. In 1978 he was in Zanzibar coaching the Navy side which reached the African Super League Finals. In the All-African Cup his team played a Ugandan side, Simba, which was President Amin's personal team. The home leg was won 1 – 0, but within the packed stadium at Entebbe, feelings ran so high among the Ugandans that the visiting coach, despite his natural combative attitude, wasn't overly disappointed when his side lost by a narrow margin. He perhaps had in mind that in the previous year's competition a game involving the home side had ended with two players being shot! That incident was doubtless also in his thoughts a few days later in Addis Ababa. Then one of his team was sent off the pitch and sat beside him on the bench. Soon afterwards another was badly hurt, which prompted the previously offending player to race onto the pitch and fling himself at his team-mate's assailant. Eric chased after him and, while struggling to restrain him, found he was surrounded by four rifle-pointing Ethiopian soldiers, one of whom snarled, 'Get off our pitch, white bastard.' And there was no doubt he was addressing Eric, for his was the only white face in the stadium. Pandemonium then broke loose. The 30,000 crowd was eventually subdued by the use of troops and tear gas, and when order was restored the referee curtailed the game by ordering a penalty shoot-out. And he got the desired result, for when the visiting 'keeper was so unwise as to save the first kick, he ordered it to be retaken!

Eric had a three-year contract but, in mid-term, war on the continent brought a halt to inter-state club matches and he wasn't sorry to return to Barnsley.

Soon afterwards he was appointed assistant commercial manager at Oakwell, and a few months later he moved onto the playing side as chief scout. He took every opportunity to involve himself with the players and in August 1983 he replaced Ian Evans as first team coach. Although unhappy about the circumstances which created the vacancy, he knew that if he didn't take the job when it was offered he would regret it for the rest of his life.

He held the position under managers Hunter, Collins and Clarke, until the latter's dismissal in November 1989. As caretaker manager, he held the reins for seven weeks, during which time, to help in a particularly difficult situation, he borrowed Brian McCord and Mark Smith – quality players who eventually signed for the club. He made no secret of a desire to become manager but he was not the board's choice, for on Thursday, 28th December, chairman John Dennis told him that Mel Machin was to be appointed on the following day.

Eric remains at Oakwell in the role of youth team manager-coach and was able to provide an element of continuity while the new regime took over. For his part, although missing the first team involvement and rush of adrenalin on Saturdays, he is relishing present responsibilities and appreciates the way the new manager made him feel wanted – and he reckons his job is next in importance to the manager's, anyway.

As a player he epitomised the best in professional football, and for nearly 10 years he was the king-pin of Barnsley sides. What he might have achieved but for the tragedy at Luton in 1965 can only be conjecture, but John Steele reckons he was the best prospect at centre half that the club has ever had – in fact, too good to be chosen as an attacker. Yet when he was in Africa in 1968 his companions – most of whom were seeing him in action for the first time because they were, in the main, from the First Division, were unanimous that he was a natural centre forward. Be that as it may, the crowd loved him. After his winning hat-trick against Watford he was overwhelmed by supporters and several minutes elapsed before he was able to fight his way to the dressing room. And on a rare occasion when he failed a Friday fitness test Steele said, 'We'll keep it quiet until tomorrow, otherwise there will be three thousand off the gate!'

In more recent times he has coached the Second Division side to the satisfaction of three managers and if he thought it possible for his career to eventually end with him as first team coach and the club in Division One he would be the happiest man in football. But perhaps the last has not been seen of Eric Winstanley as manager. And in the fullness of time his dedication may be likened to that of the man who launched him onto the Oakwell scene as a 17-year-old, in which case he too will have well deserved the accolade, 'Mister Barnsley'.

Bibliography

Rothmans Football Yearbook (annually, 1970–1990) (Rothmans/Queen Anne Press)
The Hamlyn A-Z of British Football Records by Phil Soar (1981) (Hamlyn)
Oakwell Heroes by Graham Noble (1986) (Glenwood Publications)